GoodNews
EVANGEL

2024

Phillip A. Ross

Marietta, Ohio

ISBN: 978-1-7337267-8-8
Edition: 25.7.21

Published by
Pilgrim Platform
149 E. Spring St., Marietta
Ohio, 45750
www.pilgrim-platform.org

Unless otherwise indicated Scripture has been taken from English Standard Version.

Printed in the United States of America

BOOKS BY PHILLIP A. ROSS

The Work At Zion—A Reckoning, Two-volume set, 772 pages, 1996.

Practically Christian—Applying James Today, 135 pages, 2006.

The Wisdom of Jesus Christ in the Book of Proverbs, 414 pages, 2006.

Marking God's Word—Understanding Jesus, 324 pages, 2006.

Acts of Faith—Kingdom Advancement, 326 pages, 2007.

Informal Christianity—Refining Christ's Church, 136 pages, 2007.

Engagement—Establishing Relationship in Christ, 104 pages, 1996, 2008.

It's About Time! — The Time Is Now, 40 pages. 2008.

The Big Ten—A Study of the Ten Commandments, 105 pages, 2001, 2008.

Arsy Varsy—Reclaiming The Gospel in First Corinthians, 406 pages, 2008.

Varsy Arsy—Proclaiming The Gospel in Second Corinthians, 356 pages, 2009.

Colossians—Christos Singularis, 278 pages, 2010.

Rock Mountain Creed—The Sermon on the Mount, 310 pages, 2011.

The True Mystery of the Mystical Presence, 355 pages, 2011.

Peter's Vision of Christ's Purpose in First Peter, 340 pages, 2011.

Peter's Vision of The End in Second Peter, 184 pages, 2012.

The Religious History of Nineteenth Century Marietta, Thomas Jefferson Summers, 124 pages, 1903, 2012 (editor).

Conflict of Ages—The Great Debate of the Moral Relations of God and Man, Edward Beecher, 489 pages, 1853, 2012 (editor).

Concord Of Ages—The Individual And Organic Harmony Of God And Man, Edward Beecher, D. D., 524 pages, 1860, 2013 (editor).

Ephesians—Recovering the Vision of a Sustainable Church in Christ, 417 pages, 2013.

Galatians: Backstory/Christory, 315 pages, 2015.

Poet Tree—Root, Branch & Sap, 72 pages, 2013.

Inside Out Woman—Collected Poetry, Doris M. Ross, 195 pages, 2014 (editor).

God's Great Plan for the World, 305 pages, 2019.

John's Miracles—Seeing Beyond Our Expectations, 210 pages, 2019.

Essays on Church—Ordinary Christianity for the World, 385 pages, 2020.

Thessalonians—Thorn, Thistle, and Throne, 160 pages, 2021.

Institutes of The Christian Religion, Emanuel V. Gerhart, 9 volumes, 2023 (editor).

Goodnews—Evangel 2022, 187 pages, 2023

Goodnews—Evangel 2023, 318 pages, 2024

Goodnews—Evangel 2024, 322 pages, 2024

Goodnews—Reformation Reloaded, forthcoming, 2025

The Heritage of St. Paul's Evangelical Church, 108 pages, 2024

For Renewal

TABLE OF CONTENTS

INTRODUCTION

This is the third collection of sermons from St. Paul's. They are being published as part of the ongoing renewal of St. Paul's. We are an old Church, 186 years old at the time. Founded in 1839 by German immigrants to Marietta, Ohio. Renewal is an ongoing process, one that we began a long time ago.

St. Paul's has been part of five denominations over her history, three in the past 30 years. A lot of people have the idea that a church is planted and maintains or should maintain its general theological character forever. And that is partly true, which means that it is also partly false.

The Roman Catholic Church would have us believe that it has consistently maintained the Tradition that it began, that it has been consistently and continually faithful for over two thousand years. But actual history belies that story. In fact, the Roman Catholic Church is a conglomerate of traditions, full of ebbs and flows, ups and downs. And in fact, that is simply the truth of all history.

Compare the growth and history of any institution and you will find various ebbs and flows with two steps forward and one step back. The truth is that growth happens in spurts, and we learn from our mistakes—hopefully. At least that is the ideal, which stands more as a goal than an accomplishment.

However, institutions like to craft narratives that are positive, up-lifting, and impressive in order to maintain the impression of success because such narratives help sell the institution to the public. Stories of success, worldly success, are attractive, or so we think. People like reading about success and dynamic social and business turn-arounds that are full of warm fuzzies and inspirational accomplishments.

We forget or ignore or just don't understand that the Bible is not like that. The Bible is actually the long story of human failure. Take the Old Testament for instance. There we find the story of God who gathers a particular people and inserts Himself into their story. It began with Abraham and ended in Egyptian slavery. So God chose Moses to free His people from Pharaoh, and sent them into the wilderness, which nearly killed them. So He chose David and Solomon to build a kingdom, which became the greatest empire in the world at that time, only to fall into a civil war that lasted centuries. And it finally came to a cataclysmic end in A.D. 70 as Rome destroyed Jerusalem and the Temple, and scattered the people.

And that end was involved the beginning of the New Testament story of Jesus Christ. Jesus came to free God's people from slavery to sin, which all of the Old Testament rules and practices failed to do. But Jesus died a convicted criminal on the cross, an instrument of horrific torture.

Are you getting the picture? The story of the Bible is horrifically tragic, except for the overwhelming, ongoing, and audacious hope that God will eventually prevail. And that is our hope at St. Paul's! And because we share that hope, we also share in God's tragic story of His involvement in human history. We are willing to air our laundry in public for two major reasons. First, truth is important, and our story is rough in places. We don't have everything right, but we are working on it. And second, the Bible is our model.

You can read our story in *The Heritage of St. Paul's Evangelical Church*, by Phillip A. Ross, Pilgrim Platform Books, Marietta, Ohio, 2024. The *GoodNews* collections of sermons are adjuncts to that story. These sermon collections provide various lessons and corrections to our theology, our ongoing understanding of God's mission and teachings.

The most recent renewal, which began in the 1990s and took us out of the United Church of Christ (UCC), into and then out of the Lutheran Churches In Mission (LCIM), and finally into the Evangelical Association of Reformed and Congregational Churches, where we believe we have arrived at our beginning point, our German heritage —but updated. Or we should say *updating* because it is a process.

We began as German Evangelicals. The Germans were the first evangelicals as a result of Luther's rift with the Roman Catholic Church. Germany was soon ablaze with various ideas of church revival and reform. By the 1700s there were three branches of Christianity in Germany: Roman Catholic, Lutheran, and Evangelical, which was essentially a collection of Calvinists. During this same period there was a strong desire to unite the Lutherans and the Evangelicals, though it never quite coalesced.

And this was the founding spirit of St. Paul's. We were affiliated with the Evangelical church in Germany. In 1879 we affiliated with the German Evangelical Synod of North America. In 1943 we changed our official name to *St. Paul's Evangelical and Reformed Church*, reflecting the merger of the Evangelical Synod of North America and the German Reformed Church, also known as the Evangelical And Reformed Church or the E&R. Then in 1961 we changed the name again, this time to *St. Paul's United Church of Christ*, reflecting the merger of the Evangelical and Reformed church with the Congregational Christian Churches into the United Church of Christ (UCC). Our tradition and people have always been unity minded, seeking other Christians and churches with which to cooperate in the greater Christian mission.

By the time that the 1990s rolled around we found that the the UCC had abandoned it mission of Christian unity and was actively promoting what the Bible calls sin in the church and society. This created a decade of strife as St. Paul's balked at the plans and programs of the UCC. The church was divided about these concerns and many people left, which then set the wheels of renewal in motion.

Rev. Steve Dennis, who had served as an Interim Minister at St. Luke's Lutheran Church, just down the street, was hired as Pastor. Pastor Dennis as a member of the Lutheran Churches In Mission LCIM), a small conservative reform group related to the Lutheran Church In America. Pastor Dennis hoped to draw St. Paul's into the LCIM. When Pastor Dennis left, St. Paul's turned to the LCIM to help us find a pastor. A candidate was selected, and rejected.

Tom Hendershot, who grew up in the area, had just retired from serving in the U.S. Army as a Chaplain. He had returned to the area to care for his aging mother. Pastor Tom was hired several months later, and after several years helped St. Paul's find its way into the Evangelical Association. The general thrust of renewal has continued as St.

Paul's has reacquainted herself with her own roots. And this is the renewal that is still in progress.

This renewal has led to the discovery of what is known as Mercersburg Theology, the theology and teaching of John Williamson Nevin and Philip Schaff at the German Reformed seminary at Mercersburg, Pennsylvania in the 1800s. However, that theology was not new, but was a restatement of the original Calvinistic theology of the Protestant Reformation. It followed the path of the European Reformation in distinction from the English Reformation, which was a later development.

Well, as interesting as all of this theology is, it doesn't connect with ordinary church people. So I have chosen to reveal the biblical connections of this theology rather than to dialog with the various theologians. Church people are looking to understand the Bible, not the history of theology. So in these pages you will find my effort to express various elements of Mercersburg theology, the original theology of the Protestant Reformation, in sermons rather than through theological argument. In these pages I have selected Scripture from the Lectionary in an effort to allow the theology to simply flow from the various stories in the Bible without any effort to arrange or present the theology in any particular way.

In addition, I have not provided a strict Mercersburg theology, but have dealt with Mercersburg ideas as they have presented themselves through the Lectionary. Nor have I pointed out specific Mercersburg distinctives. Rather, I am simply reading the Lectionary from a Mercersburg perspective. Had I not alerted you to this, you likely wouldn't notice it because much of what was unique in the 1800s about this theology has simply been accepted and woven into faithful, contemporary, historic Protestantism. And I pray that it will speak to you.

Phillip A. Ross
Marietta, Ohio
March 2025

CHANGED

4 John appeared, baptizing in the wilderness and proclaiming a baptism of repentance for the forgiveness of sins. 5 And all the country of Judea and all Jerusalem were going out to him and were being baptized by him in the river Jordan, confessing their sins. 6 Now John was clothed with camel's hair and wore a leather belt around his waist and ate locusts and wild honey. 7 And he preached, saying, "After me comes he who is mightier than I, the strap of whose sandals I am not worthy to stoop down and untie. 8 I have baptized you with water, but he will baptize you with the Holy Spirit." 9 In those days Jesus came from Nazareth of Galilee and was baptized by John in the Jordan. 10 And when he came up out of the water, immediately he saw the heavens being torn open and the Spirit descending on him like a dove. 11 And a voice came from heaven, "You are my beloved Son; with you I am well pleased." —Mark 1:4-11

And it happened that while Apollos was at Corinth, Paul passed through the inland country and came to Ephesus. There he found some disciples. 2 And he said to them, "Did you receive the Holy Spirit when you believed?" And they said, "No, we have not even heard that there is a Holy Spirit." 3 And he said, "Into what then were you baptized?" They said, "Into John's baptism." 4 And Paul said, "John baptized with the baptism of repentance, telling the people to believe in the one who was to come after him, that is, Jesus." 5 On hearing this, they were baptized in the name of the Lord Jesus. 6 And when Paul had laid his hands on them, the Holy Spirit came on them, and they began speaking in tongues and prophesying. 7 There were about twelve men in all. —Acts 19:1-7

From the birth of Christ the Lectionary takes us to baptism because baptism symbolizes another kind of birth—the birth of

1

new life in Christ. The celebration of the birth of Christ is also a celebration of the birth of *new life* in Christ. In the same way that the baby Jesus came to the existing world, a world that was already very old, and to a nation that had already been functioning for many thousands of years, Jesus did not come to create a new kind of physical human being, nor a new nation. Rather, He came to renew humanity, to renew the nation of God's people.

To use a computer analogy: He came to refurbish an existing computer, to replace parts that were still functioning with improved parts that were more efficient and more powerful, and to provide an improved operating system. The refurbished product would, then, be better than the old one, even when the old one was still operating. The nature of the machine would be the same, only better—more efficient, more powerful, and easier to use once you learned the new operating system. You couldn't tell the difference between the old computer and the new computer by looking at them. The difference could only be perceived by learning and using the new computer. Let's define the difference between the two computers, the old one and the refurbished one, as baptism. We'll say that the new system was baptized, but the old system was not.

The ceremony of baptism symbolizes a washing, cleansing, or forgiveness of sin, where the forgiveness of sin means no longer being controlled by sin. In our analogy we will call it a new operating system. In this example sin is the old operating system, and the washing, cleansing, and forgiveness is the replacement of old parts with new parts, including a new operating system. When you got your refurbished computer back from the shop that refurbished it, it would look the same. Maybe a little cleaner, but otherwise the same. You could tell the difference only by using it.

The gospel of Mark does not tell the story about Jesus' birth. Mark begins the story of Jesus with John the Baptist. Similarly the gospel of John begins with creation, but then avoids Jesus' birth and immediately jumps to John the Baptist. We are familiar with John's prologue because it is often read during the Christmas season:

"In the beginning was the Word, and the Word was with God, and the Word was God. He was in the beginning with God All things were made through him, and without him was not any thing made that was made. In him was life, and the life was the light of men. The light shines in the darkness, and the darkness has not overcome it. There was a man sent from God, whose name was John. He came as a witness, to bear witness about the light, that all might believe through him. He was not the light, but came to bear witness about the light" (John 1:1-8).

Matthew and Luke begin with the birth of Jesus, but Mark and John begin with John the Baptist. The four gospel stories about Jesus, then, tie Jesus' birth to the new birth in Christ of God's people. The two stories are about the one reality: about God in Christ in us; about us being in Christ, who is in God. The two stories about Jesus and John are really one story. Mark said that John came

"proclaiming a baptism of repentance for the forgiveness of sins" (v. 4).

John the Baptist prepared the way by calling people to repentance, where repentance is the turning away from sin and turning to God for forgiveness of sins. Repentance had to precede baptism, and thus baptism was not the means by which sins were forgiven but rather was a sign indicating that one had repented.

The gospel begins with forgiveness only in the sense that God sent Jesus Christ to provide forgiveness. God begins the process by providing forgiveness through Jesus. God's forgiveness is like a class action suit, where a manufacturer is sued by many people for damages caused by their product.

This analogy is not exactly right because in such a case the manufacturer is being sued for a defective product. But God has not provided a defective product. The defectiveness of the product is caused by Satan, not God. So we could say that the class action suit is against Satan. But the point is that the class action suit only involves people who sign on as litigants. If someone doesn't know about the class action suit, the result of the case will not involve them, even if it could. In order to recover damages people have to sign on to the

class action suit. Only then will they receive compensation. Notice
also that the outcome of such a class action suit does not involve anything that the damaged person has to do, other than agree to be part
of it. The attorneys do all the work. And in this example, Jesus is our
attorney.

The gospel and the forgiveness are still free, though to actually
receive forgiveness, people need to acknowledge that they are a
damaged party, and sign on as a litigant. The acknowledgement of
damage is the acknowledgement of sin. But acknowledging sin is
not enough. People still need to sign on to the class action suit,
which is, for the purposes of this analogy: repentance. Like all analogies this class action suit analogy is not perfect, and it fails at several
points. The general idea is that people have been damaged by sin,
and can be repaired or refurbished by Christ. But to benefit from
God's forgiveness, people still need to sign on, or take their machine
to the shop, if I can mix metaphors and an analogies. God has provided the forgiveness, and Jesus does all of the work, yet we still need
to sign on in order to benefit.

The active ingredient here is the Holy Spirit. John baptizes with
water in a symbolical way, but Jesus baptizes with the Holy Spirit in
a real way. Notice that in the story Jesus submits to John's baptism.
Jesus, the superior, submits to John, the inferior. Why? John himself
doesn't understand this and admits that he is not worthy enough to
tie Jesus' sandals, much less baptize Him. But he baptizes Jesus anyway. Why? By submitting to John's baptism, Jesus brought together
the symbol and the reality. Why? Why link the symbolism of water
baptism with the reality of Holy Spirit baptism?

Jesus links them because it is necessary that the symbolic action
of water baptism is more than a ceremony. It is a sacrament because
the ceremony is necessary, but not sufficient. Because the reality of
Holy Spirit baptism must be acknowledged by all three parties involved: the person being baptized, the community that witnesses the
baptism, and the Holy Spirit, who makes it real. All three of these
parties must be actively involved in baptism for it to be a sacrament.

It is immaterial whether the process involves dunking, dipping,
sprinkling, or pouring. The age of the person being baptized is also

immaterial because it is the Holy Spirit alone who makes it real, and the Holy Spirit is not bound by time. The baptism is only real, only complete when the Holy Spirit makes it real. The same thing is true generally about faithfulness: we can make all kinds of promises to God, but those promises mean nothing unless and until they are kept. An unkept promise is worthless.

Who is able to keep the promise of Jesus Christ to redeem the world? Only Jesus Himself can keep such a promise. Our only job is to acknowledge that we are in His care, that He has our back. He alone will keep His promise. In the class action suit analogy, He is the attorney. We are simply litigants. The suit proceeds on our behalf. We cannot determine the outcome. The outcome is in the hands of our attorney, Jesus Christ.

When Paul was in Ephesus he encountered some disciples. This means that the gospel (good news of Jesus Christ) had gotten to Ephesus before Paul did. It means that Paul didn't plant the gospel in Ephesus, it was already there. Rather, Paul corrected the gospel in Ephesus. Paul asked them,

> "'Did you receive the Holy Spirit when you believed?' And they said, 'No, we have not even heard that there is a Holy Spirit.' And he said, 'Into what then were you baptized?' They said, 'Into John's baptism.' And Paul said, 'John baptized with the baptism of repentance, telling the people to believe in the one who was to come after him, that is, Jesus'" (vs. 2-4).

Paul didn't ask them about their baptism, but about their *belief*. They had been ceremonially baptized with water, but knew nothing about the Holy Spirit. Here we see that the symbol (water baptism) was separate from the reality (Holy Spirit baptism). Here we see that the symbol and the reality can be separated, but when they are the result is ineffectual. Paul's correction in Ephesus was to unite the symbol and the reality, to tie them together. The ceremony alone is not sufficient. But the story is not over.

> "On hearing this, they were baptized in the name of the Lord Jesus. And when Paul had laid his hands on them, the Holy Spirit came on

them, and they began speaking in tongues and prophesying" (vs. 5-6).

When John the Baptist baptized people, he didn't yet know for sure that Jesus was the Messiah. John only confirmed that later, when he was in prison. This means that John had not been baptizing in the name of Jesus. So they were then baptized in the name of the Lord Jesus. And having been baptized in Jesus' name, Paul

"laid his hands on them (and) the Holy Spirit came on them" (v. 7).

Here we see the uniting of the symbol (water baptism) and the reality (Holy Spirit baptism). That's what makes it a sacrament.

At this point we fall prey to our modern Charismatic assumptions. When we read that "they began speaking in tongues and prophesying" we think that Paul meant what modern Charismatics mean by "speaking in tongues." *Bibbidi-Bobbidi-Boo!* Every time we read about tongues in the Bible, people today think in modern Charismatic terms—even non-charismatics think this way. But it is unlikely that that is what Paul had in mind. The old traditional understanding of *tongues* is that it means *foreign languages.*

I doubt that they began speaking in languages that they didn't previously know, or in some sort of heavenly language that only the Holy Spirit knows. Rather, some of them were probably gentiles. And when they "got" the Holy Spirit, when they understood what Paul had been talking about, they probably began discussing it in their own native languages. When people get the Holy Spirit, when they understand the reality of the Holy Spirit, they are then able to discuss God meaningfully in their native language. I think this is what it means.

In addition, prophesying is not forecasting the future, unless preaching is forecasting the future. And in a sense it is because the future is in God's hands. Rather, they simply began speaking to one another in their native languages and preaching the good news of Jesus Christ to one another. They understood and shared the reality of the Holy Spirit in their native language. But when people from several different foreign lands began to do this, it probably sounded like confusion as many people were speaking different languages at the same time.

The reality of baptism and new birth in Christ provides a new understanding of Jesus Christ and the Bible. While some insights come all at once, others take decades to unfold in the lives of believers. Baptism is the beginning of this process of spiritual growth.

SEEING WHAT YOU HEAR

3 Now the boy Samuel was ministering to the Lord in the presence of Eli. And the word of the Lord was rare in those days; there was no frequent vision. 2 At that time Eli, whose eyesight had begun to grow dim so that he could not see, was lying down in his own place. 3 The lamp of God had not yet gone out, and Samuel was lying down in the temple of the Lord, where the ark of God was. 4 Then the Lord called Samuel, and he said, "Here I am!" 5 and ran to Eli and said, "Here I am, for you called me." But he said, "I did not call; lie down again." So he went and lay down. 6 And the Lord called again, "Samuel!" and Samuel arose and went to Eli and said, "Here I am, for you called me." But he said, "I did not call, my son; lie down again." 7 Now Samuel did not yet know the Lord, and the word of the Lord had not yet been revealed to him. 8 And the Lord called Samuel again the third time. And he arose and went to Eli and said, "Here I am, for you called me." Then Eli perceived that the Lord was calling the boy. 9 Therefore Eli said to Samuel, "Go, lie down, and if he calls you, you shall say, 'Speak, Lord, for your servant hears.'" So Samuel went and lay down in his place. 10 And the Lord came and stood, calling as at other times, "Samuel! Samuel!" And Samuel said, "Speak, for your servant hears."

—1 Samuel 3:1-10

43 The next day Jesus decided to go to Galilee. He found Philip and said to him, "Follow me." 44 Now Philip was from Bethsaida, the city of Andrew and Peter. 45 Philip found Nathanael and said to him, "We have found him of whom Moses in the Law and also the prophets wrote, Jesus of Nazareth, the son of Joseph." 46 Nathanael said to him, "Can anything good come out of Nazareth?" Philip said to him, "Come and see." 47 Jesus saw Nathanael coming toward him and said of him, "Behold, an Israelite indeed, in whom there is no deceit!" 48 Nathanael said to him, "How do you know me?" Jesus answered him, "Before Philip called you, when you were under the fig tree, I saw you." 49 Nathanael answered him, "Rabbi, you are the Son of God! You are the King of Israel!" 50 Jesus answered him, "Because I said to you, 'I saw you under the fig tree,' do you believe? You will see greater things than these." 51 And he said to him, "Truly, truly, I say to you, you will see heaven opened, and the angels of God ascending and descending on the Son of Man."

—John 1:43-51

The Lectionary reading in 1 Samuel stopped at verse 10. But what the Lord actually said to Samuel, the content of the message, is extremely important.

"Then the Lord said to Samuel, 'Behold, I am about to do a thing in Israel at which the two ears of everyone who hears it will tingle. On that day I will fulfill against Eli all that I have spoken concerning his house, from beginning to end. And I declare to him that I am about to punish his house forever, for the iniquity that he knew, because his sons were blaspheming God, and he did not restrain them. Therefore I swear to the house of Eli that the iniquity of Eli's house shall not be atoned for by sacrifice or offering forever.' Samuel lay until morning; then he opened the doors of the house of the Lord. And Samuel was afraid to tell the vision to Eli" (1 Samuel 3:11-15).

The Lord told Samuel that he could not trust Eli; he could not trust the religious establishment of his day. That's a very distressing message, but is all too common in the Bible.

But I'm getting ahead of the story. This reading is about the end of the ministry of Eli, when the Lord was going to do a new thing. Samuel was the first to hear about that new thing. The context of the message is important. Eli was a priest and a judge of the Israelites in the city of Shiloh, which was the last place that the Tabernacle was erected in ancient Israel.

The tabernacle was the tent used as the mobile place of worship as Israel wandered in the desert. Shiloh was the last place they put up the tent, and so Shiloh became the center of Israelite worship until it was abandoned when King David made Jerusalem the center of worship.

When Hannah came to Shiloh to pray for a son, Eli mistakenly accused her of drunkenness, but when she protested her innocence, Eli wished her well. Hannah's eventual child was named *Samuel*, who was raised by Eli, the last priest of the Tabernacle in Shiloh. Eli failed to rein in the abusive behavior of his own sons, who also functioned as priests at Shiloh. As a result of their behavior Eli's sons died at the Battle of Aphek where the Ark of the Covenant was captured by the Philistines. When Eli heard the news of the captured Ark, he fell from his seat, broke his neck, and died.

Notice that when Samuel was a boy, Eli's vision was poor. Eli was not seeing things clearly, and the "the word of the Lord was rare in those days" (v. 1). Eli didn't have it. God had departed from Eli and Shiloh. Samuel was Eli's understudy, his developing protege. And the first thing that Samuel learned about Eli was that Eli was not faithful. That's a hard lesson to learn.

When someone you are supposed to look up to, or some institution, like your church or your government, that is supposed to engender your trust and support is proven to be unfaithful and untrustworthy, it is a bitter pill to swallow. It's hard to believe, hard to accept. Our first response is disbelief. *Surely that is not true,* we think. *There must be some mistake, some sort of misunderstanding or miscommunication.* We don't want to believe it because believing it upsets our entire world. Suddenly everything that we thought was true comes into question. If that person or institution is untrustworthy, and I have built my whole life on the basis of its trustworthiness, then everything that I thought was true suddenly comes into doubt. This is the kind of thing that results in a serious faith crisis.

And that was the situation for Samuel. Samuel could either trust his superior, Eli, whom he had grown to love and respect; or he could trust that inner voice that spoke to him about right and wrong —the voice that spoke to him in the night. Human history was at an inflection point between Eli and Samuel. That was the message that Samuel received that night.

But it wasn't just that history was about to change the world, but that Samuel had a key role to play in that unfolding change. Because the Lord had spoken directly to Samuel, Samuel was no longer a by-

stander watching history unfold. Samuel was being called into service. Samuel had a role to play, and there was no script to follow. He
would need to learn how to listen to the voice of the Lord in his
own life. And this would be more difficult because of the situation
with Eli, Samuel would need to buck tradition, to oppose the social
momentum of tradition. There would be conflict and disagreement.
The only way forward for Samuel would be to learn to hear the
voice of the Lord amid the contradicting voices of tradition. The
way things had always been done would need to change.

Samuel would not only need to learn to hear the voice of the
Lord himself, he would need to teach others how to hear the voice of
the Lord, how to discern God's truth in the cacophony of competing
voices.

"And Samuel was afraid to tell the vision to Eli" (v. 15).

Eli was a prominent figure in Samaritan religious tradition. The
Samaritans attributed the schism between their community and the
Jerusalem Jews to Eli's ministry at Shiloh. The Samaritans, following
Eli, believed that the original Israelite sacred site was Mount Gerizim, which is mentioned in the Bible as the place where Israel first
entered the Promised Land after the Exodus. It was there that the Israelites performed ceremonies of blessings, as they had been instructed by Moses. Mount Gerizim was sacred to the Samaritans,
who regarded it, rather than the Temple Mount in Jerusalem, as the
location chosen by God for a holy temple. In the Samaritan tradition,
Mount Gerizim was the oldest and most central mountain in the
world. It towered above the Great Flood and they believed that it
provided the landing place for Noah after the flood. It is also where
they believe Abraham almost sacrificed his son Isaac.

Jews, on the other hand, considered the location of Isaac's near-
sacrifice to be Mount Moriah, traditionally identified by them as the
Temple Mount.

Mount Gerizim continues to be the center of Samaritan religion
to this day. Passover is still celebrated today by the Samaritans with a
lamb sacrifice on Mount Gerizim. Today, about half of the remaining Samaritans live in close proximity to Gerizim, mostly in the small

village of Kiryat Luza at the foot of the mountain. All of this is to say that listening to the voice of the Lord is consequential. Samuel's ministry was consequential.

When the people wanted a king like the other nations, they went to Samuel. Samuel told them that he thought it was a bad idea, but he would ask the Lord. The Lord agreed with Samuel: it was a bad idea. But if that's what they wanted, the Lord would give it to them. Samuel then anointed King Saul, and the rest is history. And Israel's kingship idea was proven to be a bad idea. That story is the story of the Old Testament, which ended with the destruction of Jerusalem and the Temple in A.D. 70.

The Lectionary pairs the story of Eli and Samuel with John 14, when Jesus called Philip and Nathanael. While Samuel heard a voice in the night, Philip heard the actual voice of Jesus Christ in the flesh who said to him in particular, "Follow me."

I've always found it amazing that in the gospels Jesus says, "Follow me," and people seem to drop what they are doing and follow him. I suppose that when the Lord speaks we are compelled to listen. Then again, a lot of people don't listen to the Lord, or don't hear Him today. Hearing God seems to be a matter of hearing the truth, or believing the truth when you hear it. How is it that we know something to be true when we hear it? Or how is it that we know something to be false? My own experience is that the truth is compelling, irresistible.

When Samuel first heard God's voice, he didn't believe that it was God. He thought it was Eli calling him. He kept hearing it, and he kept thinking that it was Eli calling him. Only when Eli told him to stop coming to him and to listen to what the voice of the Lord had to say, did Samuel hear the message. And what did Samuel do with the message he heard from God. Nothing! He kept it to himself because he was afraid. He was afraid that Eli wouldn't like the message, and he was afraid for Eli because the message opposed Eli. The message was that Eli had abandoned God.

When Philip heard Jesus call him, he seems to have believed right away, and he immediately told Nathanael about Jesus. Maybe he asked Nathanael to go with him to see Jesus as a kind of second opinion. Nathanael didn't believe it at first. *If the Lord God was going to come to earth, why would He go to Nazareth?* Nathanael said that Philip was mistaken. Philip said, *Come and see for yourself.* He did, and an interesting thing happened.

Upon meeting Jesus Nathanael asked, "How do you *know* me?" Not how did you *meet* me? *How is it that you know who I am?* Jesus answered him,

"Before Philip called you, when you were under the fig tree, I saw you" (v. 48).

Immediately Nathanael responded,

"Rabbi, you are the Son of God! You are the King of Israel! (v. 49)"

What happened here? There are two sides or two perspectives related to this one event, this seeing. One is *seeing* and the other is *being seen.* Nathanael went to see Jesus for himself, and when he did, Jesus saw him. It was then that Jesus saw Nathanael, meaning that there was a mutual seeing and a being seen. Nathanael saw Jesus and Jesus saw Nathanael. There was a mutual meeting of souls that happened. Each one could see truth, honesty, in the other.

When Jesus first saw Nathanael, He said that there was no deceit in Nathanael. Jesus saw that Nathanael was an seriously honest person, a person who would not tolerate deceit. And Nathanael saw the same thing in Jesus. Each saw the honesty of the other.

It's a hard thing to put into words, but sometimes when you meet someone you feel like you have known them for a long time. It's a kind of a "love at first sight" kind of thing. I think that's what happened between Jesus and Nathanael. Everyone doesn't have this kind of experience with Jesus. Some people require more time and attention by the Lord to bring them around.

Faithfulness happens in a lot of different ways, but the result is always the same. At some point, you just "get" Jesus. You understand Him, you trust Him, and you know that He understands you. He sees you and you see Him.

ORDINARY FAITHFULNESS

*14 Now after John was arrested, Jesus came into Galilee, proclaiming
the gospel of God, 15 and saying, "The time is fulfilled, and the
kingdom of God is at hand; repent and believe in the gospel." 16
Passing alongside the Sea of Galilee, he saw Simon and Andrew the
brother of Simon casting a net into the sea, for they were fishermen.
17 And Jesus said to them, "Follow me, and I will make you become
fishers of men." 18 And immediately they left their nets and followed
him. 19 And going on a little farther, he saw James the son of
Zebedee and John his brother, who were in their boat mending the
nets. 20 And immediately he called them, and they left their father
Zebedee in the boat with the hired servants and followed him.*
—Mark 1:14-20

*17 Only let each person lead the life that the Lord has assigned to
him, and to which God has called him. This is my rule in all the
churches. 18 Was anyone at the time of his call already circumcised?
Let him not seek to remove the marks of circumcision. Was anyone
at the time of his call uncircumcised? Let him not seek circumcision.
19 For neither circumcision counts for anything nor uncircumcision,
but keeping the commandments of God. 20 Each one should remain
in the condition in which he was called. 21 Were you a bondservant
when called? Do not be concerned about it. (But if you can gain your
freedom, avail yourself of the opportunity.) 22 For he who was
called in the Lord as a bondservant is a freedman of the Lord. Likewise he who was free when called is a bondservant of Christ. 23 You
were bought with a price; do not become bondservants of men. 24 So,
brothers, in whatever condition each was called, there let him remain
with God.*   *—1 Corinthians 7:17-24*

The Lectionary always provides four readings: Old Testament, Psalms, Gospels, and New Testament. We can use them all, or pick and choose. The Old Testament lesson for today is the story of Jonah, but we have dealt with that before. So, I chose a Gospel and a New Testament lesson. But keep in mind that each reading supports the common theme for the day. Today's theme we could call "New Believers" or "New Beliefs."

Jonah had a hard time believing that God could change people. The Gospel lesson today is about the beginning of Jesus ministry. Mark doesn't mention the birth of Jesus, but begins with the stories of John the Baptist and Jesus as adults. John had been preaching in Judea and Jerusalem, in the southern part of Israel.

> "Now after John was arrested, Jesus came into Galilee, proclaiming the gospel of God" (v. 14).

Galilee is in the northern part of Israel, and Shiloh, the worship center of the Samaritans, was in Galilee. Prior to this, Jesus was tempted in the wilderness, and following that temptation Jesus began His public ministry.

Matthew tells us that John the Baptist and Jesus had the same message:

> "Repent, for the kingdom of heaven is at hand" (Matthew 3:2) *from John*; "Repent, for the kingdom of heaven is at hand" (Matthew 4:17), *from Jesus*.

Mark recorded the message as,

> "The time is fulfilled, and the kingdom of God is at hand; repent and believe in the gospel" (v. 15).

Mark said that Jesus added the idea that "the time is fulfilled." The general idea is that God had given the law through Moses. The law was given to Israel as a representative human group, and the law had run its course.

The story of the Old Testament is the story of Israel engaging God's law. It's a long story with a lot of twists and turns, but by the time Jesus came on the scene Israel was in the depths of corruption and occupied by Rome. Israel was in need of renewal—*again*. Over the centuries Israel had experienced several cycles of corruption and renewal. But over time the renewals always ended in corruption. Corruption and renewal was a well established historical pattern that repeated century after century.

Jesus' comment that the time was fulfilled, meant that God was going to break out of that Old Testament pattern of renewal and corruption by doing a new thing. God was about to do a new thing, to change the boom and bust cycle of faithlessness and revival. The old remedies weren't working. Something new was needed. And, Jesus said that the time for something new is *now!*

Simon and Andrew were fishing. They were at work, fishing was their job, not their hobby.

> "And Jesus said to them, 'Follow me, and I will make you become fishers of men.' And immediately they left their nets and followed him" (vs. 17-18).

Immediately, they dropped everything and followed Jesus! No doubts, no questions, no excuses. But note also that Jesus did not ask them to follow him. He *commanded* them. People don't respond well to commands today. Is that because we are Americans, or because we are modern, or because we are human? The same thing happened with James and John. Jesus called them, and they immediately went.

Today Christianity is all about the choice people make rather than on the mission of Christ. And when it's about our choice, it's about us, and not about Jesus. Today we bend over backwards to get people to choose Jesus. Sure, there is a choice involved; Christianity cannot be imposed, it must be taken up willingly. But when we put all of our time and effort on getting people in the door, we don't spend much time and effort on getting the message, the mission, out the door. Our attention is inward focused on the church, on the building, on our programs, on ourselves.

Clearly, we can't ignore the church or the building or our programs. But historically, American mission efforts have not been directed at our neighbors or our own communities. Rather, we send missionaries away; we send them overseas. We send our missionaries to other countries. And I'm not saying that we should not do that! I'm just saying that historically in American churches we haven't spent much time and effort on promoting the mission of Jesus Christ locally, in our own communities.

When we think about local missions we tend to think about feeding the hungry, housing the homeless, counseling the distressed, collecting money to help someone else who is doing something good, etc. And again, those are all good things. I'm not saying that we should not do those things. We should! What I am saying is that we need to think about Jesus' mission. What did Jesus say that His mission was? He said,

> "The time is fulfilled, and the kingdom of God is at hand; repent and believe in the gospel" (v. 15).

He said that it was—and still is—time to take advantage of an opportunity, a reality. What was/is the opportunity, that reality?

The kingdom of God has come on earth. That's what He meant. So, what is the kingdom of God? First and foremost, it is a kingdom where God rules as king. It's a place, but it is more than any particular place. It's a realm. It's a community or territory over which a sovereign rules; a kingdom; an area or sphere, as of knowledge or activity. A synonym is *field*, as in *field of study*. The kingdom of God is wherever God is honored as king.

The thing about a king in this world is that ordinary people rarely have any personal dealings, contact, or relationship with the king. They just know his name, and know that he's in charge. He makes the laws. But the thing about the kingdom of God is that ordinary people do have regular dealings, contact, and relationship with God, the King, through prayer, worship, study, and service. In the kingdom of God ordinary people know and honor the King by knowing and honoring His laws.

And how does this happen? How do the kingdoms of the world become the kingdom of God? Jesus said, "repent and believe in the gospel" (Matthew 1:15). *Repent* and *believe*. The current dictionary defines *repent* as to feel sorry, self-reproachful, or contrite for past

conduct; regret or be conscience-stricken about a past action, attitude, etc. But that is not what the Bible means by repent!

In Greek the word is μετάνοια, which means or refers to changing one's mind. So, having changed your mind, it is true that you
might feel bad or sorry about your previous beliefs. Or you might
feel very good about your new state of mind. We should be more
glad about our new beliefs than we are sad about our old beliefs. The
point is that Christian repentance does not focus on one's old mind,
or on feeling bad, sad, mad, or guilty about your previous beliefs and
behaviors. Rather, Christian repentance focuses on one's new mind,
one's new outlook, on the future not the past. Christians are not defined by their past. They are defined by the future that Christ has se-
cured for them, for us. We must not lament the past; rather, we must
celebrate the future. And how do we celebrate the future?

By believing, believing the Bible, believing God, believing Jesus.
To *believe* means to accept as true or real; to expect or suppose; to
think. To believe something is to assume that it is true, to be convinced that it is true and trustworthy. But it's still not a real belief
until you act on it. For instance, you might believe that a chair is
strong enough to support you. But that belief doesn't become a confirmed belief until you actually sit on it. By sitting on it you prove
the belief to be trustworthy. Sometimes we call that process of confirmation, that process of proving a belief "faith." Faith is the active
element of belief. Faith, actions of faithfulness, prove and establish
beliefs.

In support of this idea the Lectionary leads us to 1 Corinthians 7
where Paul wrote:

> "Only let each person lead the life that the Lord has assigned to him,
> and to which God has called him. This is my rule in all the churches"
> (v. 17).

Here Paul said that we are to practice faithfulness where we are, in
whatever situation we are currently in. We don't need to go somewhere else, we don't need any props. As the Nike ad says, "Just do
it®".

Verse 17 is one of the most important and least understood teachings of Jesus—and Paul. It's little understood because people are afraid of it. *Koinophobia* is the fear of being ordinary. More specifically, it is the fear of leading an ordinary, normal, common life. Teenagers today are often afraid of being ordinary, being normal. They dream of becoming famous, being great or different in some way. Our society is obsessed with being different, unique, and even famous. We are awash in movies and stories about superheros, of beating the odds. The idea of gambling is about beating the odds, about being the one-in-a-million who wins big. And gambling has become a major industry in America. It is so big that even governments are involved in sharing the profits. Lotteries and casinos are regulated, which means that they are taxed. The government gets a cut.

The psychology behind lotteries is the psychology of beating the odds, of being that one special person who wins big. Honestly, you are more likely to be struck by lightning than winning big. Of course, the lottery is structured so that there are many little wins, enough to keep people hoping—and playing.

Koinophobia is the opposite of faithfulness. To be faithful is to be like Jesus, to manifest His character qualities in your own life. A faithful society is where being like Jesus is common, ordinary. When most people make a serious effort to be like Jesus society becomes increasingly Christian—faithful. People become increasingly loving, joyful, peaceful, patient, kind, good, faithful, gentle, and self-controlled. Imagine how the world would be if most people made a serious effort to be like Jesus. What would it take for that to happen?

Do we need to eliminate slavery? Or eliminate poverty? Do we all have to don white robes and practice meditation? Or become vegetarians? Or monks? Or live in seclusion? Do we need to become missionaries and move to a foreign country? Do we have to go to seminary?

No! People don't have to do any of that! So what would it take? Seriously. Listen again to what Paul said:

"Was anyone at the time of his call already circumcised? Let him not seek to remove the marks of circumcision. Was anyone at the time of his call uncircumcised? Let him not seek circumcision. For neither circumcision counts for anything nor uncircumcision, but keeping the commandments of God. Each one should remain in the condition in which he was called. Were you a bondservant when called? Do not be concerned about it. (But if you can gain your freedom, avail yourself of the opportunity.) For he who was called in the Lord as a bondservant is a freedman of the Lord. Likewise he who was free when called is a bondservant of Christ. You were bought with a price; do not become bondservants of men. So, brothers, in whatever condition each was called, there let him remain with God" (vs. 18-24).

We don't have to do anything special. We just need to be ordinary Christians. We just need to love Jesus. And Paul defined that love like this:

"Love is patient and kind; love does not envy or boast; it is not arrogant or rude. It does not insist on its own way; it is not irritable or resentful; it does not rejoice at wrongdoing, but rejoices with the truth. Love bears all things, believes all things, hopes all things, endures all things" (1 Corinthians 13:4-7).

Let's be like Jesus.

GOD SPEAKS

15 "The Lord your God will raise up for you a prophet like me from among you, from your brothers—it is to him you shall listen— 16 just as you desired of the Lord your God at Horeb on the day of the assembly, when you said, 'Let me not hear again the voice of the Lord my God or see this great fire any more, lest I die.' 17 And the Lord said to me, 'They are right in what they have spoken. 18 I will raise up for them a prophet like you from among their brothers. And I will put my words in his mouth, and he shall speak to them all that I command him. 19 And whoever will not listen to my words that he shall speak in my name, I myself will require it of him. 20 But the prophet who presumes to speak a word in my name that I have not commanded him to speak, or who speaks in the name of other gods, that same prophet shall die.'   —Deuteronomy 18:15-20

21 And they went into Capernaum, and immediately on the Sabbath he entered the synagogue and was teaching. 22 And they were astonished at his teaching, for he taught them as one who had authority, and not as the scribes. 23 And immediately there was in their synagogue a man with an unclean spirit. And he cried out, 24 "What have you to do with us, Jesus of Nazareth? Have you come to destroy us? I know who you are—the Holy One of God." 25 But Jesus rebuked him, saying, "Be silent, and come out of him!" 26 And the unclean spirit, convulsing him and crying out with a loud voice, came out of him. 27 And they were all amazed, so that they questioned among themselves, saying, "What is this? A new teaching with authority! He commands even the unclean spirits, and they obey him." 28 And at once his fame spread everywhere throughout all the surrounding region of Galilee.   —Mark 1:21-28

Moses was telling Israel what God would do in the future. God had brought Israel out of Egypt, provided the Ten Commandments, and was further instructing Israel on the kind of society He was creating for them. Deuteronomy is known as the book of the law because it describes how Israel was to live, and cautioned Israel not to imitate the nations that God was displacing.

It is important for us to understand this because it runs counter to our current woke culture where everyone and every society is supposed to be equal. God doesn't believe in that kind of equality because He knows that some cultures, some ways of being, are better than others. Some ways of being human are healthier, happier, more productive, more loving, and can provide greater human flourishing than others. We can see this in the verses just before today's reading:

> "When you come into the land that the Lord your God is giving you, you shall not learn to follow the abominable practices of those nations. There shall not be found among you anyone who burns his son or his daughter as an offering, anyone who practices divination or tells fortunes or interprets omens, or a sorcerer or a charmer or a medium or a necromancer or one who inquires of the dead, for whoever does these things is an abomination to the Lord" (Deuteronomy 18:9-12).

At this point Moses said that God would provide another prophet, another law giver like himself, like Moses, who would provide further instruction at that time. The truth is that there were then a succession of prophets who provided guidance to Israel over the next couple thousand years. Those prophets and their words are recorded in the Bible. And because those prophets were in the future beyond Moses, Moses provided some instruction on how to identify them; so that Israel could tell the difference between true prophets and false prophets, true teaching from false teaching.

The first thing that Moses said was that true prophets would come from the people of Israel. They would be like Moses; they would not be foreigners or aliens. They would be found among God's people. And those prophets would speak for God and would not contradict anything that God or Moses had already said. There would always be continuity in God's message. And if any so called prophet spoke anything that conflicted with God's message, that prophet "shall die." Death of the prophet is the consequence for speaking against God, saying something that was opposed to God's message given to Moses, given in the Bible. God always speaks the truth, even when people don't recognize it.

But this raises a question: how can people recognize God's truth? And this question applies equally to people who do know God's truth and to people who don't know God's truth. It applies to everyone.

> "Jesus said to the Jews who had believed him, 'If you abide in my word, you are truly my disciples, and you will know the truth, and the truth will set you free.'" (John 18:31-32).

To whom was Jesus speaking? To those who believed Him. So, is believing in Jesus enough to guarantee that we will recognize God's truth? No. There is a condition: *if you abide in my word,* said Jesus. In the Greek the word translated as *if* could also be translated as *when,* i.e., *when* you abide in my word. So, in order to recognize God's truth we must abide in Jesus' word. We must live in obedience to Jesus. And all who abide in Jesus' word are true disciples.

To be a disciple is to live with a discipline, a rule, a practice. Disciples endeavor to be like their master, to inhabit His beliefs and character. Then, as disciples do this, they will come to know God's truth.

God's truth is not simply a doctrine, not a principle, or a code of ethics. God's truth is a Person. Jesus also said,

> "I am the way, and the truth, and the life. No one comes to the Father except through me" (John 14:6).

Jesus Christ is the truth that speaks, which means that all truth is God's truth. Wherever truth is found, it's source is God through Jesus, who sent the Holy Spirit. Of course, some doctrine, some teaching is truth, some is not. Some principles are right, some are wrong. And some ethical systems are better than others. Not everyone knows the truth, but everyone can know Him if/when (or *as*) they abide in Him.

Early in the gospel, Mark tells a story about a time when Jesus went to Capernaum. Capernaum was in the far north of Israel, in Samaria, on the sea of Galilee. Jesus entered a synagogue in Capernaum, which was at the opposite end of Israel from Jerusalem, in the north. Jesus began teaching at the Capernaum synagogue, and the Capernaumites

> "were astonished at his teaching, for he taught them as one who had authority, and not as the scribes" (v. 22).

Jesus was teaching something different from what the Capernaumite scribes had been teaching. Keep in mind that Capernaum was in the northern part of Samaria. So while Jesus was teaching something different from what the Capernaumites were used to, a local Capernaumite in the congregation began making a fuss. Mark said that he had an "unclean heart." Likely, he was objecting. We don't know exactly what happened, but it seems that he interrupted Jesus. A local person interrupted Jesus, a traveling Rabbi who was teaching something unexpected by the locals. The local Capernaumite said that Jesus' teaching had nothing to do with them, with Capernaum. And asked, "Have you come to destroy us?" (v. 24).

That's an odd question, unless it had to do with the long standing, historical, religious feud between Israel and Samaria. Remember that Jesus' ministry was aimed at healing that conflict, that disagreement. The man who had objected to Jesus, who had the unclean heart then recognized Jesus as "the Holy One of God" (v. 24). Here we see that, although the Samaritans did not agree with the Jerusalem Israelites about a lot of things, this local man, no doubt a Samaritan, with the unclean heart, recognized Jesus as the Holy One of God. This means that people don't have to be perfectly faithful, or know all the right doctrines and beliefs about God, in order to recognized the truth of Jesus Christ.

For instance, a guy from a different church from the other side of town who didn't believe like we believe can recognize the truth of Jesus Christ. He can know that Jesus was speaking God's words.

Which is interesting because Jesus immediately rebuked him. Did the rebuke change the guy's mind about Jesus? No! As the Capernaumite recognized the truth of Jesus Christ, Jesus told him to shut up! Jesus didn't try to reason with the guy. Jesus did not deny that He had come to destroy, or that He was the Holy One of God *because* Jesus is the Holy One of God, and He did come to destroy—but to destroy what? Jesus did not come to destroy people. People are not the enemies of the gospel. According to Paul, Ephesians 6:12,

> "For we do not wrestle against flesh and blood, but against the rulers, against the authorities, against the cosmic powers over this present darkness, against the spiritual forces of evil in the heavenly places."

Jesus came to break the hold that unclean spirits had/have on people. So, Jesus commanded the unclean spirit to come out of the man. And it did "convulsing him and crying out with a loud voice" (v. 26). That's amazing. The unclean spirit obeyed Jesus! Notice also the response of the people, the Samaritans:

> "What is this? A new teaching with authority! He commands even the unclean spirits, and they obey him" (v. 27).

They were amazed by what Jesus said and how He said it—His authority. But it wasn't that Jesus acted tough. The thing that impressed them was that the unclean spirit obeyed Jesus.

For a very long time people have believed that the basic struggle in this world is between good spirits and bad spirits, between good and evil. And because the struggle has continued throughout history people conclude that good and evil must be fairly equally matched, equally strong. Otherwise one or the other would have prevailed. But what they witnessed that day was that Jesus was in command of both good and evil spirits. The evil spirit, the unclean spirit, obeyed Jesus.

This means that Jesus Christ is sovereign. He is in control. The obedience of the unclean spirit proved Jesus' authority. His authority was more than words. It was/is real! The story established Jesus authority, that's the point.

"And at once his fame spread everywhere throughout all the surrounding region of Galilee" (v. 28).

So, did *everyone* immediately believe the truth about Jesus Christ? No. Some did and some didn't. What was the difference? Why do some hear and some don't? Why do some believe and some don't?

These are the wrong questions. They are wrong because their intent is to judge others. They are other-directed questions. They ask, *What's the matter with those unbelievers?!*

The real question is: do "I" (you) hear Jesus? Do "I" (you) believe? The question is personal: *how do **we** recognize the truth when we hear it?* It's not about other people, the real question is about us.

"But now I am going to him who sent me, and none of you asks me, 'Where are you going?' But because I have said these things to you, sorrow has filled your heart. Nevertheless, I tell you the truth: it is to your advantage that I go away, for if I do not go away, the Helper will not come to you. But if I go, I will send him to you. And when he comes, he will convict the world concerning sin and righteousness and judgment: concerning sin, because they do not believe in me; concerning righteousness, because I go to the Father, and you will see me no longer; concerning judgment, because the ruler of this world is judged. I still have many things to say to you, but you cannot bear them now. When the Spirit of truth comes, he will guide you into all the truth, for he will not speak on his own authority, but whatever he hears he will speak, and he will declare to you the things that are to come. He will glorify me, for he will take what is mine and declare it to you. All that the Father has is mine; therefore I said that he will take what is mine and declare it to you" (John 16:5-15).

Here's the point: people do not recognize the truth because they/we are not able. Rather, it is the Holy Spirit, the Advocate, the Helper, the Paraclete, in us who recognizes the truth. Jesus sent the Holy Spirit to inhabit us. And when He does, Jesus speaks and it is the Holy Spirit in us who hears Him.

And how do we make that happen? *We* don't. *He* does. It's not in our control. We are in His control. This is the practical understanding of God's sovereignty. In truth we all hear God speaking, but we are not all listening. People need to learn how to listen. It's not that what God says is difficult to hear. It's that people don't like what God has to say. Listening takes practice, and we practice by reading the Bible, by praying, by serving, by engaging God's Word. Practice makes perfect.

Listen up!

POSSESSION

Do you not know? Do you not hear? Has it not been told you from the beginning? Have you not understood from the foundations of the earth? 22 It is he who sits above the circle of the earth, and its inhabitants are like grasshoppers; who stretches out the heavens like a curtain, and spreads them like a tent to dwell in; 23 who brings princes to nothing, and makes the rulers of the earth as emptiness. 24 Scarcely are they planted, scarcely sown, scarcely has their stem taken root in the earth, when he blows on them, and they wither, and the tempest carries them off like stubble. 25 To whom then will you compare me, that I should be like him? says the Holy One. 26 Lift up your eyes on high and see: who created these? He who brings out their host by number, calling them all by name; by the greatness of his might and because he is strong in power, not one is missing. 27 Why do you say, O Jacob, and speak, O Israel, "My way is hidden from the Lord, and my right is disregarded by my God"? 28 Have you not known? Have you not heard? The Lord is the everlasting God, the Creator of the ends of the earth. He does not faint or grow weary; his understanding is unsearchable. 29 He gives power to the faint, and to him who has no might he increases strength. 30 Even youths shall faint and be weary, and young men shall fall exhausted; 31 but they who wait for the Lord shall renew their strength; they shall mount up with wings like eagles; they shall run and not be weary; they shall walk and not faint. —Isaiah 40:21-31

29 And immediately he left the synagogue and entered the house of Simon and Andrew, with James and John. 30 Now Simon's mother-in-law lay ill with a fever, and immediately they told him about her. 31 And he came and took her by the hand and lifted her up, and the fever left her, and she began to serve them. 32 That evening at sundown they brought to him all who were sick or oppressed by demons. 33 And the whole city was gathered together at the door. 34 And he healed many who were sick with various diseases, and cast out many demons. And he would not permit the demons to speak, because they knew him. 35 And rising very early in the morning, while it was still dark, he departed and went out to a desolate place, and there he prayed. 36 And Simon and those who were with him searched for him, 37 and they found him and said to him, "Everyone is looking for you." 38 And he said to them, "Let us go on to the next towns, that I may preach there also, for that is why I came out." 39 And he went throughout all Galilee, preaching in their synagogues and casting out demons.   *—Mark 1:29-39*

Isaiah 40 is a famous, often quoted chapter of the Bible. We need see it all in context. It begins, "Comfort, comfort my people, says your God." Isaiah was prophesying God's forgiveness, telling Israel that her warfare had ended, that her iniquity was pardoned, and that God knew that Israel had suffered "double for all her sins." Verse 3 is very familiar,

> "A voice cries: 'In the wilderness prepare the way of the Lord; make straight in the desert a highway for our God.'"

Verse 6 continues,

> "A voice says, 'Cry!' And I said, 'What shall I cry?' All flesh is grass, and all its beauty is like the flower of the field. The grass withers, the flower fades when the breath of the Lord blows on it."

Human life is but a moment. It's brief, and fades like flowers in the Fall. In contrast, God is great! Verse 10 speaks of God:

> "Behold, the Lord God comes with might, and his arm rules for him; behold, his reward is with him, and his recompense before him. He will tend his flock like a shepherd; he will gather the lambs in his arms; he will carry them in his bosom, and gently lead those that are with young."

The next few verses are reminiscent of Job when Isaiah said:

> "Who has measured the Spirit of the Lord, or what man shows him his counsel? Whom did (God) consult, and who made him under-

stand? Who taught him the path of justice, and taught him knowledge, and showed him the way of understanding? Behold, the nations are like a drop from a bucket, and are accounted as the dust on
the scales; behold, (God) takes up the coastlands like fine dust."

God complains that Israel worships idols made of gold rather
than the only real God who made everything. In verse 21, then, Isaiah, speaking for God, calls people *idiots*. God calls people who worship idols *idiots*! He knows that people are familiar with Him, the
God of the Bible (of his day). God looks upon people as insects, as
little creatures without power or significance compared to Himself.
He chastises Israel for the foolishness of idol worship, of not knowing the difference between trinkets and God. And Isaiah concludes
this section by touting God's power.

> "Have you not known? Have you not heard? He does not faint or
> grow weary; his understanding is unsearchable. He gives power to
> the faint, and to him who has no might he increases strength. Even
> youths shall faint and be weary, and young men shall fall exhausted;
> but they who wait for the Lord shall renew their strength; they shall
> mount up with wings like eagles; they shall run and not be weary;
> they shall walk and not faint" (vs. 28-31).

It's a grand section of Scripture that gives us hope and encouragement because, in spite of our sin and insignificance, God provides
strength, hope, purpose, and direction to His people. So, if people
have strength, hope, purpose, and direction, it is because God has
given it to them.

And how does God give people strength, hope, purpose, and direction? He inhabits them. He creates life habits in them that produce strength, hope, purpose, and direction. And this is precisely
what Jesus was doing.

Mark tells us about Jesus' visit to Capernaum. He preached in the
local synagogue, and created a stir.

> "And immediately he left the synagogue and entered the house of Si-
> mon and Andrew" (v. 29).

Simon Peter's mother-in-law was sick with a fever, and Jesus healed her. So they brought lots of sick people to Jesus. They also brought people who were oppressed by demons.

The idea of demon possession has a long and complex history. Exactly what it is, is unknown because the Greek word is general and not specific. It includes a lot of different ideas. The general sense is that it indicates someone who is not in their "right mind." It is similar yet different than delirium that accompanies high fever and other kinds of illnesses. By saying that it indicates someone who is not in their "right mind" suggests that there is a "right mind" that people can be in. And the gospel is about returning people to their "right mind," and that "right mind" is the mind of Jesus Christ.

There are a lot of different words in Greek that are translated as *mind*. Depending on its usage *heart* can mean *mind*, where the heart is thought of as the center of one's being. There is also a word that indicates a "gut feeling," which also refers to mind. Nonetheless, Christ's mission of salvation, redemption, and reconciliation is all about getting people into their "right mind." It's about seeing the world rightly, seeing it though God's eyes. It's about knowing the world, knowing life like God knows it.

Jesus was in Capernaum, an historic town in Samaria, and because Jesus' mission included healing the conflict between Jerusalem and Samaria. While He was there Jesus healed people—likely, Samaritans—of demon possession. And how did He do that?

Possession means ownership. So we could say that the demons claimed possession of people, possession of the Samaritans. And Paul tells us that Jesus purchased His people, and by purchasing them He saved them out of demon possession into His possession. Here's how Paul described it:

"Christ redeemed us from the curse of the law" (Galatians 3:13).

To redeem is to obtain possession of something. You don't have or own it, and when it is redeemed you do have or own it. The Bible reminds us that Jesus purchased a people for His own possession.

To purchase something is to take possession of it, to own it. It no longer belongs to the seller. The Bible says that Christ has paid the price for His people. He bought us. He owns us. His purchase of His people has been paid in full. We are His possession. He can do with us whatever He wants with us. And He wants our health, happiness, wholeness. He wants us to live in our "right mind," which is His mind.

Jesus "would not permit the demons to speak, because they knew him" (v. 34). This is quite curious. It's an odd detail. So why not let the demons speak? There could be several reasons Jesus did not allow the demons to speak. One reason He stated: "because they knew him." One demon had previously identified Jesus as the "Holy one of God." So they were aware of His divine status. They knew and believed that He was the Son of God. Demons are minions of Satan, and Satan is the father of lies. So demons are liars.

One of the most important things Jesus did was to prevent the spread of false information. He knew that if the demons could speak, they would be able to spread lies and chaos. By not permitting them to speak, Jesus was able to keep confusion and false information about Him to a minimum. If they could speak, knowing that He was the holy one of God, they could use that truth to foment their lies. Lies always work best when they are hidden in statements that are true. Rat poison is 99.4% rat food to insure that the rats will eat it. By forbidding them to speak He also demonstrated His authority over them.

In the midst of all of this healing and demon management Jesus found time to pray.

> "And rising very early in the morning, while it was still dark, he departed and went out to a desolate place, and there he prayed." (v. 35).

Jesus' ministry was busy and intense and tiring; He needed rest. So He went off by Himself to pray. He was tired and needed rest so He prayed. There is an important lesson here: Prayer is not simply rest. He didn't simply take a "prayer nap." Sure, He was tired, and no doubt slept some. But we must not conflate prayer with sleep. He needed more than sleep. He needed the refreshment of prayer.

Prayer is not an inactivity like recharging your batteries. Sleep does that, but sleep is not prayer. Prayer is an active involvement with God, an active conversation wherein the person who prays finds new encouragement, enthusiasm, and new motivation for the accomplishment of God's will in their life. That's what Jesus needed after dealing with a myriad of demons. Interacting with demons—liars—is exhausting. So, Jesus needed some down time, some alone time, some rest. But He also needed God's encouragement, enthusiasm, and motivation to continue. And He got it! Which meant that He could continue

> "throughout all Galilee, preaching in their synagogues and casting out demons (v. 39)."

He was ministering to and correcting Samaritans in Galilee, healing the historic breach between Jerusalem and Samaria.

> "For I am not ashamed of the gospel, for it is the power of God for salvation to everyone who believes, to the Jew first and also to the Greek" (Romans 1:16).

The Samaritans were Jewish, so Jesus was first healing the ancient divisions among the Jews, as Paul said. Next He would turn His attention to the Greeks, to the Gentiles, to the rest of the world. That's us. Praise God!

TRANSITION

Therefore, having this ministry by the mercy of God, we do not lose heart. 2 But we have renounced disgraceful, underhanded ways. We refuse to practice cunning or to tamper with God's word, but by the open statement of the truth we would commend ourselves to everyone's conscience in the sight of God. 3 And even if our gospel is veiled, it is veiled to those who are perishing. 4 In their case the god of this world has blinded the minds of the unbelievers, to keep them from seeing the light of the gospel of the glory of Christ, who is the image of God. 5 For what we proclaim is not ourselves, but Jesus Christ as Lord, with ourselves as your servants for Jesus' sake. 6 For God, who said, "Let light shine out of darkness," has shone in our hearts to give the light of the knowledge of the glory of God in the face of Jesus Christ.   *—2 Corinthians 4:1-6*

2 And after six days Jesus took with him Peter and James and John, and led them up a high mountain by themselves. And he was transfigured before them, 3 and his clothes became radiant, intensely white, as no one on earth could bleach them. 4 And there appeared to them Elijah with Moses, and they were talking with Jesus. 5 And Peter said to Jesus, "Rabbi, it is good that we are here. Let us make three tents, one for you and one for Moses and one for Elijah." 6 For he did not know what to say, for they were terrified. 7 And a cloud overshadowed them, and a voice came out of the cloud, "This is my beloved Son; listen to him." 8 And suddenly, looking around, they no longer saw anyone with them but Jesus only. 9 And as they were coming down the mountain, he charged them to tell no one what they had seen, until the Son of Man had risen from the dead.   *—Mark 9:2-9*

The theologians tell us that the transfiguration was a theophany. Theologians like to use fancy words. But when something out of the ordinary happens we need to use out of the ordinary words to describe it accurately. A theophany is a manifestation of God that is discernible to human beings. The easiest way to understand it is that it is a visible appearance of God, often, but not always, in human form. The Old Testament is filled with references to God appearing, or God speaking to someone. These occurrences are theophanies.

But God doesn't always appear in a "visible" form. Sometimes people hear a "still small voice." To ask whether it is a real voice, or a thought, is to ask the wrong question. The issue is not *how* God's voice is manifested to people. The issue is the *message* God communicates. It doesn't matter how it is communicated. The same thing can be said of a vision. Vision can involve physical eyeballs, but it can also just be a brain thing. Vision is defined as the faculty of sight; discernment, perception, foresight. A vision can be something seen in a dream, trance, or ecstasy; a supernatural communique. A thought or insight about something can also be described as a vision.

But the thing that makes it a theophany is that it is God conceived, God created, and God manifested. A theophany is about God. Some theologians like to distinguish between theophanies and Christophanies, where theophanies are about God, and Christophanies are about Christ. But as evangelical Christians we know that Jesus Christ is God manifest in the flesh. So the difference doesn't really make any difference.

Are theophanies rare? Again this is the wrong way to ask the question. Just because people don't see something doesn't mean that something isn't there. Most people don't think about God or Jesus much, so they don't notice the presence of God in Christ.

Nonetheless, the essential teaching of Christianity is "Immanuel!" God with us. God is with us always. God in Christ is actively involved in the world right now, and always. That's the message of the New Testament. And that means that our lives are always in a theophany or Christophany. God is present. God is communicating to us always, 24/7. But most people aren't listening. Most people aren't interested. So God's presence goes unnoticed. It's ignored. Most people live in a state of divine ignore-ance.

So, one day Jesus took Peter, James, and John up a high mountain to pray. And something weird happened. Jesus'

> "clothes became radiant, intensely white, as no one on earth could bleach them. And there appeared to them Elijah with Moses, and they were talking with Jesus" (vs. 3-4).

All we know about it is this description, this vision or story of what happened that day. As they were praying they began to see things. Were the things they saw real or imaginary? What sort of vision were they having? Again, the issue is not *how* God communicates to people. The issue is the *message* that God communicates. It doesn't matter how it is communicated. So, what was the message?

White robes signify purity. The disciples became aware of Jesus' purity in a new way, a deeper way, a more meaningful way than they had previously understood. They suddenly realized that Jesus was a very special, a very pure Person. We usually associate this with Jesus' divinity. Maybe before this they understood Jesus to be a great teacher, even a prophet. But this vision of the bright whiteness of His robes communicated His divinity. And this insight about Jesus is actually a very big deal.

Then they noticed that Jesus was talking to Elijah and Moses. This is a bit weird because Elijah and Moses had been dead for a long time, and they had no photos of them. So, how did they know it was Elijah and Moses? What we don't know is how they knew. But what we do know is that they identified them as Elijah and Moses. That was the *message* that they communicated to the other disciples when they came down from the mountain. The issue is not *how* God communicates to people. The issue is the *message* God communicates. It doesn't matter how it is communicated. So, what is the message?

Moses was the giver of the law and Elijah was a prophet. Traditionally they are understood to represent the law and prophets, which is another way to indicate the Bible. The Old Testament was often referred to as the law and the prophets. So, Jesus was in discussion with the law and the prophets, the Old Testament.

It means that the words or message of Jesus was on a par with the law and the prophets. Again, the traditional understanding of the transfiguration was that the message of Jesus Christ superseded the law and the prophets. Or we could say that the message and teaching of Jesus was—is—divinely inspired.

Then Peter sticks his foot in it.

> "Rabbi, it is good that we are here. Let us make three tents, one for you and one for Moses and one for Elijah' (v. 5).

James, and John were terrified and didn't know what to do or say. But Peter thought that they should make a shrine, or three shrines, one for each. And by saying this Peter acknowledged that Jesus was on a par with Moses and Elijah.

But turning the mountain experience into a shrine was the wrong response. And to correct the wrong response,

> "a cloud overshadowed them, and a voice came out of the cloud" (v. 7).

They didn't make shrines because the cloud overshadowed that idea. In the Old Testament God often appeared as a cloud or in the clouds. So the cloud represents God, who said: *Peter, you dummy. Quit trying to figure it out on you own. Just listen to Jesus.* So, the whole message of the transfiguration was that Jesus is divine, so listen to Him.

> "And suddenly, looking around, they no longer saw anyone with them but Jesus only" (v. 8).

Was it a dream? Was it a vision? Did it actually happen? The issue is not *how* God communicates to people. The issue is the *message* God communicates. It doesn't matter how it is communicated. What matters is the message. All of this is weird enough, but Jesus then makes the whole thing even more weird.

> "And as they were coming down the mountain, he charged them to tell no one what they had seen, until the Son of Man had risen from the dead (v. 9)."

Don't tell anyone!? Jesus told them to keep it a secret for a while. Until the Son of Man had *risen from the dead.* This is chapter 9 of Mark, so we are half way though Mark's Jesus' story. The disciples at this point had no idea about what lay ahead for them, or for Jesus. So they simply would not have had any understanding about rising from the dead. They knew that Jesus was referred to as the Son of Man, but He wasn't dead. The whole experience was weird, from beginning to end. And so the theologians call this episode, this transfiguration, a mystery. Mysteries are weird, unexplainable.

The Lectionary then couples this story with 2 Corinthians 4:1-6. These few verses in 2 Corinthians are about the light of the gospel. By coupling these stories together, the Lord is telling us to not get caught up in the mystery, in the weirdness or the darkness, the unintelligibility of the transfiguration.

People love to spend their time figuring out mysteries, solving puzzles, and imagining all sorts of weird things. We all love it! Just look at our books and movies and TV shows. Our scientists are desperately trying to figure out how we can travel in space, and it's quite puzzling. But God says that none of this speculation, this imagining, is worth anything. Paul suggests that it is a waste of time.

The ministry of the gospel is to change hearts and minds, to turn people from trivial, meaningless, and mysterious pursuits to the discovery of God's truth in Jesus Christ. But changing hearts and minds is hard. So Paul said, "do not lose heart" (v. 1). Don't give up.

The way to change hearts and minds is to model right living. Righteousness is compelling. When people see righteousness it convicts them, it shows them up as not being righteous themselves. In the light we see our flaws. Paul is saying that Christianity is not mysterious, even though there are things we don't understand. Mysteries are shrouded in darkness, but the gospel brings light, which dispels the darkness.

We are not to engage in disgraceful or underhanded ways. We should not engage in secret plans or plots to get our own way. We should always operate above board, in the open, and work without hidden schemes. So Christians are not to be cunning. To be cunning is to be crafty by using special or secret skills or knowledge. To be cunning is to be tricky and wiley. Christianity is not about any of that kind of stuff.

Nor are we to tamper with God's Word. Don't try to make the Bible say what you want it to say. Rather, let it say what God wants it to say. We should work "by the open statement of the truth" (v. 2). And doing so

> "we would commend ourselves to everyone's conscience in the sight of God" (v. 2).

Then Paul said,

> "And even if our gospel is veiled, it is veiled to those who are perishing." (v. 3).

The veiling of the gospel is interesting. The context is Exodus 34:33-35:

> "And when Moses had finished speaking with them, he put a veil over his face. Whenever Moses went in before the Lord to speak with him, he would remove the veil, until he came out. And when he came out and told the people of Israel what he was commanded, the people of Israel would see the face of Moses, that the skin of Moses' face was shining. And Moses would put the veil over his face again, until he went in to speak with him."

Moses' face was shining, similarly Jesus' garments were radiant and intensely white. This is the same truth described differently in the Old Testament than in the New Testament. Paul said that the whole truth was veiled or not fully disclosed in the Old Testament because the world was not ready to hear it.

What was veiled in the Old Testament was the truth that the law and the prophets, the temple and the traditions, were not able to convey the whole truth; that Jerusalem and the Temple would end in ruin. The whole truth would have to wait for the advent of Jesus Christ.

In 2 Corinthians 3:13-16 Paul said,

> "Not like Moses, who would put a veil over his face so that the Israelites might not gaze at the outcome of what was being brought to

an end. But their minds were hardened. For to this day, when they read the old covenant, that same veil remains unlifted, because only through Christ is it taken away. Yes, to this day whenever Moses is read a veil lies over their hearts. But when one turns to the Lord, the veil is removed."

In Christ the veil is lifted and the whole truth is revealed. And the whole truth was not the end destruction of all things, though Jerusalem and the Temple would be destroyed. And they were destroyed forty years after Jesus death. Rather, the whole truth, which is still being unfolded in history, is that God was/is in the process of renewing the world in the likeness of Jesus Christ. And He's not done.

CONCORDAT

8 Then God said to Noah and to his sons with him, 9 "Behold, I establish my covenant with you and your offspring after you, 10 and with every living creature that is with you, the birds, the livestock, and every beast of the earth with you, as many as came out of the ark; it is for every beast of the earth. 11 I establish my covenant with you, that never again shall all flesh be cut off by the waters of the flood, and never again shall there be a flood to destroy the earth." 12 And God said, "This is the sign of the covenant that I make between me and you and every living creature that is with you, for all future generations: 13 I have set my bow in the cloud, and it shall be a sign of the covenant between me and the earth. 14 When I bring clouds over the earth and the bow is seen in the clouds, 15 I will remember my covenant that is between me and you and every living creature of all flesh. And the waters shall never again become a flood to destroy all flesh. 16 When the bow is in the clouds, I will see it and remember the everlasting covenant between God and every living creature of all flesh that is on the earth." 17 God said to Noah, "This is the sign of the covenant that I have established between me and all flesh that is on the earth."   —Genesis 9:8-17*

18 For Christ also suffered once for sins, the righteous for the unrighteous, that he might bring us to God, being put to death in the flesh but made alive in the spirit, 19 in which he went and proclaimed to the spirits in prison, 20 because they formerly did not obey, when God's patience waited in the days of Noah, while the ark was being prepared, in which a few, that is, eight persons, were brought safely through water. 21 Baptism, which corresponds to this, now saves you, not as a removal of dirt from the body but as an appeal to God for a good conscience, through the resurrection of Jesus Christ, 22 who has gone into heaven and is at the right hand of God,

with angels, authorities, and powers having been subjected to him.
— 1 Peter 3:18-22

The story of Adam and Eve in the Garden is both long and complex, and at the same time short and simple. We don't know how long Adam and Eve were in the Garden before the Fall. But it seems that it wasn't very long. The precise length of time is immaterial. It's not part of the biblical story. Nonetheless, they sinned. Cain slew Able. Lamech built cities. People lived very long lives, during which sin and corruption increased; and Noah built the Ark. The great flood came and destroyed that civilization, leaving only Noah and his family. The story for today picks up at this point. And God said,

> "Behold, I establish my covenant with you…" (v. 8).

A covenant is an agreement. Unlike a contract, which is an agreement between equals, a covenant is an agreement established by a superior with an inferior. God is the superior and we are the inferiors to the agreement. A covenant is like a peace treaty following a war, where the victor sets the terms of the agreement and the vanquished agrees to the terms, or the war continues. While is seems like a one-sided agreement, it's not. If the loser doesn't agree or violates the terms, the agreement becomes void, and the war continues. Peace requires both sides to honor the agreement.

God didn't start the war, but was at war with human civilization before the Flood, and the Flood proved to be the decisive event. That entire civilization was destroyed. God won! God's covenant with Noah is really a covenant with the whole earth. Who are the parties to the covenant?

> "Behold, I establish my covenant with you and your offspring after you, and with every living creature that is with you, the birds, the livestock, and every beast of the earth with you, as many as came out of the ark; it is for every beast of the earth" (vs. 9-10).

God's covenant is with life itself, with Noah and his family, of course, but also with every living creature. Why does God include every living creature? Why not just make the covenant with people? The reason is because God is holy, and God is concerned about the holiness of the earth. God knows that human life depends on other animals for food, labor, clothing, shelter, etc. The earth provides the context for human life, and apart from our earthly context, our earthly habitat, human life is not possible. All life is interdependent. So God's covenant includes human beings and our context, our entire habitat, everything necessary for life.

In the contemporary idiom, God is holistic. Holism is the idea that the world and nature are correctly understood in terms of interacting organisms, that life itself emerges from a complex of interacting parts or systems. Here we see that at the very beginning of the biblical story God's holiness, God's wholeness. God's holistic perspective and concern is, at its root, a very modern or contemporary idea.

The term *holism* was coined by Jan Smuts (1870–1950) in his 1926 book *Holism and Evolution.*

> "Holism is the interdisciplinary idea that systems possess properties as wholes apart from the properties of their component parts. The concept of holism informs the methodology for a broad array of scientific fields and lifestyle practices. When applications of holism are said to reveal properties of a whole system beyond those of its parts, these qualities are referred to as emergent properties of that system" (from *Wikipedia*).

Following the flood, God promised not to destroy human culture again, at least not by flood. And God established the rainbow as a sign of His promise. The important thing about God's covenant with Noah is that it binds all human beings. It was not just between God and Noah's family, but was between God and all life on earth. That's important because it means that God's covenant is universal; everyone and every thing is involved.

We are all descendants of Adam and Eve, and we are all descendants of Noah. We are all family, kin. The human race is one family, one kind, one self-similar set. Self-similarity is a mathematical term. Snow flakes are an example of self-similarity. Every snow flake is included in what we call snow, yet every individual flake is unique. Humanity is also self-similar. We are all human, and we are each unique.

This idea, found in the story of Noah and the flood, is picked up by Peter. And Peter applies it to the new life brought by Christ. Peter understood that Jesus Christ was bringing a new kind of human being to life on earth. No longer *homo sapaien*, but in Christ people are becoming *homo Christos*. And, just as God's covenant with Noah included all human life, so God's covenant with Jesus Christ includes all human life in Christ. This does not mean that everyone alive automatically becomes a Christian. Peter was not teaching universalism. What it does mean is that God's intention is to include all people in Christ, except those who exclude themselves. Inclusion, therefore, requires our individual consent and agreement, or not.

The general tenor of God's covenant has remained unchanged throughout all time and history. Yes, the covenant has gone through many iterations with Abraham, Moses, Samuel, David, and the kings, etc. And now with Jesus Christ. But throughout all of this, God remains the superior who is making an agreement with an inferior— us. God sets the terms of the agreement and we agree, or not. If we agree, God's war with us ends. If we don't agree, His war with us continues. That's the essence of the covenant.

Peter was ministering and writing in these few verses about baptism. It was a few years after Jesus had spoken. Why focus on baptism? Because baptism is the initiating sacrament, the initiating covenant event. Our individual participation in God's covenant is acknowledged by our baptism.

Before the modern idea of signing on the dotted line as a way to seal agreements, people used other methods of formal agreement acknowledgment. American Indians used the idea of blood brothers; voluntarily cutting themselves and mingling their blood. In the old west a handshake sealed the deal. Baptism is a similar kind of thing. To be baptized is to become a party to the covenant. It's a kind of "joining the club." To be baptized is to become a formal member of Christ's church, Christ's body on earth.

In order to demonstrate that God's grace is freely given, and not dependent on works, to demonstrate that we do not earn our way into God's covenant, we baptize infants. God's gift of free grace comes to this world unbidden. God simply grants His grace, His forgiveness, to all humanity as a class action. This free gift of grace, granted freely to all humanity by God through Jesus Christ means that all humanity is included in God's covenant. Keep in mind that it is God's covenant and that He is the superior who sets the terms of the covenant, and we are the inferiors who now must agree and abide by the terms He has set.

The proverbial "ball" is now in our court. We are all included in God's covenant. We didn't ask to be included, and we didn't do anything that would merit our inclusion. Nonetheless, we are all included. *Unless* we choose not to comply with God. Unless we decide that we don't agree with God and His covenant. People are free to disregard God's covenant, but people are not free to escape the consequences of their own decisions and behavior.

If you have been baptized, you are formally under God's covenant. If you have not been baptized, you are informally under God's covenant. If you are a human being, you are faced with God's covenant because God is at war with humanity. God didn't start the war, Satan did. But God will finish it.

Baptism is the way that signifies our personal agreement with the terms of God's covenant. But the sacrament of baptism is not the end of the matter. It's the beginning. Baptism brings us into God's fold where we then practice or live out the terms of God's covenant. God brings new life to humanity, to individuals, through Jesus Christ. People are born, Christians are born again. And that new life is to be a life of love lived in forgiveness, in Christ.

God grants forgiveness through Jesus Christ, *because* of Jesus Christ. And the forgiveness that we get is the forgiveness that we give others. We get what we give. It would be nice is forgiveness were just a "one and done" thing, but it's not. And it's not because we continue to sin. And because we continue to sin, we continue to need God's forgiveness. And because other people continue to sin we need to continue to forgive other people. Again, the forgiveness that we get is commensurate with the forgiveness that we give. Jesus said,

"if you forgive others their trespasses, your heavenly Father will also forgive you, but if you do not forgive others their trespasses, neither will your Father forgive your trespasses" (Matthew 6:14-15).

So baptism is necessary for our salvation, but not sufficient. Baptism is not the end, it's the beginning. And that is why infant baptism requires confirmation. This is where many churches have dropped the ball. Confirmation is an educational process wherein those who were baptized as an infant learn about Christianity and then choose to own the covenant for themselves.

I've taught many confirmation classes over the decades, and even where churches have a strong tradition of confirmation, many of the kids who participate are not there because they want to be. Rather, they are there because their parents told them that have to be there. And that is the wrong motivation. You can't be a Christian because your parents want you to be. You have to want it yourself.

Churches and Christians across the board need to reengage the confirmation process, whether people are baptized as adults or infants. Christianity has been around for a long time, and its history is important. Christian history is God's ongoing story in the world. Confirmation is an educational process that helps Christians understand and mature in the faith. It's a life long process, not something that people can graduate from. Apart from confirmation, a process of education and sanctification, Christians tend to remain immature. It doesn't need to be a formal program of the church, though that can help. But it does need to be a serious effort by individual Christians.

Maybe we should call it *conformation* rather than confirmation because as Christians we are called to conform to Christ, to imitate Christ as best we can with the guidance of God's Holy Spirit.

RIGHTEOUS FAITH

*When Abram was ninety-nine years old the Lord appeared to
Abram and said to him, "I am God Almighty; walk before me, and
be blameless, 2 that I may make my covenant between me and you,
and may multiply you greatly." 3 Then Abram fell on his face. And
God said to him, 4 "Behold, my covenant is with you, and you shall
be the father of a multitude of nations. 5 No longer shall your name
be called Abram, but your name shall be Abraham, for I have made
you the father of a multitude of nations. 6 I will make you exceedingly fruitful, and I will make you into nations, and kings shall come
from you. 7 And I will establish my covenant between me and you
and your offspring after you throughout their generations for an everlasting covenant, to be God to you and to your offspring after you.
… 15 And God said to Abraham, "As for Sarai your wife, you
shall not call her name Sarai, but Sarah shall be her name. 16 I will
bless her, and moreover, I will give you a son by her. I will bless her,
and she shall become nations; kings of peoples shall come from her."*
—Genesis 17:1-7, 15-16

*13 For the promise to Abraham and his offspring that he would be
heir of the world did not come through the law but through the righteousness of faith. 14 For if it is the adherents of the law who are to
be the heirs, faith is null and the promise is void. 15 For the law
brings wrath, but where there is no law there is no transgression. 16
That is why it depends on faith, in order that the promise may rest
on grace and be guaranteed to all his offspring—not only to the ad-
herent of the law but also to the one who shares the faith of Abraham, who is the father of us all, 17 as it is written, "I have made you
the father of many nations"—in the presence of the God in whom he
believed, who gives life to the dead and calls into existence the things
that do not exist. 18 In hope he believed against hope, that he should
become the father of many nations, as he had been told, "So shall*

*your offspring be." 19 He did not weaken in faith when he considered
his own body, which was as good as dead (since he was about a hundred years old), or when he considered the barrenness of Sarah's
womb. 20 No unbelief made him waver concerning the promise of
God, but he grew strong in his faith as he gave glory to God, 21
fully convinced that God was able to do what he had promised. 22
That is why his faith was "counted to him as righteousness." 23 But
the words "it was counted to him" were not written for his sake
alone, 24 but for ours also. It will be counted to us who believe in
him who raised from the dead Jesus our Lord, 25 who was delivered
up for our trespasses and raised for our justification.*

—*Romans 4:13-25*

L ast week we saw that God's covenant with Noah was actually a
covenant with all life on earth, human and nonhuman.

"Behold, I establish my covenant with you and your offspring after
you, and with every living creature that is with you, the birds, the
livestock, and every beast of the earth with you, as many as came out
of the ark; it is for every beast of the earth" (Genesis 9: 9–10).

God's covenant is with life itself, with Noah and his family, of
course, but also with every living creature. Some people know that
they are in covenant with God and some people don't know that
they are in covenant with God. But the covenant or law of God does
not require our acknowledgment. The same thing is true in our
courts: ignorance of the law is no defense.

Today we look at God's covenant with Abraham. It is a different
version of the same covenant. Let's look closely at what God said
about it.

"I am God Almighty; walk before me, and be blameless, that I may
make my covenant between me and you…" (vs. 1-2).

At first sight it looks like works-righteousness, that God is requiring
Abraham to be righteous as a condition of the covenant. As if God
said: *be blameless or righteous so that I can make my covenant with you.*

And if we limit ourselves to these words, it does say that. But that was not all that God said.

Next Abraham fell on his face, which means that Abraham recognized the divinity of God who was speaking to him, and responded appropriately. He acknowledged God's power and authority, and yielded to that authority. We can call that receiving the Holy Spirit because that's what it was, that's how it happens. God speaks and we respond. God commands and we obey—ideally, anyway.

Next we see that, with Abraham's response, God issues His covenant. Abraham responded, and before Abraham had a chance to do anything else, God covenanted with him. The covenant is ratified before any works of righteousness are performed. Thus the covenant with Abraham is a covenant of grace, freely given and freely received. The fact that Abraham acknowledged and received it is important because it makes all the difference in the world to Abraham. But those who do not acknowledge God's covenant do not escape it. Ignorance of the law does not absolve people from the demands of the law. You still get a ticket even if you didn't see the speed limit sign.

God's covenant comes with a demand, and that demand was revealed at the outset of God's message:

> "I am God Almighty; walk before me, and be blameless, that I may make my covenant between me and you..." (vs. 1-2).

How does God's demand for righteousness, God's requirement, work? God promises to provide justice if we live in obedience to Him. And justice provides fairness and equity for all. God treats all people equally. God's grace is equally given, but failure to respond brings consequences. Grace and judgment are set before all people.

So, if we want justice, we need to live according to God's righteousness. It's not that our living in righteousness *causes* God to give us grace. But rather that God's free gift of grace causes us to *want* to live in righteousness, though we fail to do so. Usually when people call for justice, what they actually want is revenge. But revenge is not justice. People usually look to the government, the law, to pro-

vide justice. But neither the government nor the law are able to provide justice because justice is not something that people *get*; justice is
something that people *give*. Ask any lawyer if the law is about justice.
It's not, it's about the legal process. Justice is a different thing.

When everyone lives according to God's demand for righteousness (blamelessness), justice will prevail because when all people live
in righteousness there will be no infractions. Without blame there
will be no need for courts or adjudication. Today we hear people
chant: *"No justice, no peace!"* as people protest in the streets about
some infraction. What they are saying is that they will disturb the
peace of society until society or the government gives them justice,
by which they actually mean revenge. The justice they want is an
eye for an eye and a tooth for a tooth. But that's not justice! That's
revenge.

We need to change the chant to *"Know justice, know peace!"*
where knowing justice means knowing and obeying God's demand
for righteousness. Justice is the state or condition of living in God's
righteousness.

The other thing to notice is that God promised that He would
make Abraham "the father of a multitude of nations" (v. 4). God
promised to make Abraham "exceedingly fruitful." And God's promise was not only to Abraham, but to him and his offspring after him.
That promise was not just to Abraham, but was also given to Sarah.

> "I will bless her, and moreover, I will give you a son by her. I will
> bless her, and she shall become nations; kings of peoples shall come
> from her" (v. 16).

Here we see that God was planning to provide for a very large
population of people. And all of those people who would compose
that large population would be bound by God's covenant.

Today, the people who claim Abraham as their ancestral father
include Jews, Christians, and Muslims. These people have acknowledge God's covenant, God's demand for righteous living. And that
acknowledgment makes these people more guilty for disobedience to
God's demand. But God's plan was that these people would model
righteous living for the rest of the world. God's covenant was not

given to the biological lineage of Abraham and Sarah, but to all who freely receive God's free grace, like Abraham did, to Abraham's spiritual lineage. So, how's that going? What do we expect God to think of our world today?

Paul then provides further commentary about God's covenant with Abraham. Paul wrote about God's promise to Abraham. And what was God's promise to Abraham? It was a two-fold promise: God would provide righteous guidance, and God would drastically increase Abraham's "children," those who would claim Abraham as their ancestral father.

At this point in history, in 2024 A.D., God has fulfilled both parts of His promise. Christ has come and provided righteous guidance, and the world is bursting with the children of Abraham. But at the time that Paul wrote these words, there were very few children of Abraham, and Paul was clarifying Christ's righteous guidance. The point that Paul was making was that living according to God's law, the law that Moses brought, was never intended to result in human righteousness. The function of the law was to point out human sin. It was to show us our own lack of righteousness. Paul said that "the law brings wrath" (v. 15).

If we don't know what righteousness requires of us, we will think that we are naturally righteous in all that we do because we have no standard by which to correctly judge ourselves. We will interpret God's law to suit ourselves, to justify our own behavior. So God provided a standard: Jesus Christ. And God has provided for the sustainability of a very large population on earth. The lesson of the Old Testament is that people are incapable of living in simple obedience to God's law, God's righteousness.

People don't obey rules. Rather, we bend the rules to match our desire so that we can think of ourselves as righteous people, which we are not. We are sinners and are unable in and of ourselves to extract ourselves from sin. Sin is like quicksand. The more we struggle against it, the deeper we sink into it. And if we just stop struggling, we only sink more slowly. We cannot get ourselves out of it. We need help.

God sent Jesus Christ to be our standard of righteousness. And Jesus Christ sent His Holy Spirit to provide both counsel and ability. So when we listen to the counsel of the Holy Spirit, and depend on the strength and energy of the Spirit, we can be free of the quicksand. But it doesn't happen all at once. The initial acknowledgement of God happens all at once as we surrender to God. But living in that surrender takes time to unfold. Paul said that Abraham, who lived at the very beginning of this process, simply believed God. Abraham believed that God would do as He said He would do.

And believing that, Abraham was able to begin walking in faith, walking in God's righteousness. But not all at once, and not perfectly! Abraham continued to mess up, continued to sin, and to disobey God. But his belief also began to manifest. Believing in God was difficult for Abraham. At the time that God promised to make him the father of many nations Abraham and Sarah were without children. And they were old! Very old. They would start a family in their old age. Imagine having and raising a baby when you are 100 years old!

At that time the fulfillment of God's promise was a long way off. A very long way off. Paul said that,

"In hope (Abraham) believed against hope that he would become the father of many nations..." (v. 18).

Abraham believed without any evidence. And that is the model of faithfulness! The reason that people are called to believe without any evidence is that believers become the evidence for the reality of God's existence. How so? Belief in God changes lives, and those changed lives become the evidence for the reality of God.

Now you may not be swayed by someone else's belief or testimony. But when we believe in God ourselves, and act on that belief as if it is true, we see how God changes our own life, then our own changed life becomes evidence of God's reality to us. Because we are changed, we know God is real.

Today, the reality that God has provided a very large population of Abraham's children is upon us. I'm not saying that the return of Christ is near. But I am saying that no other generation in history has been as close to Christ's return as we are. But that's always been true. However, the fact that it has always been true doesn't discount the fact that it is true today for us. Christ is coming, and we need to be prepared.

KNOW BETTER

And God spoke all these words, saying, 2 "I am the Lord your God, who brought you out of the land of Egypt, out of the house of slavery. 3 "You shall have no other gods before me. 4 "You shall not make for yourself a carved image, or any likeness of anything that is in heaven above, or that is in the earth beneath, or that is in the water under the earth. 5 You shall not bow down to them or serve them, for I the Lord your God am a jealous God, visiting the iniquity of the fathers on the children to the third and the fourth generation of those who hate me, 6 but showing steadfast love to thousands of those who love me and keep my commandments. 7 "You shall not take the name of the Lord your God in vain, for the Lord will not hold him guiltless who takes his name in vain. 8 "Remember the Sabbath day, to keep it holy. 9 Six days you shall labor, and do all your work, 10 but the seventh day is a Sabbath to the Lord your God. On it you shall not do any work, you, or your son, or your daughter, your male servant, or your female servant, or your livestock, or the sojourner who is within your gates. 11 For in six days the Lord made heaven and earth, the sea, and all that is in them, and rested on the seventh day. Therefore the Lord blessed the Sabbath day and made it holy. 12 "Honor your father and your mother, that your days may be long in the land that the Lord your God is giving you. 13 "You shall not murder. 14 "You shall not commit adultery. 15 "You shall not steal. 16 "You shall not bear false witness against your neighbor. 17 "You shall not covet your neighbor's house; you shall not covet your neighbor's wife, or his male servant, or his female servant, or his ox, or his donkey, or anything that is your neighbor's. —"*Exodus 20:1-17*

18 For the word of the cross is folly to those who are perishing, but to us who are being saved it is the power of God. 19 For it is written, "I will destroy the wisdom of the wise, and the discernment of the discerning I will thwart." 20 Where is the one who is wise?

Where is the scribe? Where is the debater of this age? Has not God made foolish the wisdom of the world? 21 For since, in the wisdom of God, the world did not know God through wisdom, it pleased God through the folly of what we preach to save those who believe. 22 For Jews demand signs and Greeks seek wisdom, 23 but we preach Christ crucified, a stumbling block to Jews and folly to Gentiles, 24 but to those who are called, both Jews and Greeks, Christ the power of God and the wisdom of God. 25 For the foolishness of God is wiser than men, and the weakness of God is stronger than men.   *—1 Corinthians 1:18-25*

The Ten Commandments are the original expression of God's law. Let's put this in the context of God's covenant, which we've been talking about the past couple of weeks. God's covenant with Noah was a covenant with the whole world, all living things, which means all people everywhere. God's covenant with Abraham was a covenant of grace because it was given and ratified prior to Abraham doing anything.

Thus, God's law has been given as an act of grace, an act of love. God is concerned for the well-being of humanity. God's law was given to Moses or through Moses, so we also see that God covenanted with Moses. The essence of God's covenant with Moses is found in Deuteronomy 28. Again, it is the same universal covenant, given with additional clarity.

"And if you faithfully obey the voice of the Lord your God, being careful to do all his commandments that I command you today, the Lord your God will set you high above all the nations of the earth. 2 And all these blessings shall come upon you and overtake you, if you obey the voice of the Lord your God. 3 Blessed shall you be in the city, and blessed shall you be in the field."

Obedience results in blessings.

5 "But if you will not obey the voice of the Lord your God or be careful to do all his commandments and his statutes that I command you today, then all these curses shall come upon you and overtake

you. 16 Cursed shall you be in the city, and cursed shall you be in
the field."

Disobedience results in curses.

Here we are thrown again into the idea of works-righteousness,
where it looks like people need to earn God's blessing by their obedience. And this is a formidable argument that continues to domi-
nate in the Old Testament and is still held among "faithful" Jews
today, Jews who do not recognize the validity of the New Testament. From this perspective, human behavior is the fulcrum that
moves God's grace, mercy, and blessings. The idea is that God re-
sponds to us as we respond to Him. We get what we deserve. This
idea is known the world over as karma. God gives people what they
deserve.

However, this perspective falls short of God's actual gift and His
intention. It falls short because it does not consider the viability of
the New Testament. If all we had was the Old Testament, this perspective would be logically consistent, or true. Had we lived in the
time of the Old Testament, prior to Christ, we would have done no
better than the Jews did.

But with the coming of Christ and God's new covenant with Jesus Christ, which is really the same as the old covenant, but with a
more inclusive perspective and additional clarity, we are able to understand God's covenant more fully. In the light of Christ given
through the New Testament we see that we have been given God's
Holy Spirit, who provides for us what we cannot provide for ourselves. This gift of God's grace provides God's blessings prior to our
obedience, which then opens a channel in which we can respond to
God's love as best as we are able, with God's Holy Spirit making up
for what we lack.

To fully understand this we need to understand why God has
given His law, the Ten Commandments. Are the Ten Commandments arbitrary instructions from an uptight potentate? Not at all! Is
God trying to cramp our style because He is jealous of our freedom?
No. God is jealous, but not jealous of our freedom. God is jealous
because He loves us, and because He loves us, He wants what is best

for us. He wants us to prosper, to thrive, to be fruitful, productive, happy. And when something gets in the way of this, God gets jealous and wants to remove it.

God has given us His law because we are ignorant of our actual situation. The sin of Adam and Eve dominates this world—still. It's not that God is not here, He is! But apart from the power and presence of the Holy Spirit in our own individual lives, we deny Him. We ignore God. We don't recognize His presence. We are blind to Him. Paul says that we are slaves to sin. And this is the context in which God has given us His law. God's law is a hand of mercy extended to extract slaves from the condition of their slavery.

For the most part, people don't even know that they are slaves. They just think that that's the way the world is. People have accepted the fact of their slavery, and many have even come to embrace it. They think: *if that's the way the world is, then let's just make the best of it as it is.* This is a compromise position of living in slavery because people don't see any option. And it's true that if there is no option, we must make the best of what we have. And prior to Jesus, the option was veiled, unclear.

God had given the law prior to Jesus, and the law does provide an option. However, the option of obedience to the law was not in the reach of humanity prior to Jesus. Old Testament Israel tried to live according to the law, but the record of the Old Testament is a record of their failure. Time and again they failed to be obedient to the law, and suffered the consequences. Over and over again, a boom and bust cycle of revival and relapse played out century after century.

It's not the the law is bad. It's not! It's good! But slaves to sin are unable to live in obedience to God's law because they don't want to. They don't know how to because they prefer their addiction to sin. They prefer their sin because they are used to it. They have grown comfortable with sin. So comfortable that they just think that that's the way the world is. But that's not the way the world is. That's not the way that God made the world. God made the world for the joy of His people.

And in order to restore that joy God had to step into the world Himself, personally, and fix it. He needed to provide access to the

Christ option. First, the Christ option was presented in the life, ministry, death, and resurrection of Jesus Christ. Then that option was made real, made accessible by God's Holy Spirit, which was poured out on all flesh.

"And it shall come to pass afterward, that I will pour out my Spirit on all flesh; your sons and your daughters shall prophesy, your old men shall dream dreams, and your young men shall see visions. Even on the male and female servants in those days I will pour out my Spirit" (Joel 2:28-29).

This pouring out of the Spirit happened with Jesus Christ, when Jesus sent His Spirit into the world.

"If you love me, keep my commands. And I will ask the Father, and he will give you another advocate to help you and be with you forever—the Spirit of truth. The world cannot accept him, because it neither sees him nor knows him. But you know him, for he lives with you and will be in you. I will not leave you as orphans; I will come to you. Before long, the world will not see me anymore, but you will see me. Because I live, you also will live. On that day you will realize that I am in my Father, and you are in me, and I am in you. Whoever has my commands and keeps them is the one who loves me. The one who loves me will be loved by my Father, and I too will love them and show myself to them" (John 14:15).

So obedience to God's law is now a real option. Not that we can do it perfectly! But that God can do it adequately through us by the power and presence of His Holy Spirit. And Jesus simplified the law. He summed it up in two commandments: love God and love one another.

Can it really be that simple? It can. But simple doesn't mean easy. Yet, sinners deny the simplicity of the gospel. And it's hard to blame them, considering the many difficulties that the Bible has produced over the history of the world. It is the most disputed book in history. Countless wars have been fought over it. Countless people have died in its service and because of various misunderstandings about it. The Bible is at the heart of the world's longest running conflict, which is playing out today in Gaza.

So, how can it be simple? People tie themselves into knots trying to figure it out. Paul said,

> "For the word of the cross is folly to those who are perishing, but to us who are being saved it is the power of God" (v. 18).

Love God and love one another. It sounds easy, but it's harder than it sounds. It begins with loving God. How do we love God? Jesus said, "If you love me, keep my commands," which brings us back to the Ten Commandments. To love God is to want to please God, and God wants our obedience. And God will be satisfied with our desire to be obedient. He knows that perfect obedience is currently beyond us. So He is satisfied with our honest desire to live in obedience, as best as we are able, according to our honest effort. He's satisfied with that because our ability to live in obedience will grow and mature over time. And God knows that. So He is patient because He loves us. Like anything, we begin with small steps. The Ten Commandments provide ten small steps:

1. You shall have no other gods, only the God of the Bible.
2. You shall not worship other things, not love things more than you love God.
3. You shall not misuse God's name; honor God rightly.
4. Remember the Sabbath day, take time to grow in God.
5. Honor your father and your mother. Respect authority.
6. You shall not murder. Do no harm to others.
7. You shall not commit adultery. Sex should only happen in marriage.
8. You shall not steal.
9. You shall not lie about other people.
10. You shall not want what is not yours.

Summed up: love God and love one another. Let's try this and see what happens.

OPULENT LOVE

14 And as Moses lifted up the serpent in the wilderness, so must the Son of Man be lifted up, 15 that whoever believes in him may have eternal life. 16 "For God so loved the world, that he gave his only Son, that whoever believes in him should not perish but have eternal life. 17 For God did not send his Son into the world to condemn the world, but in order that the world might be saved through him. 18 Whoever believes in him is not condemned, but whoever does not believe is condemned already, because he has not believed in the name of the only Son of God. 19 And this is the judgment: the light has come into the world, and people loved the darkness rather than the light because their works were evil. 20 For everyone who does wicked things hates the light and does not come to the light, lest his works should be exposed. 21 But whoever does what is true comes to the light, so that it may be clearly seen that his works have been carried out in God."   *—John 3:14-21*

And you were dead in the trespasses and sins 2 in which you once walked, following the course of this world, following the prince of the power of the air, the spirit that is now at work in the sons of disobedience—3 among whom we all once lived in the passions of our flesh, carrying out the desires of the body and the mind, and were by nature children of wrath, like the rest of mankind. 4 But God, being rich in mercy, because of the great love with which he loved us, 5 even when we were dead in our trespasses, made us alive together with Christ— by grace you have been saved—6 and raised us up with him and seated us with him in the heavenly places in Christ Jesus, 7 so that in the coming ages he might show the immeasurable riches of his grace in kindness toward us in Christ Jesus. 8 For by grace you have been saved through faith. And this is not your own doing; it is the gift of God, 9 not a result of works, so that no one may boast. 10 For we are his workmanship, created in Christ Jesus for good works, which

God prepared beforehand, that we should walk in them.
                                                    —*Ephesians 2:1-10*

Jesus was talking to Nicodemus about being born again in John 3. Jesus explained the whole theology of the cross to Nicodemus, but the explanation was cloaked in the story of Moses and the serpents. Let's remind ourselves of that story.

> "From Mount Hor they set out by the way to the Red Sea, to go around the land of Edom. And the people became impatient on the way. And the people spoke against God and against Moses, 'Why have you brought us up out of Egypt to die in the wilderness? For there is no food and no water, and we loathe this worthless food.' Then the Lord sent fiery serpents among the people, and they bit the people, so that many people of Israel died. And the people came to Moses and said, 'We have sinned, for we have spoken against the Lord and against you. Pray to the Lord, that he take away the serpents from us.' So Moses prayed for the people. And the Lord said to Moses, 'Make a fiery serpent and set it on a pole, and everyone who is bitten, when he sees it, shall live.' So Moses made a bronze serpent and set it on a pole. And if a serpent bit anyone, he would look at the bronze serpent and live" (Numbers 21:4-9).

The people again got discouraged, and in their unbelief they murmured against Moses for bringing them into the wilderness. They had already forgotten that it was their own sin that caused them to be there, and they tried to blame Moses for it. As a judgment against the people for their sin, God sent poisonous serpents into the camp, and people began to die. This showed the people that they were the ones in sin.

In response they came to Moses to confess that sin and ask for God's mercy. God then instructed Moses to make a bronze serpent and put it on a pole so the people could look at it and be healed. God was teaching the people about faith. It is totally illogical to think that looking at a bronze image could heal anyone from snakebite, but that is exactly what God told them to do. It required an act of faith in God's plan to be healed, and the serpent on the pole was a reminder of their sin, which originated with the serpent in the Garden and had brought about their suffering. The serpent was symbolic of their sin and its consequences (the poisonous bites) that God used to chastise the people for their unbelief.

Here we see that the people must look at or confront or admit or confess their own sin as a prerequisite to salvation. If you don't think you sin, you don't think you need salvation. Jesus' conclusion comes in John 3:36,

> "Whoever believes in the Son has eternal life; whoever does not obey the Son shall not see life, but the wrath of God remains on him."

Notice the transition from *believe* to *obey*. Why does God do this?

> "For God so loved the world, that he gave his only Son, that whoever believes in him should not perish but have eternal life." (v. 16).

God loves the *world*. The Greek word is *kosmos*, which suggests world affairs, the aggregate of earthly things; earthly goods, endowments, riches, advantages, pleasures, etc. God doesn't love what we sinners have done with the world; He loves what the world could be in Christ.

Salvation comes from seeing Christ on the the cross, but it's the kind of seeing that involves more than looking. Salvation comes from understanding why Christ was on the cross, not why He was sentenced to suffer the cross, but why He volunteered to give Himself to the cross. Christ was on the cross to atone for our sin. We must see the cross through the eyes of sin. We must understand that our sin put Christ on the cross. It's our fault! The answer to the question: *who crucified Christ?* is: *We are responsible!* You and I! It's our fault! He did it for *us*. He did it to redeem our faulty character. He did it for our correction. He didn't do it for our condemnation.

> "For God did not send his Son into the world to condemn the world, but in order that the world might be saved through him" (v. 17).

The world is obsessed with sin. To be obsessed is to be influenced or controlled by a powerful force such as a strong emotion. To be obsessed is to be driven, to be compelled by something that is beyond our control. To be obsessed is to be preoccupied with something. Sin is the obsession of the world. And Christ came to break the grip of our obsession with sin. And since an obsession is a function of the mind, the counter of an obsession also involves the mind: *belief*.

To overcome an obsession, we need believe differently. We need a change of mind, a change of commitment, a change of belief.

> "Whoever believes in him is not condemned, but whoever does not believe is condemned already, because he has not believed in the name of the only Son of God" (v. 18).

Jesus said,

> "I am the light of the world. Whoever follows me will not walk in darkness, but will have the light of life" (John 8:12).

Light reveals what is unseen in the dark. And this seeing what is in the darkness is what is happening in our contemporary world right now.

Everyone who pays any attention to the news today is concerned about what they see. It doesn't matter if you are liberal or conservative, left or right. Each side blames the other, and only sees the world through their own eyes. But both sides are seeing sin and corruption—not their own, but the sin and corruption of the other side. But if we can step back from the fray and look at the larger context that includes both sides, we can conclude that we are in an historical time of sin and corruption. Neither side is guiltless! One side may be more guilty, but both are guilty.

Jesus tells us that the light reveals whatever is in the darkness. Thus, my thesis is that the light of Christ is currently increasing in the world today, and that light is showing us our collective sin, our corporate sin. And while each side blames the other side, each side appears to be blind to their own sin. And yet, each side has a viable point to make. It's always easier to see the sins of others than to see our own sin. People tend to be blind to their own sins and faults.

But here's the thing: We are currently face to face with an opportunity, an opportunity that comes because of the increasing light of Christ in our world. The light of Christ is revealing the contemporary condition of the world. We are able to see the world, to see what has been previously hidden in the darkness of the world. At first sight we see the sins of others because that is our natural tendency. But if we can persist in the light, we will be able to see our own sin, as well. The challenge before us is for each side to publicly confess its own sin, to see itself—ourselves—in the light of Christ. Just as individual confession of sin opens the door of salvation, so national confession of sin will open the door to national healing.

> "For everyone who does wicked things hates the light and does not come to the light, lest his works should be exposed. But whoever does what is true comes to the light, so that it may be clearly seen that his works have been carried out in God" (vs. 20-21).

There are only two possible responses to the increasing light of Christ in the world: confession or damnation, admit the truth or deny the truth. Paul said that every Christian was once

> "dead in the trespasses and sin in which (we) once walked" (vs. 1-2).

Every Christians knows what it is like to be an unsaved sinner, but unsaved sinners do not yet know what it is like to be a Christian.

Today Christians are in the minority, which means that the majority of people today are still

> "following the course of this world, following the prince of the power of the air, the spirit that is now at work in the sons of disobedience—among whom we all once lived in the passions of our flesh, carrying out the desires of the body and the mind, and were by nature children of wrath, like the rest of mankind" (vs. 2-3).

Jesus said that Satan is the father of liars, that deceit is Satan's most effective weapon. We tend to think all lying is intentional deceit because if it is unintentional, it is more likely to be an error, a mistake, rather than a lie. But what happens when Satan deceives us about ourselves. Deceit happens in darkness because darkness obscures or hides the truth. When we are self-deceived, when we believe things about ourselves that are not true, when we think more of ourselves than we should, more than is warranted, we fail to see the whole truth. When we are committed to a narrative that is not true, we are blind to the truth.

We certainly fail to see ourselves as others see us. Remember that it is easier to see the sins and faults of others than to see our own sins and faults. When we are self-deceived, self-deluded, we are blind to our own sins and faults. To be self-deluded is to believe things about ourselves or about the world that are not true. When self-deluded people speak, they think that their delusions are true. Are they lying? They don't think so.

The only way to fix self-delusion is confession. And confession comes through exposure to the light because the light reveals the truth. And Jesus Christ is the light of the world!

"I am the way and the truth and the life" (John 14:6).

Paul goes on to say that Christians have been raised up in Christ and seated with Christ in the "heavenly places in Christ Jesus" (v. 6). Christians are saved in Christ. Paul said that the church is the body of Christ, which means that we are each a part or a member of Christ's body on earth. Paul also said that Christ's ministry, Christ's mission, is a mission of reconciliation. Christ reconciles individuals to God, and He also reconciles Christians to one another.

To reconcile is to resolve disputes. So, if Christ's mission is to resolve humanity's dispute with God (or God's with humanity), then the mission of Christ's church is to resolve disputes between Christians. Of course no reconciliation is possible until individuals are first reconciled with God (which Jesus does). This means that reconciliation among Christians is the incomplete mission of Christ's church on earth.

Let me repeat myself: We are currently face to face with an opportunity, an opportunity that comes because of the increasing light of Christ in our world. It looks like the sin of the world is increasing. But what if it is actually the light of Christ that is increasing, and because the light of Christ is increasing, we are able to see the sin of the world more clearly, more fully. What if we acknowledge the light of Christ, examine ourselves more closely in that light, and simply confess our own sin.

What would that look like if we did it nationally? Lord, make it so. Amen.

ETERNAL PRIEST

31 "Behold, the days are coming, declares the Lord, when I will make a new covenant with the house of Israel and the house of Judah, 32 not like the covenant that I made with their fathers on the day when I took them by the hand to bring them out of the land of Egypt, my covenant that they broke, though I was their husband, declares the Lord. 33 For this is the covenant that I will make with the house of Israel after those days, declares the Lord: I will put my law within them, and I will write it on their hearts. And I will be their God, and they shall be my people. 34 And no longer shall each one teach his neighbor and each his brother, saying, 'Know the Lord,' for they shall all know me, from the least of them to the greatest, declares the Lord. For I will forgive their iniquity, and I will remember their sin no more."   *—Jeremiah 31:31-34*

5 So also Christ did not exalt himself to be made a high priest, but was appointed by him who said to him, "You are my Son, today I have begotten you"; 6 as he says also in another place, "You are a priest forever, after the order of Melchizedek." 7 In the days of his flesh, Jesus offered up prayers and supplications, with loud cries and tears, to him who was able to save him from death, and he was heard because of his reverence. 8 Although he was a son, he learned obedience through what he suffered. 9 And being made perfect, he became the source of eternal salvation to all who obey him, 10 being designated by God a high priest after the order of Melchizedek.   *—Hebrews 5:5-10*

L et's begin with the second reading in order to put the first in its proper context. Paul compared Christ to Melchizedek, whom we first encounter in Genesis 14. Lot, Abram's nephew, had been captured when Sodom was defeated in a war involving several kings.

Sodom was looted, and Lot taken as a prisoner/slave. Abram learned about it and went to rescue Lot.

> "Now when Abram heard that his brother was taken captive, he armed his three hundred and eighteen trained servants who were born in his own house, and went in pursuit as far as Dan. He divided his forces against them by night, and he and his servants attacked them and pursued them as far as Hobah, which is north of Damascus. So he brought back all the goods, and also brought back his brother Lot and his goods, as well as the women and the people" (Genesis 14:14-16).

Abram then had possession of Lot and the booty that had been stolen from Sodom. He then met with the king of Sodom. At this point Melchizedek is inserted into the story. It appears that Melchizedek was the mediator between Abram and the king of Sodom.

> "Then Melchizedek king of Salem brought out bread and wine; he was the priest of God Most High. And he blessed him and said: 'Blessed be Abram of God Most High, Possessor of heaven and earth; And blessed be God Most High, Who has delivered your enemies into your hand.' And he gave him a tithe of all" (Genesis 14:18-20).

Notice three things: 1) Melchizedek officiated a ritual of peace with 2) bread and wine, and blessed Abram, who then 3) gave ten percent, a tithe, of his war booty to Melchizedek. Abram tithed to Melchizedek, suggesting Melchizedek's superiority. We might think of the tithe as a tax. Abram was a visitor on the land where Melchizedek ruled.

One other point tells us about Abram's character: The king of Sodom told Abram to return the "persons, and take the goods for" himself. But Abram refused and returned both persons and goods to the king of Sodom because he didn't want to cause any future ill-feelings between himself and the king of Sodom. Abram only wanted Lot and his family, which he got.

This, then is the only story of Melchizedek that we have. Let me point out here that Melchizedek is not the name of a person, but is a title or an office. Melchizedek, composed to two words, *melchi* and *zedek*, literally means *king of righteousness*. And this title belonged to the king of Salem, the area in which they were. Note also that the word *salem* means *peace*, and that the central city of the biblical story, Jerusalem, is composed of two words, *jeru* and *salem*, and literally means *city of peace*. All of this then means that Melchizedek was the central Old Testament figure in the long narrative of Abram in the Old Testament. Melchizedek's office or role is at the heart of everything.

But this did not become known or understood until Jesus Christ came as Messiah, and the New Testament writers clarified the relationship between Melchizedek and Jesus Christ. The centrality of Melchizedek was the point that the author of Hebrews was talking about. He said that Jesus Christ was

> "designated by God a high priest after the order of Melchizedek" (v. 10).

This link between Melchizedek and Christ provides the link between the Old Testament and the New Testament. It's importance is central to the role that Jesus Christ plays in the history of the world.

Again, Melchizedek is not the name of a person, but is a title or office. And similarly, Christ is not the name of a person but is a title or office. Melchizedek is the *king of righteousness*, and Jesus Christ is the *Lord of righteousness*. It's the same office under a different name or title, in a different language.

Jesus Christ is referred to as the High Priest, but He is not a Priest in the order of Aaron or Levi, the two orders of priests in the Old Testament Temple establishment. The High Priest of the Old Testament Temple establishment was an Aaronic Priest. The point is that Jesus Christ outranks the High Priest of the Old Testament.

It is also important to understand the role of righteousness in all of this. Paul says much about righteousness in Romans 3-7. As I've said before, righteousness and justice seem different in the English, but are the same word in Hebrew. Recall the various discussions of Paul about justification (the root of which is *justice*) and righteousness.

Abraham was justified by faith, and justification by faith is the central doctrine or belief or teaching of evangelical Christianity. It is also central to the New Covenant of the New Testament, which brings us to the reading from Jeremiah 31.

The time difference between Abraham and Jeremiah is about 1300 years. The time difference between Moses and Jeremiah is about 750 years. This means that Jeremiah's prophecy about the new covenant, was about 1300 years after God's covenant with Abraham, and about 750 years after God's covenant with Moses. The point is that Israel had been living with God's covenant(s) for a very long time, and that Jeremiah's observation was that it was *not* working.

The covenant of God's law, which was a written covenant captured in the words of the Old Testament, wasn't working. Corruption was rampant during the time of Jeremiah. Jeremiah was prophesying a new covenant that would actually be the return to an older covenant. Jeremiah's prophecy looked both to the past and to the future at the same time.

Abraham had been justified by faith, which means that Abraham's faith had been written on his heart.

> "For this is the covenant that I will make with the house of Israel after those days, declares the Lord: I will put my law within them, and I will write it on their hearts" (v. 33).

What does it mean that the law is to be written on hearts? There are two parts to this idea: 1) it applies to all human beings because God's covenant is with all humanity, and 2) it applies to born again Christians in a special way.

How does it apply to all human beings? All human beings have an innate sense of good and evil. It is not a well-focused sense, but is a dull, general sense. And it triggers what we call guilt because, while we know that we should be good, we don't know what qualifies as good.

When people do something wrong, evil, bad, or unfair, they feel a sense of guilt. The secular philosophers acknowledge this when they speak of "categorical imperatives" or the sense of "oughtness," as in, *I ought to do this or that.* A *categorical imperative*, a term coined by the German philosopher Immanuel Kant, is a rule of moral conduct that is unconditional or absolute for all people at all times. It has no conditions. "Thou shalt not steal," for example, is absolute, and not dependent on conditions. In contrast, a conditional imperative would be: "Do not steal if you want to be popular." A categorical imperative is an absolute value, and should not tolerate any exceptions.

The violation of a categorical imperative or absolute value results in the feeling of guilt. We know that we should not do this or that, or that we really should do something. When human behavior is not in line with an absolute value, people feel guilt. Guilt is felt when there is a breach of conduct, especially violating some law that involves a penalty, and communicates the sense of having done something wrong. It also arises when we know that we deserve blame for some offense or from our inadequacy to some task.

Guilt is a universal human experience. Not everyone feels remorse, or a sufficient degree of remorse. Some people feel proud when they break the law; it makes them feel superior to others who don't have the courage to break the law. Nonetheless, they know that they are breaking the law. The problem is that laws have no effect on such people. They ignore the law. So passing laws has no effect on them.

The purpose of guilt is to bring people to a sense of remorse that is sufficient to change their behavior. A change of behavior is called repentance. This is the good side of guilt. Guilt can motivate people to change their behavior, to improve themselves. The bad side of guilt comes when people feel guilt, but do not change their behavior. They simply wallow in their guilt. They don't feel remorse. And this response to guilt leads to depression, defeat, and apathy.

The second part of the law being written on our hearts applies to Christians, to those who are born again in Christ. Here the idea of the law being written on our hearts means that the individual has an active, personal relationship with God through the Holy Spirit in Christ that produces a kind of mental activity that we call prayer. It also means that Christians have a way to handle their guilt: through confession (speaking to God) and forgiveness (listening to God).

Prayer is simply a personal conversation with God that involves both speaking and listening. In prayer we speak our concerns to God, and we listen to God's concerns. And how do we know what God's concerns are? We read about them in His book, the Bible. It is interesting to realize that the new covenant with Jesus Christ is the same as the old covenant with Abraham, who considered Melchizedek to be his Lord. The Lord of Abraham was the king of righteousness, who is the eternal king of peace, Jesus Christ.

Jeremiah's prophecy about a new covenant reached back to Abraham and Melchizedek and forward to Jesus Christ. When will this covenant be complete? Jeremiah said,

> "And no longer shall each one teach his neighbor and each his brother, saying, 'Know the Lord,' for they shall all know me, from the least of them to the greatest, declares the Lord. For I will forgive their iniquity, and I will remember their sin no more (v. 34)."

Some day preachers will no longer need to instruct people to know the Lord, when everyone knows the Lord. The kingdom of God will be complete when everyone knows the Lord, when we can all read the law on our hearts and know the will of God by reading and understanding the Bible faithfully ourselves—not as individuals, but as the community of God in Christ.

It seems to me that that day is still a long way off, and that there is much work to do in the meantime.

GOSPEL POLICY

*The Lord God has given me the tongue of those who are taught, that
I may know how to sustain with a word to him who is weary.
Morning by morning he awakens; he awakens my ear to hear as
those who are taught. 5 The Lord God has opened my ear, and I was
not rebellious; I turned not backward. 6 I gave my back to those who
strike, and my cheeks to those who pull out the beard; I hid not my
face from disgrace and spitting. 7 But the Lord God helps me; therefore I have not been disgraced; therefore I have set my face like a
flint, and I know that I shall not be put to shame. 8 He who vindi-
cates me is near. Who will contend with me? Let us stand up together. Who is my adversary? Let him come near to me. 9 Behold,
the Lord God helps me; who will declare me guilty? Behold, all of
them will wear out like a garment; the moth will eat them up.*
—Isaiah 50:4-9

*12 The next day the large crowd that had come to the feast heard
that Jesus was coming to Jerusalem. 13 So they took branches of
palm trees and went out to meet him, crying out, "Hosanna! Blessed
is he who comes in the name of the Lord, even the King of Israel!"
14 And Jesus found a young donkey and sat on it, just as it is written, 15 "Fear not, daughter of Zion; behold, your king is coming, sitting on a donkey's colt!" 16 His disciples did not understand these
things at first, but when Jesus was glorified, then they remembered
that these things had been written about him and had been done to
him.* *—John 12:12-16*

Have you ever been reading something, and you find your
mind wandering, and suddenly realize that you have been
actually reading the words on the page, but have no idea of what
you just read? You've been going through the motions of reading:

holding the book or magazine, your eyes following each line, and you can hear the words in your mind as you read them, but your mind is somewhere else. Isaiah is talking about the opposite experience. He has found that he understands God. God was providing him with a kind of understanding that he had never thought of before.

If you are like me, you have a twenty-four-seven dialog going on in your head. People call it thinking, and it is. But sometimes it seems more like listening. Mine is a conversation. It's not a voice per say, but the ideas are clear, and on occasion I'm surprised by what I think, in the sense that suddenly I understand something that I didn't understand before. Or I understand something in a new way. I first noticed this when I was in junior high school. I had a running dialog with myself about all sorts of things. I decided that I would frame it as a dialog with God. Some people call it prayer. Some people call it talking to yourself.

Prayer is a process of interaction with God through His Holy Spirit. I found that I could ask questions, and I would get answers that would sometimes surprise me. The answers were in my own inner voice, yet it seemed like I was interacting with someone else. Maybe I'm just weird! And I probably am. At any rate, these verses from Isaiah remind me of this experience, and they confirm for me that my experience of this phenomenon is real, that is it meaningful and important.

Isaiah said that he could "hear as those who are taught" (v. 4). If you are being taught something, the voice doing the teaching is not your own—and yet when you are thinking, it is! Isaiah said that the "Lord God has opened my ear" (v. 5). Jesus often speaks of those who have "ears to hear" at the end of a difficult saying or parable (Matthew 11:15; Mark 4:9, 23). What does He mean? Who is He referring to? Everyone has ears on the sides of their heads, but not everyone understood what Jesus was talking about.

When Jesus addressed those who have ears to hear, He was saying that not everyone would understand Him. He was also suggesting that understanding is a gift from God. Understanding the gospel is not a function of intelligence. We cannot boast in our intelligence because understanding is a gift that doesn't depend on intelligence. It doesn't depend on education, age, ethnicity, language, or status, either.

Jesus was calling for people to pay attention. By speaking in parables Jesus sought to gain people's attention, to get them thinking and wondering, to start a dialog. People love stories, and the parables depicted events and characters that they could relate to. But unless they were willing to tune out other distractions His words would only be empty stories. People needed more than physical ears, however keen they were; they needed ears to hear, they needed the Holy Spirit in their lives to help them hear the truth.

Isaiah found that he was able to hear or understand things that were unpopular, things that would cause him to be persecuted for, if he shared them. Yet, he was compelled to speak the truth in spite of the fact that doing so would bring him harm. He knew that the truth would ultimately prevail. It always does, though it usually takes longer than we expect. Today we understand Isaiah to have prefigured or predicted the suffering of Jesus Christ during Holy Week. And Isaiah was also persecuted for the truth he spoke, just as Jesus was.

I suppose we could say that truth is an acquired taste. It takes some getting used to. People generally don't like it because it usually contradicts what they think they believe. God's truth, like God's law, reveals our sinfulness, our weaknesses, our failings. No one likes to be proven wrong, and especially not publicly. So our godless response to truth is an emotional revulsion. We reject it, or dismiss it, or belittle it. And it takes the power and presence of the Holy Spirit through regeneration to give us new ears, to consider a hard truth, and to accept it. When we accept something as true, it changes our thinking. It causes us to reorient ourselves, to rearrange our thoughts and beliefs to make room for this new truth that we didn't understand before. We could call this process *repentance*.

Palm Sunday is the day when we remember that Jesus rode into Jerusalem as a king, but on a donkey. He was lauded as the king of Israel by the people. Because the people called Him *king*, the Romans and the Temple establishment felt threatened. We know that there

was much political unrest at the time, that Rome dominated
Jerusalem, and that the faithful Israelites were looking for the return
of Israel's national glory. They hoped that Jesus would be a kind of
king like David. They hoped that He would reestablish Israel's national greatness.

We could say that Jesus stepped into politics that day, or that the
people thrust Him into politics by calling him king. Either way, Jesus collided with the political establishment that day. And that day
then led to His mock trial, conviction, and death on the cross.

Holy Week began as the events of this week in His life lead to
the cross and His death. We find the story of Jesus riding into
Jerusalem in John 12. Two forces were at play: Jesus and the people.
Jesus set His face to go to Jerusalem during the high holy days of
Passover. He didn't need to do that, but it was His decision that
brought Him to Jerusalem that day.

And when the people heard that He was coming, they did what
they could to give Him a royal welcome. The people were poor and
couldn't provide a fancy reception. But they did what they could.
They laid palm branches before His path as a traditional acknowledgement of His kingship. The people didn't need to do that, but
they did because they recognized something special about Jesus, and
hoped that He would fulfill their dreams of Israel's greatness. Because
the people acknowledged Jesus as a king, the politicians saw Jesus as
a political rival.

Large crowds greeted Him, waving palm branches and welcom-
ing Him with shouts of acclamation. They welcomed their king and
hoped that he would lead a revolt against the Romans, who were oc-
cupying their nation. Even His closest disciples expected it (Mark
10:37). This wasn't the first time that this expectation broke out. Earlier, in John 6 we read that some disciples had been planning to
make Jesus king by force. But when Jesus found out about it, He
"withdrew again to a mountain by himself" (John 6:15). It was not
Jesus' intention to become a worldly king.

We know that Jesus is King of the universe, but we also know
that His Kingship is of a different kind. Political kings are ruled and
fueled by politics. What drives politics is popular sentiment. Politi-

cians gauge popular sentiment by taking polls. Before modern polling, they depended on other people in society who would "read the people," who understood what various groups of people were thinking and feeling about various issues. Politicians try to sway popular opinion in their favor, or try to ride the various waves of popular opinion to shape their governmental decisions.

Political kings have power; they have wealth; and they lord over others. They impose their will on others. They do this by making laws or using other kinds of force. Kings use force, trickery, bullying, and murder to get their way. But these are not the ways of Jesus. Jesus is King, but not a worldly, political king.

The Kingdom of God functions differently. When Pilate asked, "Are you the king of the Jews?" (John 18:33). Jesus answered,

> "My kingdom is not of this world. If my kingdom were of this world, my servants would have been fighting, that I might not be delivered over to the Jews. But my kingdom is not from the world" (John 18:36).

The decisions and governance of Jesus are not dependent on popular opinion. Jesus doesn't govern by polls. When Pilate found that Jesus was not trying to stir up a rebellion, he told the Sanhedrin that he had no reason to charge Jesus with sedition. Were the Romans and the Temple establishment justified in their belief that Jesus was a political threat to them? Yes and no.

God's intention has always been to change the world, to rid the world of sin, to free people from their bondage to sin. Is Jesus a threat to people who love their sin? Well… yes He is! But He's not a threat to their happiness or well-being. He is a threat to their love of sin. Jesus has come to put an end to sin, so people who love their sin feel threatened because Jesus wants to take away what they think they love, to free them from sin.

But what they don't know is that the love of sin is not real love. What they don't know is that what Jesus gives to people is so superior to the love of sin that there is really no comparison. What Jesus gives is so much greater than our paltry love of sin. Our attachment to sin isn't love, it's habit. People are comfortable with their habits, and are afraid of the unknown. So people hold on to what they know. The old saying is "better the devil you know than the devil you don't know." It means that something bad and familiar is better than something bad and unknown. And because sinners don't know the goodness of God, they assume that God, being true and faithful, will give them what they deserve. And they know what they deserve! And so they are afraid.

But what they don't know is the grace of God, the forgiveness of God, the goodness of God, who faithfully bestows His grace and mercy to those who love and honor Him, to a thousand generations. What they don't know is the true story of the Bible, the true story of human history. What people need to know is the good news of Jesus Christ who is Lord and Savior of humanity. A lot of people think that they know it, but they don't. They mistake their own desires for the will of God.

Maybe we can help with that. Maybe you can help someone understand Jesus better. Let's pray for an opportunity.

Beyond Resurrection

On this mountain the Lord of hosts will make for all peoples a feast of rich food, a feast of well-aged wine, of rich food full of marrow, of aged wine well refined. 7 And he will swallow up on this mountain the covering that is cast over all peoples, the veil that is spread over all nations. 8 He will swallow up death forever; and the Lord God will wipe away tears from all faces, and the reproach of his people he will take away from all the earth, for the Lord has spoken. 9 It will be said on that day, "Behold, this is our God; we have waited for him, that he might save us. This is the Lord; we have waited for him; let us be glad and rejoice in his salvation."   —Isaiah 25:6-9

34 So Peter opened his mouth and said: "Truly I understand that God shows no partiality, 35 but in every nation anyone who fears him and does what is right is acceptable to him. 36 As for the word that he sent to Israel, preaching good news of peace through Jesus Christ (he is Lord of all), 37 you yourselves know what happened throughout all Judea, beginning from Galilee after the baptism that John proclaimed: 38 how God anointed Jesus of Nazareth with the Holy Spirit and with power. He went about doing good and healing all who were oppressed by the devil, for God was with him. 39 And we are witnesses of all that he did both in the country of the Jews and in Jerusalem. They put him to death by hanging him on a tree, 40 but God raised him on the third day and made him to appear, 41 not to all the people but to us who had been chosen by God as witnesses, who ate and drank with him after he rose from the dead. 42 And he commanded us to preach to the people and to testify that he is the one appointed by God to be judge of the living and the dead. 43 To him all the prophets bear witness that everyone who believes in him receives forgiveness of sins through his name."   —Acts 10:34-43

Isaiah preached seven hundred years before Jesus. Jesus lived more than two thousand years ago. The things we remember and celebrate in the Bible happened a very long time ago. Why is that important? They are important because we still remember and celebrate them. But we don't remember them like we remember things that actually happened to us in our lives. We have no actual experience of biblical events, so our memories are of stories told and retold.

We are separated from the actual events of the Bible by thousands of years. Our connection to the actual events of the Bible is literary. We read about those events. Our memories are not imaginary, but neither are they experiential. They are historical memories. Our memories of those events are filtered by time, and by thousands of years of retelling and analysis.

Do we today have any actual experience of the biblical stories? Do we have any real connection to the distant past? Or to Jesus? Are they just stories we tell? Do we actually believe that these ancient stories are real in any way? Resurrection? Really? Is our connection with these stories just a matter of thinking? How many Christians throughout history actually had any personal experience with Jesus Christ in the flesh, the historical Person who lived a couple thousand years ago? Very few.

Given that there are two billion Christians alive today and assuming that a thousand people had some actual experience of the resurrected Jesus in the flesh, that means that 0.0000005 percent of Christians have had any actual experience of Jesus as an actual man. That means that 99.9999995 percent of Christians have a different kind of connection, a different kind of experience with Jesus, assuming that Christians do have an actual experiential connection with Jesus Christ.

The Bible places a lot of importance on the reality of Jesus' resurrection, especially on Easter. And Christian history has expended a lot of ink defending the resurrection idea. And so today we Christians believe it to be true, yet we have no actual, personal experience of a resurrection. All we have are stories, testimonies, and analysis. Yet, we believe! Why? Unbelievers and skeptics don't believe it. Why not? Because they have no personal experience of any kind that supports the idea. Do we? It's easy to understand why those who actually encountered the resurrected Jesus in the flesh believed. They simply trusted their own experience. But how did people believe after Jesus' ascension? After He left this world the second time?

Earlier Jesus told His disciples how things would play out after His death, after His ascension.

> "I will ask the Father, and he will give you another Helper, to be with you forever, even the Spirit of truth, whom the world cannot receive, because it neither sees him nor knows him. You know him, for he dwells with you and will be in you" (John 14:16-17).

Jesus sent the Holy Spirit to be with His people. And who is the Holy Spirit? This question can only be answered in the light of the Trinity. God is Father, Son, and Holy Spirit. Three persons, one essence. This is a very odd answer. What is it supposed to mean?

A person is defined as "an individual of specified character; the composite of characteristics that make up an individual personality or a self." A Trinitarian Person, if we can speak of such a thing, is three unique sets of personal characteristics. But it is important to say that we are not talking about one person who has three sets of unique characteristics, but we are talking about three unique, overlapping Persons. The Trinitarian Godhead is not one Person, but is three individual and unique Persons. To say that they are individual means that they are not divided, they are in unity, yet they are not identical. What unifies these Persons is their common essence. So what's an essence?

The definition of essence talks about permanent characteristics as opposed to temporary or accidental characteristics. Essence is the defining or most significant element, quality, aspect, or characteristic of a thing or person. Essence is also the smell of a thing. Perfume has an essence. This is important because it suggests that an essence is not something physical, but is more like a classification, category, of something of a higher order. Essence is contrasted with substance, which suggests something physical, some actual, some underlying substrate. Thus, the primary difference between essence and substance is the difference between the physical and the spiritual. We

could call the spiritual realm the realm of ideas, but not really, because the spiritual is more than just thought or thinking. There is a
spiritual reality that is different from the material reality and more
than the ideas of abstract thought.

Putting all of this together, the Trinity is three unique manifestations of Persons who share one essence. What they share is a spiritual unity, spiritual commonality, a spiritual center. They are
manifestations of the same Spirit. In addition, we need to remember
that the Persons of the Trinity are always together in unity. Where
one is they all are. And that means that when Jesus sent the Holy
Spirit to be with His people in His absence, He was sending Himself
manifest in another Person. The Holy Spirit is also a Person. So
when people have experience of the Holy Spirit they have experience of the Person of Jesus Christ as well.

Paul discovered this on the road to Damascus, when he met the
resurrected Jesus in the Person of the Holy Spirit. Paul not only actually met the resurrected Jesus in the Person of the Holy Spirit, but
that same Holy Spirit then took up residence is Paul's own heart, in
his own inner being. The Holy Spirit is the link between Jesus Christ
and Paul. This link is not only between Jesus Christ and Paul, but—
He, the Holy Spirit—experientially links all Christians to Jesus Christ
and to one another.

What all Christians in all places and in all times have in common
is the Holy Spirit, who brings them into union with the Father
through the Son. The connection between all Christians is the
power and presence of the Holy Spirit who has been dispatched to
bring about the resurrection of all humanity one day.

In the meantime, the Holy Spirit brings about the regeneration
of individuals on earth as the first step toward the final resurrection.
The church on earth is, then, the stepping stone to heaven. Christians are saved into the church, the body of Christ on earth, as a pre-
liminary to our final union with Christ on earth as it is in heaven.
Isaiah prophesied about this:

"He will swallow up death forever; and the Lord God will wipe away tears from all faces, and the reproach of his people he will take away from all the earth, for the Lord has spoken" (v. 8).

In Acts Peter testified that this was exactly what was happening. God has

"anointed Jesus of Nazareth with the Holy Spirit and with power" (v. 38).

At that time Jesus did not appear to all people, but only to those who had been chosen as witnesses, those who ate and drank with Him after He rose from the dead (v. 41). Only a few people had that experience. But as it turns out Paul had essentially the same experience as they had through his encounter with the risen Christ on the Damascus road. Paul had no faithful contact with Jesus in the flesh, only with the resurrected Jesus. So, Paul is more like us today.

The Holy Spirit utterly changed Paul. He became a different person that day, a new person. His old person died, and his new person was born. But Paul's physical body did not die, his person, the composite of characteristics that made up his individual personality or his self underwent a radical change. Technically, Paul was not a new person, he was a *renewed* person. His character changed. He did not become a different person; he became a better human being, an improved person.

If we can compare Paul's experience with computer language, Paul didn't experience a reboot, he was give a new operating system. His name changed from Saul, to Paul; and his character changed from Saul into the likeness of Jesus Christ. He spent the rest of his life growing into the fruits of the Spirit, the characteristics of Jesus Christ.

Today, as important and significant as the resurrection of Jesus Christ is for the world, Christians the world over understand the resurrection of Jesus Christ because of the reality of the Holy Spirit in their own lives. As important as the testimony of others is, and especially the testimony of those first Christians who experienced Jesus in the flesh, Christians today don't rely on the testimony of others. We rely on the reality of the Holy Spirit in our own lives. Of course, not everyone has a knock down experience of the Holy Spirit like Paul had. Nor is that kind of experience necessary.

Most people do not remember the trauma of their own physical birth. But they do know that they were born. The same thing is true among born again Christians. Remembering the past, the birth event, is not nearly as important as focusing on the future, the ongoing life in Christ. Remembering the day or moment of your conversion is not as important as celebrating the spiritual fruits of your life today. The time and circumstances of your conversion are not as important as what you have become as a result of your conversion. The time and circumstances of your birth do not determine the content of your character. Your growth and maturity in Christ determine your character. What happened in the past is gone. What is important now is what lies before us today and in the future. God's future is full of promise and hope.

Let's lean into God's future in Christ with all our might! Lord, make it so, amen.

QUALM BEFORE THE STORM

And he said to me, "Son of man, stand on your feet, and I will speak with you." 2 And as he spoke to me, the Spirit entered into me and set me on my feet, and I heard him speaking to me. 3 And he said to me, "Son of man, I send you to the people of Israel, to nations of rebels, who have rebelled against me. They and their fathers have transgressed against me to this very day. 4 The descendants also are impudent and stubborn: I send you to them, and you shall say to them, 'Thus says the Lord God.' 5 And whether they hear or refuse to hear (for they are a rebellious house) they will know that a prophet has been among them. —Ezekiel 2:1-5

He went away from there and came to his hometown, and his disciples followed him. 2 And on the Sabbath he began to teach in the synagogue, and many who heard him were astonished, saying, "Where did this man get these things? What is the wisdom given to him? How are such mighty works done by his hands? 3 Is not this the carpenter, the son of Mary and brother of James and Joses and Judas and Simon? And are not his sisters here with us?" And they took offense at him. 4 And Jesus said to them, "A prophet is not without honor, except in his hometown and among his relatives and in his own household." 5 And he could do no mighty work there, except that he laid his hands on a few sick people and healed them. 6 And he marveled because of their unbelief. And he went about among the villages teaching. 7 And he called the twelve and began to send them out two by two, and gave them authority over the unclean spirits. 8 He charged them to take nothing for their journey except a staff—no bread, no bag, no money in their belts—9 but to wear sandals and not put on two tunics. 10 And he said to them, "Whenever you enter a house, stay there until you depart from there. 11 And if any place will not receive you and they will not listen to you, when you leave, shake off the dust that is on your feet as a testimony

against them." 12 So they went out and proclaimed that people
should repent. 13 And they cast out many demons and anointed with
oil many who were sick and healed them. —Mark 6:1-13

Ezekiel lived during one of the most tumultuous times of Israel. The kingdom had experienced a civil war and was hopelessly divided. Assyrians had previously conquered the Northern kingdom, and the Southern kingdom of Judah was about to be defeated. The Babylonian Empire had conquered the ancient world and made Israel's kings pay tribute. Babylon was like a mob boss, in that as long as you paid him off, you wouldn't run into trouble. But trouble came when Israel's king decided to not pay their tribute. Trouble ensued and rather than trusting in the Lord to deliver them from the Babylonians, Judah made an alliance with Egypt, the same Egypt who had previously enslaved Israel, and whom they were commanded to avoid. Nonetheless, the Babylonians successfully laid siege to Jerusalem and took most of its inhabitants captive.

Ezekiel lived during the godly reign of King Josiah, who had rediscovered Moses' law, the Deuteronomy scroll that had been lost. and instituted successful reforms in Israel. Ezekiel was born toward the end of Josiah's reign, and the kings following Josiah were not faithful. So Ezekiel knew about faithfulness, and also had witnessed much unfaithfulness by the Temple authorities. Many false Priests and prophets said that Israel would be safe from the Babylonians, but they were not. Babylon sacked Israel and carried off most of the upper class Israelites to Babylon.

Ezekiel's call didn't come until late in his life. He was about thirty. Ezekiel died in his fifties, like most people at the time. Ezekiel's book has three sections: It begins with a strange vision of God involving wheels within wheels suggesting God's glory. It then anticipates the destruction of Jerusalem and the Temple, and explains this as being God's punishment for Israel's faithlessness. And the book closes with the promise of a new beginning and the promise of a new Temple, which anticipated Israel's return from Babylon and the rebuilding of the Temple.

The reading from chapter 2 is about Ezekiel's call. It is a clear description of Ezekiel hearing God's voice, and is important for two reasons: 1) It describes the reality of God giving a message to Ezekiel. And 2) it provides an example for all of God's people because God's message applies to all of people.

What does it mean to hear God's voice? For Ezekiel it was like God was speaking to him in the flesh. The apostles and a few others actually heard Jesus speak in the flesh. But 99.999% of Christians hear God in other ways. For us this hearing isn't physical. For us to hear means to understand and to obey. When I was a child my mom would give me some instruction, and then say, "Did you hear me?" By which she meant: *did I understand that she was issuing a command?*

Some very important things happen in these few verses.

> "And as he spoke to me, the Spirit entered into me and set me on my feet, and I heard him speaking to me" (v. 2).

The Spirit entered into Ezekiel. This is clearly an example of being born again in the Old Testament. When we place our faith in Christ, a divine transaction takes place (2 Corinthians 5:21). At the moment of repentance and faith, the Holy Spirit breathes new life into us. Jesus said,

> "I will ask the Father, and he will give you another Helper, to be with you forever, even the Spirit of truth, whom the world cannot receive, because it neither sees him nor knows him. You know him, for he dwells with you and will be in you" (John 14:16-17).

When that happens we can commune with God's Spirit as He assures us that we belong to Him (Romans 8:16). This was the kind of thing that Ezekiel experienced. God had a message for Israel. God's message was twofold:

1. They were in Babylonian captivity because they had rebelled against God. They had not been faithful, and the destruction of Jerusalem was a consequence of their faithlessness.
2. And God would restore them to faithfulness and reestablish Jerusalem and the Temple.

All of that happened five hundred years before Christ. Israel did return to Jerusalem and rebuild the Temple. And that rebuilt Temple, the Second Temple, was the Temple when Jesus was born. The story of Jesus happened during the time of the Second Temple.

The reading from Mark 6 is to be understood in the light of Ezekiel's prophecy to rebuild the Temple after Israel's disastrous faithlessness five hundred years earlier. Israel's faithlessness destroyed the Temple, God's faithfulness rebuilt it. Into this situation, this historical context, came Jesus Christ. The last verse from our reading from Ezekiel said,

> "And whether they hear or refuse to hear (for they are a rebellious house) they will know that a prophet has been among them" (v. 5).

Whether or not people heard God's message, whether or not they believed, God wanted people to know that a prophet had spoken.

This is odd because we tend to think that God's message or Jesus' salvation is just for believers, that the message doesn't apply to nonbelievers. But God wanted both believers and nonbelievers to know the message of the prophets, and in our day, the message of Jesus Christ. We are not used to thinking like this. We are used to thinking that God's message is for believers—and it is! But God also has a message for unbelievers. God's message is that faithfulness has consequences, and faithlessness also has consequences.

In 1948 Richard Weaver published a book called *Ideas Have Consequences*. It's a philosophical work that deals with the harmful effects of nominalism on Western civilization, since this doctrine gained prominence in the Late Middle Ages. The book provides a course of action through which Weaver believes that the West can be rescued from its decline. Nominalism is the theory that ideas are not real, that ideas are only abstractions, the there is no real connection between words and reality. Weaver argues that ideas are as real as the wind: we can't physically see them, but we can see their effects on the world. We can't see the wind blowing, but we can see the trees moving.

Faith is an idea. It's not a thing. It's a belief. Our beliefs are ideas. The issue is whether faith is real or not. Nominalism says *no*. It's just an idea. The Bible defines faith as confidence in what we hope for and the assurance that the Lord is real. Faith is trusting in God's promises, God's Word. Are promises real? They are if we keep them. God's promises are real because God is faithful. He keeps His promises.

The Hebrew word for *faith* means "support." Faith is the Lord's support, and support is what holds a thing together, what makes it strong. A wall without support will fall. A people without faith will fail. Regardless of what we think, God always knows best. God knows more than we do. God is stronger than we are. And God's ways are not our ways. Our Father knows best.

When we hear God, when we listen to the Holy Spirit, which means when we understand and obey biblical truth, we have faith. And when we don't, we don't. Both hearing and not hearing have real consequences.

One day Jesus taught in his hometown. He taught among people he knew, people who knew him. These were people who had grown up in the Second Temple, the Temple that had been rebuilt hundreds of years earlier because of God's promise to Ezekiel to restore Israel to faithfulness. At the time Israel was filled with Messianic expectations. The Old Testament had promised that a great prophet would return and reestablish the glory of God in Israel. Israel had been waiting for Messiah for hundreds of years.

It seems that if Jesus was to be trusted anywhere, surely He would be most trusted in His hometown, among people who knew Him. They would have known His honesty and integrity. They would have know that He was not a charlatan. But they didn't! Why not? Maybe it was because they didn't understand His message. What was His message?

"Jesus began to preach, saying, 'Repent, for the kingdom of heaven is at hand'" (Matthew 4:17).

Repent! Change your ways, change your beliefs.

Ideas have consequences. The message that people like is that the consequence of faithfulness is salvation. It's not that our faithfulness alone will save us, but that believing in our own salvation brings about our faithfulness through our obedience, partial and hesitant as it is. We are not saved *because* we are faithful, because we are not. We're working on it! Rather, we respond to God's salvation with the desire to become faithful. Our desires change.

But the message that people don't like is that the consequence of faithlessness is damnation. And again, it's not that our faithlessness produces damnation, but rather that believing in our own damnation brings about our faithlessness, our lack of desire to be obedient. If we fail to believe in the power of God's salvation, we continue in the power of Satan's damnation. Our minds are not changed.

Here's how it works: if we believe that God loves us, that God has already saved us, we find that we actually want to love and obey God's Word in gratitude. When we believe or understand that God loves us first, in the midst of all of our sinfulness, we respond to God's love for us with our love for Him. But when we believe or think that God does not love us first, that we have to prove our love for God before He will save us, we respond to what we think is God's lack of love for us in all of our sinfulness. We respond to our perception of God's lack of love for us with a lack of love for Him. And so, it all hinges on our belief, our faith, on the idea that God really loves us in spite of our sinfulness.

If we believe that God loves us, and He does, we respond positively and grow in obedience. Our belief does not make it true. It's just true already! And that truth makes us willing. But if we don't believe that God loves us, even though He actually does, we respond negatively, and continue in disobedience. Our belief doesn't mean that God doesn't love us. Our lack of belief doesn't make God hate us, but neither does it eliminate our sin. And our unforgiven sin, the sin that we cling to, that we will not give up, condemns us. And because we continue to believe that we are condemned, we give up hope, and are unwilling to obey God.

Ideas have consequences. There is a storm on the horizon. Will God see you through it? Do you believe that He will? Or do you believe that He won't? Ideas have consequences.

Pent & Repent

36 As they were talking about these things, Jesus himself stood among them, and said to them, "Peace to you!" 37 But they were startled and frightened and thought they saw a spirit. 38 And he said to them, "Why are you troubled, and why do doubts arise in your hearts? 39 See my hands and my feet, that it is I myself. Touch me, and see. For a spirit does not have flesh and bones as you see that I have." 40 And when he had said this, he showed them his hands and his feet. 41 And while they still disbelieved for joy and were marveling, he said to them, "Have you anything here to eat?" 42 They gave him a piece of broiled fish, 43 and he took it and ate before them. 44 Then he said to them, "These are my words that I spoke to you while I was still with you, that everything written about me in the Law of Moses and the Prophets and the Psalms must be fulfilled." 45 Then he opened their minds to understand the Scriptures, 46 and said to them, "Thus it is written, that the Christ should suffer and on the third day rise from the dead, 47 and that repentance for the forgiveness of sins should be proclaimed in his name to all nations, beginning from Jerusalem. 48 You are witnesses of these things." —Luke 24:36-48

12 And when Peter saw it he addressed the people: "Men of Israel, why do you wonder at this, or why do you stare at us, as though by our own power or piety we have made him walk? 13 The God of Abraham, the God of Isaac, and the God of Jacob, the God of our fathers, glorified his servant Jesus, whom you delivered over and denied in the presence of Pilate, when he had decided to release him. 14 But you denied the Holy and Righteous One, and asked for a murderer to be granted to you, 15 and you killed the Author of life, whom God raised from the dead. To this we are witnesses. 16 And his name—by faith in his name—has made this man strong whom you see and know, and the faith that is through Jesus has given the

man this perfect health in the presence of you all. 17 "And now,
brothers, I know that you acted in ignorance, as did also your rulers.
18 But what God foretold by the mouth of all the prophets, that his
Christ would suffer, he thus fulfilled. 19 Repent therefore, and turn
back, that your sins may be blotted out.   —*Acts 3:12-19*

Let's look closely at Luke's report of Jesus' resurrection appearance to the disciples in the Upper Room. Luke did not include the story about Thomas. Rather, Luke's concern was that Jesus' resurrection was real. The resurrected Jesus was not a spirit, nor was He resurrected into heaven, but He was resurrected into His human body on earth. He ate with them because He knew that they knew that ghosts don't eat. His eating proved to them that His resurrection body was just like their bodies.

The fact that Jesus remained human is important because it makes the story real. It's not a ghost story. Jesus told them that His death and resurrection were part of the fulfillment of the Old Testament prophecy. And He

"he opened their minds to understand the Scriptures" (v. 45).

This is Luke's way of saying that Jesus gave them the Holy Spirit. Luke also talked about the power of forgiveness:

"that repentance for the forgiveness of sins should be proclaimed in his name to all nations" (v. 47).

Notice how Luke phrased it: "repentance for the forgiveness of sins." He tied repentance and forgiveness together.

The Acts reading follows the story of the healing of a man, lame from birth, who had been healed by the name of Jesus. Peter said to him,

"I have no silver and gold, but what I do have I give to you. In the name of Jesus Christ of Nazareth, rise up and walk!" (v. 6).

The people who witnessed the healing were "utterly astounded" as they gathered on Solomon's portico to see the man themselves. Peter used that occasion to preach to the gathered crowd. He began by denying that the disciples had any power to heal. The power was not theirs, but belonged to

> "the God of Abraham, the God of Isaac, and the God of Jacob, the God of our fathers" (v. 13).

That power had healed the man in order to glorify

> "Jesus, whom you delivered over and denied in the presence of Pilate" (v. 13).

Peter simultaneously gave glory to God for the healing, and accused the gathered Jews of crucifying Jesus. He began his sermon by accusing his audience.

Preaching like this is not taught in the seminaries. You don't begin by accusing your audience. Start with a joke or a story to gain rapport with them. Help them identify with you, to see that you are like them, because people listen to people who are like them. Make no more than three points. Tell them what you are going to tell them. Then tell them. And then tell them what you told them. This will help them remember what you said.

But that's not what Peter did! Peter began by accusing them of killing Jesus Christ, the Son of God, the Son of the God of Abraham, Isaac, and Jacob—their God! By doing so they publicly denied their own God before Pilate by demanding the release of Barabbas and the condemnation of Jesus. "You killed the Author of life!" (v. 15), he cried. I imagine Peter scowling and shaking his finger at them.

In the previous chapter we talked about the keys to the kingdom, the power of forgiveness, and how Thomas had been converted when Jesus forgave him for his disbelief. The power of forgiveness is the power of the gospel. Forgiveness is the essential message of the gospel and was given to the disciples when Jesus breathed on them, when He breathed the breath of new life into them, when they were filled with the power of the Holy Spirit. Forgiveness is the key!

But here Peter in his very first sermon accused his audience of having murdered the Lord of Life! Did Peter not get the memo?! Did Peter forget to share the power of forgiveness? Maybe he forgot in the excitement of the healing and the confusion on the portico as people gathered to see the miracle for themselves. Maybe. But no, that's not what was going on. Peter's sermon was perfectly faithful to the gospel of Jesus Christ. How so?

In the last chapter we saw that the action or power of the gospel did not come from giving forgiveness, but came from receiving forgiveness. The gospel is not a matter of going around and randomly telling people that they have been forgiven by the grace and mercy of Jesus Christ. The message of forgiveness falls flat when people think that they don't need it, or that it is given to everyone for everything.

If I have not harmed anyone, if I have not defamed, defrauded, or belittled anyone, or think that I haven't, I don't need to be forgiven. And if I acknowledge my sin, but believe that God has already given forgiveness to everyone for everything, then I don't need to receive anything. The message of forgiveness only has application to the guilty who know that they are guilty. Apart from real guilt, forgiveness can safely be ignored.

It seems to me that this happens a lot today. People see the message of forgiveness plastered on billboards, hear it broadcast over the radio waves, and shared from pulpits, with no effect. The preaching of the gospel falls flat, it fails to reach the ears of most people today. Why is the message of the gospel not prospering today?

There is no question that the church today doesn't have the kind of power or effect that this sermon of Peter had on his audience. Why is that? Are people less guilty today than people were in Peter's day? Did Peter do something that pastors are not doing today? How is Peter's message different than messages from pulpits today? Peter said,

> "you denied the Holy and Righteous One, and asked for a murderer to be granted to you, and you killed the Author of life, whom God raised from the dead. To this we are witnesses" (vs. 14–15).

Peter said that Jesus' death revealed two things: 1) that they killed Jesus, and 2) that God raised Jesus from the dead. These two messages need to be held together. Either one without the other is powerless. To simply accuse people won't move the gospel forward.

The message that Jesus died for our sins, while true, is inadequate. It doesn't connect with people who are outside of the church, people who do not already identify as Christian. A common response is: *That's great! I'm glad that works for you;* or *Jesus is a crutch, which is fine for people who need a crutch. But I don't need it. I'm fine.* The message of forgiveness by itself doesn't connect. People have become numb to it. It's like a commercial that you've seen a thousand times. People quit listening to it. People just don't hear it because they don't need it, or don't think that they need it.

Peter continued by telling his audience how the lame man had been healed. Faith in the name of Jesus Christ

> "has made this man strong whom you see and know, and the faith that is through Jesus has given the man this perfect health in the presence of you all" (v. 16).

Peter pointed out the real source of the man's healing—faith in Jesus Christ. What was it about this particular man who had been lame from birth that allowed him to receive the healing power of forgiveness?

It is important to understand that forgiveness is the power of the gospel, and to see how forgiveness played into this man's healing. And it is not obvious, and particularly not obvious simply from the Lectionary reading. This is because the Lectionary reading does not include the whole story. To see the whole story we need to read all of chapter three.

The story began when the man asked Peter and John for money (alms). He was begging people as they went into the Temple. Verse 4 is very odd:

> "And Peter directed his gaze at him, as did John, and said, 'Look at us.'"

Peter said, *We don't have any money, but we have something that might help.*

"And (the man) fixed his attention on (Peter and John), expecting to receive something from them" (v. 4)

Notice two things: Peter and John *looked deeply* at the man, and the man expected to receive something. The man had no hope. He had given up on life and resigned himself to a life of begging. The man was stuck in a rut. Peter and John saw beyond the man's lameness; they saw the reality of his hopelessness. And the man knew that they saw him for what he was, that he had given up on life!

If it is true that the gospel moves through the power of forgiveness, then forgiveness must have played a roll in the man's healing. But we don't see it directly. But neither does the recorded story tell us everything that happened that day. Therefore we must assume that Peter and John effectively shared the gospel of forgiveness with the man. In other words, we assume that the man heard the gospel of forgiveness because that's the only way that the gospel moves in someone's life.

And hearing it means that he acknowledged his own personal guilt. And that was the moment of his healing. That's it! The moment of healing, the moment of hearing, the moment of receiving forgiveness, the moment of receiving the gospel, the good news of salvation comes through the acknowledgement of our own personal guilt so that we can see that God's forgiveness actually applies to *us*. It's easy to say the words. It's easy to think about the idea. But the real admission of one's own personal guilt is a hard, personal moment. It's a hard thing to admit if it's real.

The first step of Alcoholics Anonymous (AA) applies here: 1. *We admitted we were powerless over alcohol—that our lives have become unmanageable.* We need a Sinner's Anonymous Twelve Step program that would say: 1. We admitted we were powerless over (insert personal sin here)—that our lives have become unmanageable. 2. We came to believe that a Power greater than ourselves could restore us to sanity. AA doesn't want to offend anyone or scare people away, so they don't name the Power. But it's Jesus Christ. We know that.

This is the moment of change, the moment of repentance. Repentance is not about feeling bad, though feeling bad is inevitable because of the mess we have made of things. Repentance is about the end of the person you thought you were, and the beginning of the person that God knows you to be.

The Lectionary reading leaves the story with the call for repentance. But there is more to the story, and I commend it to you. Take a moment and read the rest of chapter three so that you can see that Peter's initial accusation was accurate and that they did receive God's forgiveness and repent. Peter's sermon worked. People heard the gospel and were changed.

Maybe there's a message for us in that.

WHAT AUTHORITY?

"I am the good shepherd. The good shepherd lays down his life for the sheep. 12 He who is a hired hand and not a shepherd, who does not own the sheep, sees the wolf coming and leaves the sheep and flees, and the wolf snatches them and scatters them. 13 He flees because he is a hired hand and cares nothing for the sheep. 14 I am the good shepherd. I know my own and my own know me, 15 just as the Father knows me and I know the Father; and I lay down my life for the sheep. 16 And I have other sheep that are not of this fold. I must bring them also, and they will listen to my voice. So there will be one flock, one shepherd. 17 For this reason the Father loves me, because I lay down my life that I may take it up again. 18 No one takes it from me, but I lay it down of my own accord. I have authority to lay it down, and I have authority to take it up again. This charge I have received from my Father." —John 10:11-18

On the next day their rulers and elders and scribes gathered together in Jerusalem, 6 with Annas the high priest and Caiaphas and John and Alexander, and all who were of the high-priestly family. 7 And when they had set them in the midst, they inquired, "By what power or by what name did you do this?" 8 Then Peter, filled with the Holy Spirit, said to them, "Rulers of the people and elders, 9 if we are being examined today concerning a good deed done to a crippled man, by what means this man has been healed, 10 let it be known to all of you and to all the people of Israel that by the name of Jesus Christ of Nazareth, whom you crucified, whom God raised from the dead—by him this man is standing before you well. 11 This Jesus is the stone that was rejected by you, the builders, which has become the cornerstone. 12 And there is salvation in no one else, for there is no other name under heaven given among men by which we must be saved." —Acts 4:5-12

The story of the healing of the lame man continues as the Temple authorities hear about it and call the disciples in to explain themselves. The situation looks like a courtroom scene

> "with Annas the high priest and Caiaphas and John and Alexander, and all who were of the high-priestly family (gathered). ... they inquired, 'By what power or by what name did you do this?'" (v. 6-7).

Their concern was not for the healed man. They were not celebrating the fact that someone had been healed of a lifelong malady. Their concern was the authorization of the disciples. *Who gave you permission to do ministry in the Temple?* It's a legitimate concern. We would have the same kind of concern if someone that we did not know began preaching or teaching at St. Paul's. We would be concerned because there are existing structures of authority in place here, structures that we agree with and that we have control of. The same would be true in any church today, or in any day.

> "Then Peter, filled with the Holy Spirit, said to them..." (v. 8).

Before we look at what Peter said, we need to understand the authority and power under which Peter was operating. The primary element of His authority and power was the Holy Spirit. And the fact that it was the Holy Spirit was problematic for the Temple authorities because they had no knowledge or experience of the Holy Spirit.

And to see how the Holy Spirit functions in the church, the Lectionary takes us to John 10:11-18, where Jesus is described as the Good Shepherd, and serves as the model for church ministry. According to this model, the pastor is the shepherd of the flock, the local church. Jesus provided the model for how it is supposed to work. The good shepherd is contrasted with the hired hand, and that contrast tells us that the shepherd is not to be like a hired hand.

There are two aspects of the message here: one is for the church and one is for the shepherd. The message to the church is not about paying the pastor. Jesus was not suggesting that shepherd should not be paid. But *paid* is not the right way to understand what we should call pastoral remuneration. The problem with thinking or saying that the pastor is paid a salary is that those words turn pastoral ministry into a job. Pastoral ministry is not a job, it is a calling. We hire someone to do a job, and we then pay the person to do the job. This is a secular or worldly way of defining pastoral ministry. And if we define pastoral ministry in a secular or worldly terms, we strip it of its spiritual or godly aspects. If pastoral ministry is a job, then the pastor is a hired hand by definition.

And, indeed, this is the way that the government defines pastoral ministry. But it is not the way that the church should define it. The church should not follow the lead of the secular government, nor should the government impose its definitions of the church on the church. Traditionally, in the U.S. there is a separation between church and state. They operate in different spheres or jurisdictions. Each should stay out of the jurisdiction of the other. The contrast of jurisdictions is between the good shepherd and the hired hand. And the difference is in the attitude of both the shepherd and the church.

The shepherd is not *hired* to do a job, he is *called* to his life's work. The church is not to *pay* the pastor a salary, but is to *support* the life work of the shepherd. And the shepherd is not *called* to do a job, he is called to serve the Lord in a particular place at a particular time. In part the issue is: who does the shepherd work for? Or to whom is the shepherd responsible? Who is his boss?

The shepherd does not work for the sheep. The shepherd works for the owner of the sheep. The shepherd does not own the sheep, nor do the sheep own the shepherd. However, the primary concern of the shepherd is the well-being of the sheep. And it's a hard job because the sheep are their own worst enemies. They are forever getting themselves into trouble.

Sheep are among the dumbest animals. Maybe *dumb* is the wrong word. Let's say that they are *short-sighted*. They eat anything in front of them, so the shepherd needs to make sure that they are grazing in the right places. And they are completely defenseless. Their only real defense is to grow an impenetrable bun-

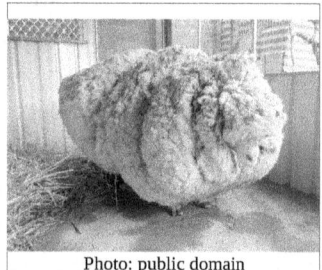
Photo: public domain

dle of wool between them and the world. An unsheared sheep is a sight to behold! Sheep need to be sheared, otherwise their unsheared wool will be the death of them.

The good shepherd defends the flock with his life. He does not abandon them when things get tough. In contrast, the hired hand works in order to get paid. He's not working for the owner or the sheep, he's working for the money. His primary concern is not about the sheep, he cares about the money. He is paid a salary to do a job. The hired hand is not engaged in a life work that is larger than himself. He is working for himself. And when the work no longer serves him, he moves on. The good shepherd does not move on. He remains with the flock no matter what. But neither does the good shepherd always give the sheep what they want because they often want what is not good for them because they feed indiscriminately. Again, sheep will graze a field bare regardless what grows there.

Sheep gather in flocks. *Flock* refers to a relatively small sheep group, a family. If the group of sheep is larger, the group may be called a mob, a fold, or a band. Herd is also used. Herd is more of a slang version, based on the word *shep-herd*, which is short for sheepherder. The sheepherder keeps the sheep united by herding them. A herd of sheep is composed of several flocks or small groups. The small group or flock is the primary group for sheep. The integrity of the various flocks are preserved in the herd.

In addition, sheep are habitual creatures. They like their habits. They are comfortable with what they know, what they are used to. And they grow used to the shepherds voice. Shepherds often sing to their sheep to comfort them. The sheep hear the voice of the shepherd and know that everything is under control. The shepherd even develops a personal relationship with the sheep. They don't object when he handles them. He can sheer them, give them a haircut. And they don't object. He inspects them often because they are always getting problematic stuff caught in their fur.

Jesus said that he has other sheep of a different fold, a different herd. For pastors that means that ministry requires more than simply tending the local flock, the local church. The pastor needs to be involved in other community groups, and to minister to people outside of the local church. He does that in order to model evangelism, be-cause all Christians are to be involved in more than their local church. We need relationships within the larger community in order to extend the ministry of the church, the ministry of the gospel.

Nonetheless, all of the various groups, flocks, and folds all belong to the one great shepherd, Jesus Christ. He is the master shepherd of all of the sheep. As a model of commitment Jesus then laid down his own life. No one took His life from Him. He voluntarily gave Him-self up for the work of His ministry. And that is the model, not only for the shepherd, but for all Christians. Jesus said,

> "I have authority to lay it (His life) down, and I have authority to take it up again" (v. 18).

And that is the authority that the first disciples had, and the au-thority that all disciples always have. Jesus is our authority. And that is the right answer to the question asked of the disciples by the Tem-ple authorities when they healed the lame man. How did they ac-quire this authority?

> "Then Peter, filled with the Holy Spirit, said to them" (v. 8).

He told them about their authority. *It is not ours,* he said, *we didn't do it.* Rather,

> "let it be known to all of you and to all the people of Israel that by the name of Jesus Christ of Nazareth, whom you crucified, whom God raised from the dead—by him this man is standing before you well" (v. 10).

Jesus is the power and authority.

> "This Jesus is the stone that was rejected by you, the builders, which has become the cornerstone. And there is salvation in no one else, for there is no other name under heaven given among men by which we must be saved" (vs. 11-12).

Jesus is the authority and the power, and you killed Him! And now you need to turn to Him to be saved. That's how the apostles preached the gospel. Maybe there is a lesson for us in that.

GENUINE GOD TALK

*9 As the Father has loved me, so have I loved you. Abide in my love.
10 If you keep my commandments, you will abide in my love, just as
I have kept my Father's commandments and abide in his love. 11
These things I have spoken to you, that my joy may be in you, and
that your joy may be full. 12 This is my commandment, that you
love one another as I have loved you. 13 Greater love has no one
than this, that someone lay down his life for his friends. 14 You are
my friends if you do what I command you. 15 No longer do I call
you servants, for the servant does not know what his master is doing;
but I have called you friends, for all that I have heard from my Father I have made known to you. 16 You did not choose me, but I
chose you and appointed you that you should go and bear fruit and
that your fruit should abide, so that whatever you ask the Father in
my name, he may give it to you. 17 These things I command you, so
that you will love one another.* —John 15:9-17

*44 While Peter was still saying these things, the Holy Spirit fell on
all who heard the word. 45 And the believers from among the circumcised who had come with Peter were amazed, because the gift of
the Holy Spirit was poured out even on the Gentiles. 46 For they
were hearing them speaking in tongues and extolling God. Then Peter declared, 47 "Can anyone withhold water for baptizing these
people, who have received the Holy Spirit just as we have?" 48 And
he commanded them to be baptized in the name of Jesus Christ.
Then they asked him to remain for some days.* —Acts 10:44-48

Let's begin with Acts, and come back to John, because in order to
understand Acts 10:44-48, we need to know what has preceded
it. What things was Peter still saying when the Holy Spirit fell? The
Lectionary jumps to the end of a series of events to provide a lesson.

But we need to understand the whole story before we can appreciate the lesson.

The story under consideration began in Acts 9. It's a story about the Holy Spirit, and it begins with Paul being confronted with Jesus Christ on the road to Damascus. The general thrust of the story is about the reception of the Holy Spirit, how that works, and what the Spirit is doing.

Paul was a very unlikely convert to Christianity. We know the story: he was the chief persecutor of Christians when Jesus showed him that he was blind, and unable to see the Truth. Jesus came into his life and showed him what he had missed in his blindness as a Pharisee. At *that* point Jesus became alive to him. The reality of Jesus' resurrection became real in his own life, and the rest is history. That was Acts 9.

Acts 10 continues the story of the movement of the Holy Spirit. Cornelius went to get Peter so he could preach to the Gentiles. Peter had a vision about clean and unclean food. In the vision was a message about Jewish law, food laws in particular. The message to Peter was that all food was clean in Christ.

God had used various cultural practices to create a separation between the Jews and the Gentiles. God had separated the Jews from the rest of the world in various cultural ways because He had a specific job for them. The coming of Jesus Christ meant the completion of that job. The message of Peter's vision was that all food was acceptable in Christ; the kosher food laws were no longer applicable because God was using Jesus Christ to bring all people together. God was tearing down the cultural walls and divisions between Jews and Gentiles. Jesus Christ was opening the gospel to all of the peoples of the world, not just the Jews.

So, Peter went with Cornelius and preached that message to the Gentiles, and the Holy Spirit fell upon them. This story is the reading from Acts today. The Gentiles received the message of salvation from the Holy Spirit in the same way that the Jews had received it. The separation between Jew and Gentile had been breached by the Holy Spirit, who had now come to both Jew and Gentile. The message about salvation in Jesus Christ was given to the Gentiles by the Holy Spirit through Peter. And the Gentiles received it with joy.

"For they were hearing them speaking with tongues and exalting God" (v. 46).

Who was hearing whom? The *Gentiles* were hearing Peter and the disciples speak about Jesus Christ. And Peter and the disciples were also hearing the Gentiles speak about Jesus Christ in language that the Gentiles understood—Greek and other languages, not Hebrew. Everyone was hearing the message about Jesus Christ through the Holy Spirit in a language that they could understand. And this is the heart of the message of the Gospel. The message comes through the preacher, but the message is not complete until it is received by the people who hear it, who understand it.

And there is more! The message of the Gospel is not complete until the people who hear it are able to speak it themselves in their own native tongue. And as the Gentiles speak it in their own languages, others are then able to hear it. When or as all of this happened, the Holy Spirit moved forward, moving out from the Jews to the world through the Gentiles. At this point we can appreciate the conclusion or lesson of this story, which is the manifestation of the Holy Spirit among the Gentiles.

John 15:9-17 then provides that lesson that reveals the essence or heart of the message of the Gospel. And what is that message? Jesus summed it up:

"As the Father has loved me, so have I loved you" (v. 9).

The message is God's love for the world. And because God loves the world, God wants the world to love Him because reciprocal love is the fullness of love. So how do we love God?

Of course, love is the feeling of attraction, care, concern, and satisfaction when we are with the one we love. But love is more than a feeling. In order to abide in God's love, we need to keep God's commandments. The purpose of all of this is "that (God's) joy may be in you, and that your joy may be full" (v. 11).

This was not a new message. It is also the message of the Old Testament. But there was a problem in the Old Testament world. The Jews had been trying to keep God's commandments for a couple thousand years, but were not able to do it. The law began with the Ten Commandments, and progressed through the 644 laws of the Old Testament, to the tithing of dill and cumin.

Jesus had accused the Temple establishment of failure:

> "Woe to you, scribes and Pharisees, hypocrites! For you tithe mint and dill and cumin, and have neglected the weightier matters of the law: justice and mercy and faithfulness. These you ought to have done, without neglecting the others" (Matthew 23:23).

God had given the law to the Jews and separated them from the cultures of the world so that they could not blame anyone else for their multiple failures to live in obedience. God knew that they would fail, but charged them to succeed, knowing that they would fail. Why would God do that? Why would God demand that people do something that they could not do, and then ask them to record their repeated efforts and failures? Is God cruel? Or is He just toying with people?

No. He has a purpose in all of this. His purpose was to demonstrate to humanity that humanity needs a Savior, that humanity needs help to keep from destroying themselves, that humanity needs guidance in order to survive long time in the world, in *this* world.

If you have children, you know that imposing rules on them doesn't work for very long. At some point in their maturity they will need to willingly respond to good advice, advice that will benefit them. Advice is rules or principles regarding behavior that is not imposed, but is recommended. Advice usually comes with reasons and justifications for doing something in particular. Advice is not a demand, it is a plea, an appeal, a petition, a recommendation, a prayer or supplication.

Does God give advice? The word *advice* is not a biblical word. It doesn't occur in the Bible. God gives commands, not advice. But we are advised to heed His commands. The reason that God doesn't give advice is that advice is defined as an opinion. And God doesn't have opinions because opinions lack the assurance of ultimate truth. God knows the Truth. Or we could say that God's opinion is the Truth. But the idea of opinion lacks the assurance of proof. And God has the proof. God's Word is the proof. The Bible is the proof.

The Old Testament is the proof that humanity is unable to live in obedience to God's law, God's commands. Israel's failure is the failure of humanity. We are all unable! Therefore, we need help. And the New Testament provides the help that we need: Jesus Christ in the flesh! So, Jesus has given us a new command:

> "This is my commandment, that you love one another as I have loved you. Greater love has no one than this, that someone lay down his life for his friends. You are my friends if you do what I command you" (vs. 12-14).

The problem is that love cannot be imposed. Love must be willingly given. So Jesus' command, though He knows it to be the absolute Truth, comes as advice to believers. He will not impose His law, His understanding of the world, but demands that His love be willingly accepted. And, of course, it cannot be willingly accepted unless we actually believe God's love and God's law to be the absolute Truth. This lesson will stand in history until it is learned. Because when we fail to learn it, we invite the consequences of our failure. What consequences?

God has shown us in the Old Testament that our failure of love and obedience leads to death and destruction. The story of Israel in the Old Testament is the story of the failure of the brightest and the best to actually love and obey God. Apart from Christ, God wiped their nation from the the face of the earth with the complete destruction of the Temple and Jerusalem in A.D. 70. The Jews lost their nation and have never been the same.

But in Christ, we like they, Gentile and Jew, have another opportunity. In Christ we can be God's friends. But it is not a friendship that we as unrepentant people have chosen. Unrepentant people want nothing to do with Jesus. Jesus said,

"You did not choose me, but I chose you and appointed you that you should go and bear fruit and that your fruit should abide, so that whatever you ask the Father in my name, he may give it to you (v. 16).

The deciding choice belongs to Jesus, not to us.

So, if you hear my voice, if you understand what I'm saying, what Christ is saying, then you understand that I am not asking you to make a choice. I'm saying that Jesus has already chosen you. So you are not faced with a choice. You, chosen by Jesus, are faced with a command:

"These things I command you, so that you will love one another" (v. 17).

I'm not calling you to make a decision. Jesus is calling you to action, to obedience!

Can you hear Him?

ANTICIPATION

15 In those days Peter stood up among the brothers (the company of persons was in all about 120) and said, 16 "Brothers, the Scripture had to be fulfilled, which the Holy Spirit spoke beforehand by the mouth of David concerning Judas, who became a guide to those who arrested Jesus. 17 For he was numbered among us and was allotted his share in this ministry. … 21 So one of the men who have accompanied us during all the time that the Lord Jesus went in and out among us, 22 beginning from the baptism of John until the day when he was taken up from us—one of these men must become with us a witness to his resurrection." 23 And they put forward two, Joseph called Barsabbas, who was also called Justus, and Matthias. 24 And they prayed and said, "You, Lord, who know the hearts of all, show which one of these two you have chosen 25 to take the place in this ministry and apostleship from which Judas turned aside to go to his own place." 26 And they cast lots for them, and the lot fell on Matthias, and he was numbered with the eleven apostles.
—Acts 1:15-17, 21-26

6 "I have manifested your name to the people whom you gave me out of the world. Yours they were, and you gave them to me, and they have kept your word. 7 Now they know that everything that you have given me is from you. 8 For I have given them the words that you gave me, and they have received them and have come to know in truth that I came from you; and they have believed that you sent me. 9 I am praying for them. I am not praying for the world but for those whom you have given me, for they are yours. 10 All mine are yours, and yours are mine, and I am glorified in them. 11 And I am no longer in the world, but they are in the world, and I am coming to you. Holy Father, keep them in your name, which you have given me, that they may be one, even as we are one. 12 While I was with them, I kept them in your name, which you have given me. I have guarded them, and not one of them has been lost except the son of destruction, that the Scripture might be fulfilled. 13 But now I am coming to you, and these things I speak in the world, that they may have my joy fulfilled in themselves. 14 I have given them your word, and the world has hated them because they are not of the world, just as I am not of the world. 15 I do not ask that you take them out of the world, but that you keep them from the evil one. 16 They are not of the world, just as I am not of the world. 17 Sanctify them in the truth; your word is truth. 18 As you sent me into the world, so I have sent them into the world. 19 And for their sake I consecrate myself, that they also may be sanctified in truth. —John 17:6-19

What is missing from the Lectionary in our Acts reading this morning is the story of Judas' death. Judas had betrayed Jesus in the garden leading to Jesus' death. The question that we are sidestepping this morning is whether Judas was obedient. Was Judas betraying Jesus, or was he being obedient? It was necessary for Jesus to die on the cross in order to fulfill the message of the gospel. And Judas facilitated that.

But we are not going to deal with that part of the story today. Rather, the story that the Lectionary provides is about the apostles. It is related to Judas because after his death Judas was missing from the apostolic roster. There had been twelve apostles and the number twelve is significant in that there were also twelve tribes of Israelites in the Old Testament. The apostolic board had twelve members, twelve positions, and with Judas' death, there was an opening. They were short a man. They needed a replacement. And they were not wrong in this assessment. They cited Psalm 109:8 to justify their action: "may another take his office!"

But there was a problem: the Psalm did not say: *elect a replacement.* Yet there was a vacancy! What were they to do? They decided to fix the problem, to fill the empty position on the board themselves. So, they elected Matthaias. They thought that they were being faithful to Scripture, which said, "may another take his office!" But they weren't. They failed to read and heed the Scripture closely.

They thought that they understood the general meaning of the words.

Their actions are reminiscent of various kings in the Old Testament: Saul, Agag, and Solomon. They thought that they were being faithful to God, to God's Word, but they were not. Over and over King Saul thought that he was being faithful to God, but he was not. His obedience to God was only partial.

In 1 Samuel 13 Saul was supposed to meet Samuel prior to a battle, so Samuel could pray and offer sacrifice before the battle. But Samuel was late. So, Saul prayed and offered the sacrifice himself. But Saul, the King, was not authorized to perform the duties of a priest. Rather than wait, Saul got impatient and got ahead of the Lord.

When Samuel arrived he chastised Saul. The Lord had instructed Saul to utterly destroy the enemy, the Amalakites. After the battle, after Samuel arrived, Samuel and Saul met. Samuel noticed that Saul had not utterly destroyed the enemy. Saul thought that he had followed God's instruction close enough. Saul won the battle. Samuel disagreed. Saul thought that he was being faithful, but he adjusted God's instruction to suit himself.

Solomon did the same kind of thing. Solomon preserved God's Word, collected and edited the books of Moses, and added the book of Proverbs. Solomon thought that he understood God's Word—and his work is commendable. But there was a problem.

> "When the Lord your God brings you into the land that you are entering to take possession of it, and clears away many nations before you, the Hittites, the Girgashites, the Amorites, the Canaanites, the Perizzites, the Hivites, and the Jebusites, seven nations more numerous and mightier than you, and when the Lord your God gives them over to you, and you defeat them, then you must devote them to complete destruction. You shall make no covenant with them and show no mercy to them. You shall not intermarry with them, giving your daughters to their sons or taking their daughters for your sons, for they would turn away your sons from following me, to serve other gods" (Deuteronomy 7:1-4).

And who did Solomon marry?

"And Solomon became allied to Pharaoh king of Egypt by marriage, and took Pharaoh's daughter, and brought her into the city of David, until he had made an end of building his own house, and the house of the Lord, and the wall of Jerusalem round about" (1 Kings 3:1).

Solomon married Pharaoh's daughter! And what did the apostles do?

"And they cast lots for them, and the lot fell on Matthias, and he was numbered with the eleven apostles" (v. 26).

They elected Matthias to the apostolic board because they had a vacancy. So, what's the problem? If Matthias was the twelveth apostle replacing Judas, then Paul was the thirteenth. And that messes up the symbolism related to the number twelve. What do we know about Matthias? Nothing. Scripture says nothing about him. We never hear about him again. But the New Testament says a lot about the apostle Paul.

What happened? The apostles got ahead of the Lord. Rather than waiting for the Lord to fill the vacancy, they thought that they needed to put someone in Judas' slot. They knew that there should be twelve apostles, not eleven. Matthias was the apostle's choice, but Paul was God's choice.

The Lectionary then points us to John 17, Jesus' prayer for His people. The first thing to notice about this prayer is that Jesus distinguished between two groups of people: God's people and worldly people. The first group are those whom God gave Jesus "out of the world" (v. 6). Those who are of Christ are no longer of the world. There is a difference between God's people and worldly people.

God's people have received Jesus' words, have come to know the truth that Jesus comes from God. Jesus did not pray for the unrepentant people, those who will not recognized that Jesus is the messiah of God. They won't listen to Him, so He doesn't listen to them. Rather, He puts His attention on those who put their attention on Him.

There is a similarity of Jesus' prayer in John 17 and the Lord's Prayer in Matthew 6. The prayers are repeatedly directed to God the Father. There is recognition of and concern for God's name. There is concern for the work of the kingdom of God. There is concern for keeping from evil.

And there are also differences: John 17 focuses on two different groups of people: God's people and worldly people. The Lord's Prayer focuses on one group: those who call God "Our Father." The central concern in John 17 is glory. The glory of the gospel is Jesus's resurrection, but resurrection requires Jesus' death on the cross. And here Jesus accepted His role to die on the cross for the glory of God.

Jesus was aware that His mantle, His mission, was being passed to His people. Not everyone will believe, but some will. And Jesus aims His prayer at believers. Jesus has given His people God's words, and they received them. Those who receive God's words know the truth about Jesus.

> "Holy Father, keep them in your name, which you have given me, that they may be one, even as we are one" (v. 11).

In the Bible, when we read the word *name*, we should think *character*. The name of a thing points to the character of the thing named. Jesus prayed that God would keep His people in God's *character*. Christians are to aspire to reflect or reproduce the characteristics of Jesus. Christians are, first and foremost, to manifest the fruits of the spirit in their own lives:

> "love, joy, peace, patience, kindness, goodness, faithfulness, gentleness, and self-control" (Galatians 5:22–23).

The purpose of doing this is Christian unity,

> "that they may be one, even as we are one" (v. 11).

Those who have survived the United Church of Christ (UCC) still hold on to this verse because it is at the heart of the gospel, and was the motto of the UCC. Christian unity is found in ordinary faithfulness, not in denominational pronouncements. Christian unity will be manifest in this world inasmuch as ordinary Christians manifest the fruits of the spirit in their own lives, in *our* own lives. Christian unity does not require denominational conformity.

Jesus was aware that His human body would soon be taken from this world. He knew and accepted that He was headed to the cross. His destination on the cross did not lessen His joy in this world. He was joyful in spite of that destiny. Even more! He was joyful because that destiny would bring salvation to the world.

He was not praying that His people would be raptured out of the world and avoid the worst pain and suffering of a world without Christ. Rather, He prayed that His people would not be taken out of this world, but that God would keep His people from the clutches of the evil one.

The action of the gospel is not escape from this world into heaven. The action of the gospel is the struggle to manifest the gospel in this world. And that struggle is

> "not against flesh and blood, but against the rulers, against the au-
> thorities, against the cosmic powers over this present darkness,
> against the spiritual forces of evil" (Ephesians 6:12).

This struggle is not optional, it is necessary. God's plan is to bring heaven to earth, to bring the kingdom of God to earth. The kingdom of God is not like the kingdoms of this world, and that still confuses a lot of people, both believers and unbelievers. God's kingdom does not come from political manipulation. It comes from gospel reproduction.

How are we to prevail in this struggle? Jesus prayed,

> "Sanctify them in the truth; your word is truth" (v. 17).

Sanctification is spiritual growth and maturity that only comes from knowing God's Word, the Bible. Our preparation for the struggle is prayer, Bible study, fellowship, and service. Our gospel weapons are Word & water, bread & wine.

And who has Jesus drafted to engage this struggle, to win this war?

> "As you sent me into the world, so I have sent them into the world"
> (v. 18).

Do you hear what I hear?

SPIRITUAL HEARING

26 "But when the Helper comes, whom I will send to you from the Father, the Spirit of truth, who proceeds from the Father, he will bear witness about me. 27 And you also will bear witness, because you have been with me from the beginning. ... 15:4 But I have said these things to you, that when their hour comes you may remember that I told them to you. I did not say these things to you from the beginning, because I was with you. 5 But now I am going to him who sent me, and none of you asks me, 'Where are you going?' 6 But because I have said these things to you, sorrow has filled your heart. 7 Nevertheless, I tell you the truth: it is to your advantage that I go away, for if I do not go away, the Helper will not come to you. But if I go, I will send him to you. 8 And when he comes, he will convict the world concerning sin and righteousness and judgment: 9 concerning sin, because they do not believe in me; 10 concerning righteousness, because I go to the Father, and you will see me no longer; 11 concerning judgment, because the ruler of this world is judged. 12 "I still have many things to say to you, but you cannot bear them now. 13 When the Spirit of truth comes, he will guide you into all the truth, for he will not speak on his own authority, but whatever he hears he will speak, and he will declare to you the things that are to come. 14 He will glorify me, for he will take what is mine and declare it to you. 15 All that the Father has is mine; therefore I said that he will take what is mine and declare it to you.   —John 15:26-27; 16:4-15

When the day of Pentecost arrived, they were all together in one place. 2 And suddenly there came from heaven a sound like a mighty rushing wind, and it filled the entire house where they were sitting. 3 And divided tongues as of fire appeared to them and rested on each one of them. 4 And they were all filled with the Holy Spirit and began to speak in other tongues as the Spirit gave them utterance. 5 Now there were dwelling in Jerusalem Jews, devout men from every

115

nation under heaven. 6 And at this sound the multitude came to-
gether, and they were bewildered, because each one was hearing them
speak in his own language. 7 And they were amazed and astonished,
saying, "Are not all these who are speaking Galileans? 8 And how is
it that we hear, each of us in his own native language? 9 Parthians
and Medes and Elamites and residents of Mesopotamia, Judea and
Cappadocia, Pontus and Asia, 10 Phrygia and Pamphylia, Egypt
and the parts of Libya belonging to Cyrene, and visitors from Rome,
11 both Jews and proselytes, Cretans and Arabians—we hear them
telling in our own tongues the mighty works of God." 12 And all
were amazed and perplexed, saying to one another, "What does this
mean?" 13 But others mocking said, "They are filled with new
wine."   —*Acts 2:1-13*

Pentecost, which is celebrated fifty days after Easter Sunday, is about the Holy Spirit coming to the apostles in the Upper Room, following Jesus' ascension. That's what the readings for today are about. It occurred during the Festival of Weeks (*Shavuot*), the Old Testament Jewish festival following the wheat harvest. The Rabbonic tradition taught that it was also the time of the giving of the Ten Commandments to Moses on Mount Sinai.

There is a lot of symbolism in all of this: It followed Jesus' ascension, when He was installed as King of the Universe. It followed the harvest of wheat. In the parable of the weeds Jesus said that at harvest we are to

> "Gather the weeds first and bind them in bundles to be burned, but gather the wheat into my barn" (Matthew 13:30).

It is the gathering of the crop of believers for salvation. And it is also a celebration of the Ten Commandments.

In that Upper Room that day something unusual happened. Before His ascension He told the disciples that He would be going away, leaving them, but not leaving them alone. Jesus had promised to send the Helper, the Holy Spirit to guide His people.

> "And when he comes, he will convict the world concerning sin and righteousness and judgment" (v. 8).

"When the Spirit of truth comes, he will guide you into all the truth, for he will not speak on his own authority, but whatever he hears he will speak, and he will declare to you the things that are to come" (v. 13).

Jesus told them that this was going to happen, and to wait for it. Then it happened:

"And suddenly there came from heaven a sound like a mighty rushing wind, and it filled the entire house where they were sitting. And divided tongues as of fire appeared to them and rested on each one of them" (vs. 2-3).

A sound like rushing wind, like wind blowing in the trees, like the sound of a crowd of people all speaking at the same time. A sound like "divided tongues as of fire" (v. 2), different tongues or distributed tongues, and *tongues* means *languages*. It was like a crowd of people speaking different languages. People's tongues were flickering like the flames of fire flicker. The idea is that they were all talking at the same time about the same thing: about Jesus!

And the tongues were not fire, but were "*as of fire*." We could also call it a hot topic. People were animated, excited, passionate. And "the Spirit gave them utterance" (v. 4), the Holy Spirit gave them the words to speak, true words about Jesus.

Luke then went on to say that there were all kinds of people there:

"Parthians and Medes and Elamites and residents of Mesopotamia, Judea and Cappadocia, Pontus and Asia, Phrygia and Pamphylia, Egypt and the parts of Libya belonging to Cyrene, and visitors from Rome, both Jews and proselytes, Cretans and Arabians" (vs. 9-11).

People speaking all kinds of languages, foreign languages (other than Hebrew), foreign tongues. And people from all of these different places who spoke all of these different languages heard people speaking the gospel, speaking about Jesus, in their own native language. Suddenly in that Upper Room that day, all sorts of different people understood what had happened to Jesus. They understood the importance of Jesus' death, Jesus' sacrifice, His substitutionary death for the sins of the world.

They understood and they accepted or received the Holy Spirit who was showing them the Truth about Jesus! And they began talking about it to their friends. And yet not everyone understood. Some did not understand and were amazed and perplexed. Apparently the Spirit had not fallen on them all. Some of them mocked the believers saying, "They are all full of sweet wine" (v. 13). Some of them thought that the believers were a bit tipsy. It's always been that way; Some believe and some don't.

But here we can see what makes the difference between believers and unbelievers, why some people understand and accept the gospel and some don't. Going back to the beginning of story of the Upper Room on that Pentecost day we see that it started all of a sudden. But why? They had gone to the Upper Room to wait. They were of "one mind" and were "devoting themselves to prayer" (Acts 1:14). Jesus had instructed them:

> "And behold, I am sending the promise of my Father upon you. But stay in the city until you are clothed with power from on high" (Luke 24:49).

Jesus told them to wait. Wait for what? Wait until they were "clothed with power from on high" (Luke 24:49). Power is ability. They were to wait until they were able. Able to do what? Able to understand the gospel, the good news about Jesus. They couldn't share their faith until they understood it themselves. No doubt, they talked about it with each other.

Following Holy Week they were drenched in the bad news of Jesus' suffering and death. Jesus, the leader of this new movement, had been killed by the authorities. The disciples were defeated, deflated, and demoralized. They didn't know what to do. Then Jesus was resurrected! And He continued to teach them. Then weeks later He ascended into heaven to take up His throne as King of the earth. And He sent the Holy Spirit to them to continue the mission.

And all at once they understood: the mission was not over, the mission was just beginning! And they could not contain themselves.

They all began talking about it to one another, talking among their friends who spoke their native tongues. It seemed like pandemonium, but it wasn't. It was actually an expression of Christian unity, of unity in Christ through the power and presence of the Holy Spirit.

Christian unity is when everyone talks truly about the same thing—Jesus Christ—in their own naive languages. When individuals do that, we call it regeneration, renewal, new life, even being born again. When people understand Jesus, they understand their own lives in a new way.

FLESH V. SPIRIT

12 So then, brothers, we are debtors, not to the flesh, to live according to the flesh. 13 For if you live according to the flesh you will die, but if by the Spirit you put to death the deeds of the body, you will live. 14 For all who are led by the Spirit of God are sons of God. 15 For you did not receive the spirit of slavery to fall back into fear, but you have received the Spirit of adoption as sons, by whom we cry, "Abba! Father!" 16 The Spirit himself bears witness with our spirit that we are children of God, 17 and if children, then heirs—heirs of God and fellow heirs with Christ, provided we suffer with him in order that we may also be glorified with him.   —Romans 8:12-17*

Now there was a man of the Pharisees named Nicodemus, a ruler of the Jews. 2 This man came to Jesus by night and said to him, "Rabbi, we know that you are a teacher come from God, for no one can do these signs that you do unless God is with him." 3 Jesus answered him, "Truly, truly, I say to you, unless one is born again he cannot see the kingdom of God." 4 Nicodemus said to him, "How can a man be born when he is old? Can he enter a second time into his mother's womb and be born?" 5 Jesus answered, "Truly, truly, I say to you, unless one is born of water and the Spirit, he cannot enter the kingdom of God. 6 That which is born of the flesh is flesh, and that which is born of the Spirit is spirit. 7 Do not marvel that I said to you, 'You must be born again.' 8 The wind blows where it wishes, and you hear its sound, but you do not know where it comes from or where it goes. So it is with everyone who is born of the Spirit." 9 Nicodemus said to him, "How can these things be?" 10 Jesus answered him, "Are you the teacher of Israel and yet you do not understand these things? 11 Truly, truly, I say to you, we speak of what we know, and bear witness to what we have seen, but you do not receive our testimony. 12 If I have told you earthly things and you do not believe, how can you believe if I tell you heavenly things? 13 No one has ascended into heaven except he who descended from heaven, the Son of Man. 14 And as Moses lifted up the serpent in the wilderness, so must the Son of Man be lifted up, 15 that whoever believes in him may have eternal life.   —*John 3:1-15*

The distinction between flesh and spirit in the Bible has given rise to way too many misunderstandings. At its root it is the difference between Christ's humanity and His divinity. And historically, this distinction is at the source of the most pernicious heresies, which deny either Christ's humanity, making Him a purely divine being devoid of humanity or flesh; or which deny Christ's divinity, making Him a purely human being devoid of divinity or His Godhood. It is the doctrine of the Trinity alone that is able to hold together Christ's humanity and His divinity without confusing the One with the other.

The way to clarify this issue is to correctly define the terms *flesh* and *spirit* at the outset of the discussion. So, let me take a stab at setting forth a clear definition of terms. We'll start with flesh. The Greek word is *sarx* and it refers to the meat of the body, which includes the basic bodily functions: eating, elimination, and reproduction. The first thing to notice about these things is that God is not opposed to them. Without them life would not be possible. So when Paul said that we should not live according to the flesh, he did not mean that we should not eat, eliminate, or reproduce. These bodily functions are absolutely necessary for life.

Nor did he mean that our natural desire for these things is bad. It is not. Life is good, and the necessary functions of life are also good. It is a blessing to have adequate food, sanitary plumbing, enjoyment, and children. God is not opposed to any of this.

The proper definition of spirit is more subtle. People tend to think of angels and ghosts, but such thinking is inadequate and will lead us astray from God's meaning, God's direction, God's instruction in these verses. The proper understanding of spirit pertains to issues and concerns of the heart and mind, things like emotions, values, ideas, and desires. The realm of the spiritual is the mind, but also more than the mind. It includes the heart, but not the muscle that pumps blood in our chest. That muscle is meat, so it is included in idea of flesh.

In the Bible the heart is the wholeness of physical and spiritual being. It represents the "gut" wisdom of feeling as opposed to the "head" wisdom of logic. The heart is compassion and understanding, but more than these, it is the will, or our most fundamental desires. It is a symbol for love and commitment. We often call it the seat of our emotions; the heart is synonymous with our affections.

When we think about spirit we tend to think in religious and churchly terms, and this is what confuses us. Paul was not thinking in those terms. We can get a better understanding of Paul if we think like a modern physicist. *Flesh* refers to the physical aspects of life and living: consumption, elimination, and reproduction. *Spirit* refers to the thinking and feeling aspects of life and living: words, language, thoughts, ideas, emotions, passions, and desires.

That which is physical is clearly defined. The spiritual elements of life are not difficult to understand, but some kinds of thinking are concerned with the purely physical, and some are concerned with the spiritual, or a higher order of consideration. When Paul said that living by the flesh leads to death, he meant that living without spiritual considerations, living by the flesh only. When our thinking is dominated by self-concern our desires and thoughts are fleshly. In contrast, when our thinking is dominated by concern for others our desires and thoughts are spiritual.

Thus, feeding ourselves and sexual gratification are fleshly desires, but love involves feeding and caring for the good of others. One is self-directed thinking, the other is other-directed thinking. Spiritual concerns involve things like: love, joy, peace, patience, kindness, goodness, faithfulness, gentleness and self-control. Spiritual things always involve other people because love always involves other people. Love is concern for others.

Notice that this definition, this distinction between flesh and spirit is not about heaven, not about angels or angelic visitations. None of that! It's about life on earth in our earthly bodies. God is not opposed to our human bodily needs and desires: food, sanitation, and reproduction. The Bible is not arguing for some sort of Buddhist escape from the needs and demands of this world. Christianity is not an ascetic discipline. This error crept into Christianity very early in its history.

As Christianity spread into India and Asia it discovered Buddhism, which had been in existence for about 500 years before the birth of Christ. Hinduism is even older. That's a long time, which means that Buddhism and Hindusim were fully developed and widely spread long before Christianity got going. As Christianity moved into India and Asia, in order to appeal to Buddhists and Hindus it began to adapt to their various cultures.

This is a normal practice of evangelism because in order to reach people with the Gospel, we need to develop common lines of thought and behavior with them. Otherwise, Christianity will seem too weird, and people will dismiss it before they understand it. Thus, an arm of Christian thinking and teaching began to mimic some of the Buddhist and Hindu ascetic disciplines because there are similar ideas in the Bible. Self-denial is a biblical teaching, as is suffering and moderation. This is not the place or time to go into all of that, but I want to point out the similarities because the ideas of self-denial and suffering can lead us to miss what Paul and John are getting at in today's readings.

Christianity is not about the denial of the joy and pleasure of ordinary life. Rather, Christianity is the celebration of the joy of life that is founded on God's Word. The kingdom of heaven is described as a sumptuous feast for all of God's people. The kingdom of heaven is a joyful, pleasurable, ecstatic realm of love and abundance.

The problem with ascetic discipline is that it is self-focused, self-centered. And love is not self-centered. A life of love is a life that is filled with concern, commitment, and service to others. Love is not self-negation, it's finding self-fulfillment in serving others. It's not self-denial, because self-denial cannot escape from self-concern. And yet the Christian life begins with death. It begins with the death of old self and the birth of the new self in Christ. It involves the mortification of the flesh, but it is not about the mortification of the flesh.

The "mortification of the flesh" is the putting to death the passions of the flesh. But at the same time it is not about the denial of the ordinary joys and pleasures of life. The central concern of Christianity is not the death of self, but life in Christ. Yet it begins with the death of the old self. But we don't focus on killing the old self, we focus on nurturing the life of the new self in Christ.

Buddhism focuses on the death of the old self by denying the ordinary elements of life: food and sex. It then goes one step further and teaches people to stop thinking about those things. They call it meditation; and it is an effort to stop thinking altogether, to still the mind. And the ultimate conclusion of Buddhism is the escape from life altogether. Buddhists believe in reincarnation, and the ultimate goal is not to be reincarnated. The goal is the end of life because they define life as suffering.

This is not Christianity. It is the opposite of Christianity. And yet, Jesus taught that we must be born again. However, Jesus was not talking about reincarnation. He was talking about new life in Christ. To understand this we must know what the Bible teaches about sin, about Adam and Eve in the garden, and the history of humanity.

Buddha said that life is suffering, and he was right. He was talking about the only life he knew, the life of sin. The history of the Old Testament is the story of sin and suffering. Buddha knew no other option, nor did Nicodemus. The prophets of the Old Testament hoped for an option, hoped for something or someone to come and put an end to the sin and suffering of the world. But all they had was a hope, an idea, a desire. That hope, that idea, that desire for the end of sin and suffering is spiritual. The Spirit of God is the hope, the idea, and the desire for the end of sin and suffering.

Concern about this Spirit is contrasted with sin, where sinful life is captured by self-concern, where that self-concern manifests as the pursuit of pleasure or the denial of pleasure. Both are completely self-concerned. Jesus provides another option, another solution, another way to frame the problem that gives rise to a different solution. Life is full of suffering, and sin is the source of suffering. The biblical solution to this problem is the end or death of sin.

And what exactly is sin? Sin is the way we live life without Christ. Sin is doing our best apart from Christ. Sin is the absolute best that humanity has to offer, with all of our wisdom, experience, and technology, but without or apart from Jesus Christ, who is Father, Son, and Holy Spirit, the all in One.

Nicodemus came to Jesus in the night so no one would see him. Nicodemus wanted what Jesus offered. Jesus said to him,

> "Truly, truly, I say to you, unless one is born again he cannot see the kingdom of God" (v. 3).

Note two things: Jesus called it "born again," and Nicodemus had no idea what He was talking about. The Greek word translated "born again" is literally born from above, or born first or born anew. Sometimes we call it a new heart, where *heart* indicates the central focus or impetus for all of our thinking, feeling, and being. Today we could also call it a new identity, or a new definition of one's self, one's person, one's persona. It involves the complete restructuring of humanity because we are social beings and our identities are dependent on one another. No one is an island. We are social beings, which means that individuals cannot know who or what they are apart from the communities in which they live.

I am a man, a married man who lives with his wife in a community composed of a neighborhood, a work or employment situation, an extended family connections, a church community, etc. in Marietta, in Ohio, in the U.S. And all of that determines what language I speak, what values I have, what relationships constrain me, what opportunities I have, etc.

To be born again is to start over, but I can't start over by myself because all of these social things work to constrain and define me. So, if I try to change who I am by myself, my wife and family (and all the rest) won't understand and will continue to treat me as they always have, drawing me back into my old life. We see this problem with alcoholics and drug users who try to reform. If they return to their old friends and communities, those old friends and communities will pull them back into their old habits. To really start over, we need a new community, new friends, new situations that will contribute to our new habits and ways of being, and not pull us back into our old habits and ways of life.

In short, we need a church, a community of people who are born again, and who will encourage our new way of life. That new way of life is life in the spirit, in the Spirit of Jesus Christ. New life in Christ is living into the Spirit of Christ by practicing the fruits of the Spirit. The struggle between flesh and spirit is aggrivated from not being in a community of support, a community whose attention is focused on life in Christ.

The old community, or life without Christ, tends toward our old habits of self-concern or sin. The old community reminds us of our old ways, and that brings tension and struggle. All of this is to say that there is more to being born again than one's own individual experience of it. The community dimension of our new life in Christ is absolutely necessary. We can't do it alone. Love requires being in relationship with other people. It means being in relationship with other Christians.

That's what Nicodemus didn't have. Maybe he became part of the new Christian community later, we don't know. But if he didn't, he couldn't be saved. We all need the love of God, but we also need the love of God's people. Church membership is an essential part of Christianity.

Don't be apart from it!

REPRESENTATIVE

*Now the boy Samuel was ministering to the Lord in the presence of
Eli. And the word of the Lord was rare in those days; there was no
frequent vision. 2 At that time Eli, whose eyesight had begun to grow
dim so that he could not see, was lying down in his own place. 3 The
lamp of God had not yet gone out, and Samuel was lying down in
the temple of the Lord, where the ark of God was. 4 Then the Lord
called Samuel, and he said, "Here I am!" 5 and ran to Eli and said,
"Here I am, for you called me." But he said, "I did not call; lie down
again." So he went and lay down. 6 And the Lord called again,
"Samuel!" and Samuel arose and went to Eli and said, "Here I am,
for you called me." But he said, "I did not call, my son; lie down
again." 7 Now Samuel did not yet know the Lord, and the word of
the Lord had not yet been revealed to him. 8 And the Lord called
Samuel again the third time. And he arose and went to Eli and said,
"Here I am, for you called me." Then Eli perceived that the Lord was
calling the boy. 9 Therefore Eli said to Samuel, "Go, lie down, and if
he calls you, you shall say, 'Speak, Lord, for your servant hears.'" So
Samuel went and lay down in his place. 10 And the Lord came and
stood, calling as at other times, "Samuel! Samuel!" And Samuel said,
"Speak, for your servant hears."*   —1 Samuel 3:1-10

*5 For what we proclaim is not ourselves, but Jesus Christ as Lord,
with ourselves as your servants for Jesus' sake. 6 For God, who said,
"Let light shine out of darkness," has shone in our hearts to give the
light of the knowledge of the glory of God in the face of Jesus Christ.
7 But we have this treasure in jars of clay, to show that the surpass-
ing power belongs to God and not to us. 8 We are afflicted in every
way, but not crushed; perplexed, but not driven to despair; 9 persecuted, but not forsaken; struck down, but not destroyed; 10 always
carrying in the body the death of Jesus, so that the life of Jesus may
also be manifested in our bodies. 11 For we who live are always be-*

ing given over to death for Jesus' sake, so that the life of Jesus also
may be manifested in our mortal flesh. 12 So death is at work in us,
but life in you.   —*2 Corinthians 4:5-12*

Hannah, Samuel's mother, was married to Elkanah, a priest. Hannah, like, Sarah and Rebecca, was barren long into her marriage. She very much wanted to have a child, so she prayed fervently. One day Hannah went up to the Tabernacle and prayed and wept (I Samuel 1:10). She prayed that God would give her a child, a son.

Eli the High Priest was sitting near the doorpost and heard her prayer. In her prayer she vowed to give her son back to God for the service. She promised that he would be a Nazarite all the days of his life. Eli thought she was drunk, but he prayed with her, blessed her, and sent her home. She had a child, named him Samuel, and when he was weaned, she brought him to the Eli to raise him as a Nazarite. Samuel entered ministry at a very young age.

The reading today is the story of Samuel's first encounter with God. The first thing to note is that Israel at the latter stages of the story of the Judges, just previous to this time, was in a state of decline.

"the word of the Lord was rare in those days; there was no frequent vision" (v. 1).

Eli, the chief judge/Priest at the time, had not been faithful. He and his own sons, who had become priests, were corrupt. The Lord was not communicating with them because they would corrupt God's Word if He did give it to them.

One night Samuel thought that he heard Eli call him. This happened several times, and each time Eli said that he had not called him. Finally, Eli told him to simply listen to the voice.

"Eli perceived that the Lord was calling the boy. Therefore Eli said to Samuel, 'Go, lie down, and if he calls you, you shall say, "Speak, Lord, for your servant hears"'" (v. 8-9).

The reading for today ends here, and the lesson is that we need to learn how to listen to God. Our prayers should involve both speaking and listening to God. The speaking is easy. It's easy to tell God our troubles and to ask for solutions. It's more difficult to listen, to hear God, because He doesn't tell us what we want to hear. He tells us what He wants us to hear. And often that includes things that we don't want to hear.

God's message to young Samuel that night was that Eli was corrupt, faithless, and that his faithlessness had corrupted his sons who were priests, and that their corruption had also infected Israel generally. Young Samuel would need to listen to the voice of God because the voice of Eli was corrupt. Samuel's teacher was not trustworthy, and God was going to use Samuel to teach Israel about the consequences of unfaithfulness. That lesson involved the kingdom of Israel, and Samuel would appoint Israel's first King, contrary to God's recommendation.

The people wanted a king like the other nations. God said that would be a bad idea, but would give them a king so that they could see why it was a bad idea. That story is the Old Testament. God was not opposed to the idea of a king, but was opposed to the idea of a faithless king, like the kings of the other nations. From that day to this day, the main problems of the world and of God's people, come from faithless kings, faithless leaders who do not listen to God's Word.

When Israel left Egypt she was led by military leaders—Joshua. During the four hundred years that the Judges ruled, Israel was trying to live according to the law, as interpreted by the various judges. And every so often the judge of the day needed to become a military leader to protect Israel from foreign invaders. A foreign nation would invade, and a judge would lead them to victory. This happened many times.

The law had been given to Moses, but the people in their wilderness years were unable to live by it. Those biblical stories are filled with distrust and misunderstanding. God had taken Israel out of Egypt in order to separate them from the corrupting influences of Egyptian culture. Their time in the wilderness showed them their own resistance to life according to the law of God. They needed to develop a culture of faithfulness to replace the culture they had learned in Egypt. The four centuries under the leadership of the Judges greatly helped to develop that culture. But the other nations of the world kept intruding on them. Foreign kings would invade, and the judges would need to revert to military procedures in order to preserve nascent Israel.

Later, during the period of the kings Israel became the dominant military force in the area, which solved the problem of foreign invaders. During the period of the kings Israel could develop God's culture into full flower. But they discovered another problem. The problem was not the faithless nations who had continued to invade Israel. The problem was the faithlessness of the Israelite kings and people themselves. The enemies of God's faithful culture in the world were not simply the faithless people of the other cultures of the world. It was the faithlessness of their own hearts.

Most of their own kings proved to be faithless, and the best of their kings were compromised at best. David, the best of their kings, was a murder and an adulterer, and was unable to raise faithful sons himself. That family failure by David then led to fighting over the succession of the crown, which again is the story of the Old Testament. God had given the law to Moses, and Israel needed to learn that the problems with the world are not the fault of other people.

During the War of 1812, the United States Navy defeated the British Navy in the Battle of Lake Erie. Master Commandant Oliver Perry wrote to Major General William Henry Harrison, "We have met the enemy and they are ours." Perry's parody of this famous battle report perfectly summarizes humanity's tendency to create our own problems. The comic strip "Pogo" then popularized this idea in the 1970s.

We began today with Samuel learning to listen to the Lord. And the Lectionary then sends us to 1 Corinthians for reflection. Paul said that "what we proclaim is not ourselves" (v. 5). To proclaim someone else is to represent them. He said that we proclaim

"Jesus Christ as Lord, with ourselves as your servants for Jesus' sake" (v. 5).

The long story of the Bible is about us—humanity—learning to live in the light of God's law, God's way, God's love. The story of the Bible is the failure to do that. Israel was a case study over a 1500 year period that ended in the destruction of the Temple and Jerusalem in A.D. 70.

The New Testament story is still in process. Jesus came just before Israel's destruction to provide a new way, a different way. Jesus came as a judgment of God on Israel, but He did not come to destroy Israel. He came to plant a seed, to show Israel and the world a better way. But the new way would require the end of the old way. The new life in Christ necessitated the end of the old life in Adam. If the old way of life does not end, the new way of life gets muddied by the lingering of the old way. A clean break is best, but a clean break seldom happens. So we live in muddied times. For the most part, we live muddied lives.

So what do we do now? In order to see through the mud we need a brighter light to shine. And what is that light?

"the knowledge of the glory of God in the face of Jesus Christ" (v. 6).

We are Christians. I'm not engaged in evangelism here. I'm not writing to heathens, I'm writing to Christians. I don't need to tell you to come to Christ. Faithlessness is not our problem. We're in church. So now what? We need representation. We need to be representatives because

"we have this treasure in jars of clay" (v. 7).

Christ is the treasure, we are the clay. Christ is worthy, we are not. But we have Christ. Our worthiness is not the jars of clay that we are. Our worthiness is the treasure we have—Jesus Christ. Jesus lived God's law in the flesh. Jesus showed us that it can be done. And how did the world respond to Jesus?

The world responded in two different ways: some understood and were faithful, and some didn't understand and were not. The faithful worked to

> "show that the surpassing power belongs to God and not to us" (v. 7).

We are not to promote ourselves or our particular church. We are to promote Jesus Christ. Faithful Christians represent Jesus Christ to the world, in the world. To represent is to present again, to make Jesus Christ present to the world. This is the calling of every Christian and every church. No one else can do it. Unbelievers most certainly can't do it.

As Christians we often find ourselves angry and frustrated by the world. We often wonder why and shake our finger at the faithlessness of the world, and chastise them for not being faithful. What's the matter with those people! We watch the news in awe, wondering why people don't know better, and blame them for their faithless ignorance. We wonder why there is no blood in those turnips!

The truth is that the world doesn't know any better. Is the problem the lack of faith by the unfaithful? Or is the problem that the faithful are not adequately re-presenting Jesus Christ to the world, in the world? Yes, it's hard. And the world doesn't want to hear it.

> "We are afflicted in every way, but not crushed; perplexed, but not driven to despair; persecuted, but not forsaken; struck down, but not destroyed; always carrying in the body the death of Jesus, so that the life of Jesus may also be manifested in our bodies" (vs. 8-10).

Too often we worry about how to best represent Jesus, and fail to just do it. The questions about how to do it are answered by the actual doing of it.

Let's do that!

WHERE ARE YOU?

8 And they heard the sound of the Lord God walking in the garden in the cool of the day, and the man and his wife hid themselves from the presence of the Lord God among the trees of the garden. 9 But the Lord God called to the man and said to him, "Where are you?" 10 And he said, "I heard the sound of you in the garden, and I was afraid, because I was naked, and I hid myself." 11 He said, "Who told you that you were naked? Have you eaten of the tree of which I commanded you not to eat?" 12 The man said, "The woman whom you gave to be with me, she gave me fruit of the tree, and I ate." 13 Then the Lord God said to the woman, "What is this that you have done?" The woman said, "The serpent deceived me, and I ate." 14 The Lord God said to the serpent, "Because you have done this, cursed are you above all livestock and above all beasts of the field; on your belly you shall go, and dust you shall eat all the days of your life. 15 I will put enmity between you and the woman, and between your offspring and her offspring; he shall bruise your head, and you shall bruise his heel." —Genesis 3:8–15

13 Since we have the same spirit of faith according to what has been written, "I believed, and so I spoke," we also believe, and so we also speak, 14 knowing that he who raised the Lord Jesus will raise us also with Jesus and bring us with you into his presence. 15 For it is all for your sake, so that as grace extends to more and more people it may increase thanksgiving, to the glory of God. 16 So we do not lose heart. Though our outer self is wasting away, our inner self is being renewed day by day. 17 For this light momentary affliction is preparing for us an eternal weight of glory beyond all comparison, 18 as we look not to the things that are seen but to the things that are unseen. For the things that are seen are transient, but the things that are unseen are eternal. 5:1 For we know that if the tent that is our

earthly home is destroyed, we have a building from God, a house not
made with hands, eternal in the heavens.   —2 Corinthians 4:13-5:1

Adam and Eve heard God and hid themselves. Why did they hide? What were they trying to hide? We need to look at what happened in the prior verses to see what they did not want God to see. In Genesis 3:1-7 we find their encounter with the serpent. The serpent is one of the most intriguing characters to be found in the Bible. According to some Bible commentators, in the story of Adam and Eve, the serpent represents evil inclination. This understanding is based the Prophet Isaiah:

> "In that day, the Lord will punish with his sword, his fierce, great and powerful sword, Leviathan the gliding serpent, Leviathan the coiling serpent; he will slay the monster of the sea" (Isaiah 27:1).

There are also positive references to the serpent:

> "The people came to Moses and said, 'We sinned when we spoke against the Lord and against you. Pray that the Lord will take the snakes away from us.' So Moses prayed for the people. The Lord said to Moses, 'Make a snake and put it up on a pole; anyone who is bitten can look at it and live'" (Numbers 21:7-9).

Here the serpent is associated with healing. The snake on a pole, *cadusus*, is the international symbol for medicine. And regarding healing, the Greek word for witchcraft is *pharmakia*, which is the root of the English *pharmacy* and the industry of pharmaceutics. Witchcraft involved the art of potions and herbs; and also fortune telling, or predicting the future, what we might also call guessing. Today we call it *prognosis*.

Putting all this altogether, then, what were Adam and Eve hiding? What did it have to do with the serpent? What had they done? God had told Adam not to eat of the tree of the knowledge of good and evil. The idea of the tree represents the determination of good and evil for themselves. It represents making moral decisions based on their own knowledge, making moral decisions, knowing good and evil apart from God's guidance. God said, don't do it!

Eve, following the advice of the serpent, said that doing so would be

"good ... and ... was a delight to the eyes, and that ... (it would) make one wise" (Genesis 3:6).

She convinced Adam that it was good, beautiful, and would help them become wise like God. They then decided that in doing so they would be helping God. They turned what God had forbidden into something that they thought would help God. They then thought that helping God was their religious duty.

Then they heard God coming near them and they panicked. But why? If they believed that they were actually doing God's will, why would they hide. What did they hide? They hid their nakedness. Their what?

Naked is used as a descriptor 104 times in Scripture. Depending on the context, it can indicate innocence, purity, defenselessness, vulnerability, helplessness, humiliation, shame, guilt, and judgment. Sometimes it indicates several of these qualities. The earlier context (Genesis 2:7) offers no indication that their being naked before God and each other had caused even the slightest embarrassment. But after they followed the serpent's advice, they became aware of their nakedness, and with it they also felt shame. Were they ashamed of their nakedness, or their disobedience? When God approached them they suddenly realized that they had done something wrong, something that God told them not to do. If there was no shame, why would they seek to cover themselves?

We tend to associate this sin with sex, but there is no reference to sex other than being naked, which could mean a variety of things. In covering their nakedness they were hiding their weakness. Being naked suggests weakness because being endoskeletal creatures (our skeletons are one the inside), our sensitive skin is on the outside and is completely exposed to the harsh conditions of the world. When we are naked, we are most weak and vulnerable. So they covered themselves with leaves, with plant material. Cotton is a plant material with which we all still use to cover ourselves.

Immediately they began blaming each other for their infraction. Satan is defined as the accuser. Accusation is Satan's *modus operandi*. Satan uses accusation to move his plan forward. Satan uses accusation as his favorite weapon. They began using Satan's weapon. As they accused each other of being the one who caused their sin, they were engaging Satan's weapon against one another and against God Himself. Their sin was not exposing their nakedness in public, nor exposing their nakedness to one another. Being naked is not a sin. God created us naked, as weak, sensitive creatures who would need protection from the harsh realities of the world.

God then protected them/us by giving them/us His Word, His command to be obedient. God was not limiting our creativity, He was protecting our weakness, our gullibility. The symbol of God's protection was leather clothing, made from an animal sacrifice. That sacrifice provided protection. Strip us naked and we are gullible to the slightest suggestion. Their sin was not believing and obeying God. In addition, their sin was engaging Satan's weapon of accusation as a defense in order to hide their guilt, their responsibility for their own actions. The coverup was worse than the crime.

Adam blamed Eve, Eve blamed the serpent. Then Adam blamed God:

> "The woman whom you gave to be with me, she gave me fruit of the tree, and I ate" (Genesis 3:12).

Adam blamed God! At that point the loving, filial relationship between Adam and God had broken. Adam did not trust God because God had given him a deceitful, wicked woman, nor did God trust Adam. That is the plain meaning of these verses.

But here's the thing: Adam blamed God where he should have blamed the serpent. God didn't make Eve believe the serpent. She did it of her own free will, and apparently she then convinced Adam that she was right. But she did not think that she was opposing God; she thought that she was serving God, helping God. She thought that the forbidden fruit would make her wise like God, or so the serpent had told her. She could find nothing about the forbidden fruit that was bad or evil. It was food; it was lovely; and it would make them wise. God wanted them to be fed, beautiful, and wise. So, she thought she was helping God. Doing so would be an act of faithfulness, she thought.

Adam and Eve had no idea how their failure to hear and obey God's Word, God's direction would play out in history. Nor is there any indication in the story that Adam and Eve repented of their sin. Adam blamed God for giving him Eve, who deceived him. And Eve then blamed the serpent.

Notice that Eve was the only one who correctly understood what had happened. She blamed the serpent. But she did not repent. She did not ask for God's forgiveness, nor did she accept any personal blame or responsibility herself. She thought it was not her fault, it was the serpent.

So God then executed judgment on them all. The serpent was cursed "above all livestock and above all beasts of the field" (Genesis 3;14). God then put enmity between the children of the serpent and the children of the woman. Enmity is a deep-seated, mutual hatred. From that day forward there would be conflict between two lines of human beings: the children of the serpent/Satan, and the children of Eve/God. There would be enmity between those who follow or believe the serpent/Satan and those who follow or believe God.

And there it is! At the very beginning of the story of humanity on earth we find that the root conflict between people is believing God, believing God's Word—or not.

The Lectionary then sends us to 2 Corinthians 4. Verse 13 includes a quote from Psalm 116:5-19:

> "Gracious is the Lord, and righteous; our God is merciful. The Lord preserves the simple; when I was brought low, he saved me. Return, O my soul, to your rest; for the Lord has dealt bountifully with you. For you have delivered my soul from death, my eyes from tears, my feet from stumbling; I will walk before the Lord in the land of the living. I believed, even when I spoke, 'I am greatly afflicted;' I said in my alarm, 'All mankind are liars.' What shall I render to the Lord for all his benefits to me? I will lift up the cup of salvation and call on the name of the Lord, I will pay my vows to the Lord in the presence of all his people. Precious in the sight of the Lord is the death of his

saints. O Lord, I am your servant; I am your servant, the son of your maidservant. You have loosed my bonds. I will offer to you the sacrifice of thanksgiving and call on the name of the Lord. I will pay my vows to the Lord in the presence of all his people, in the courts of the house of the Lord, in your midst, O Jerusalem. Praise the Lord!"

Paul has simply applied this Psalm to Christ. He was showing us how Scripture makes sense of his experience in Christ. And in the midst of difficulty, pain, and struggle Paul could persevere because he

"know(s) that he who raised the Lord Jesus will raise us also with Jesus and bring us ... into his presence" (v. 14).

As surely as God raised Jesus from the dead, so He will raise us from our death. We can be as sure as Christ was about this. We need not fear. We need not fret. We need not worry. Soon we all will be in the presence of God. This present death is but a fleeting moment against the backdrop of eternity.

Paul's suffering (and ours) is all for the sake of the church and "to the glory of God" (v. 15). Paul lived in a difficult time. The church was in labor, in the process of giving birth. It was a painful and bloody time. Paul knew that in time as grace extended to more people it would increase the ability of people to give thanks, and would increase the number of people who gave thanks. As more people became grateful to God it would become easier to be a Christian.

The fire burns brighter when the logs are piled together. Similarly, Christian fellowship doesn't simply add to the grace of thanksgiving, it multiplies it. Because of these things, said Paul, "we do not lose heart" (v. 16). Yes, times are hard, but the difficulties we face only encourage us to greater faithfulness. The gospel of Jesus Christ cannot be defeated because difficulties only increase the resolve of the faithful by reminding us that

"we were buried therefore with him by baptism into death, in order that, just as Christ was raised from the dead by the glory of the Father, we too might walk in newness of life" (Romans 6:4).

This is who we are as Christians. We are not who we think we are. In Christ we are who God has created us to be. When God draws near you, and He always does, don't hide. Don't cover up your sin. Don't blame others.

I think I hear the Lord calling now,"Where are you?"

GOD'S PLAN

22 Thus says the Lord God: "I myself will take a sprig from the lofty top of the cedar and will set it out. I will break off from the topmost of its young twigs a tender one, and I myself will plant it on a high and lofty mountain. 23 On the mountain height of Israel will I plant it, that it may bear branches and produce fruit and become a noble cedar. And under it will dwell every kind of bird; in the shade of its branches birds of every sort will nest. 24 And all the trees of the field shall know that I am the Lord; I bring low the high tree, and make high the low tree, dry up the green tree, and make the dry tree flourish. I am the Lord; I have spoken, and I will do it."

—Ezekiel 17:22-24

6 So we are always of good courage. We know that while we are at home in the body we are away from the Lord, 7 for we walk by faith, not by sight. 8 Yes, we are of good courage, and we would rather be away from the body and at home with the Lord. 9 So whether we are at home or away, we make it our aim to please him. 10 For we must all appear before the judgment seat of Christ, so that each one may receive what is due for what he has done in the body, whether good or evil. 11 Therefore, knowing the fear of the Lord, we persuade others. But what we are is known to God, and I hope it is known also to your conscience. 12 We are not commending ourselves to you again but giving you cause to boast about us, so that you may be able to answer those who boast about outward appearance and not about what is in the heart. 13 For if we are beside ourselves, it is for God; if we are in our right mind, it is for you. 14 For the love of Christ controls us, because we have concluded this: that one has died for all, therefore all have died; 15 and he died for all, that those who live might no longer live for themselves but for him who for their sake died and was raised. 16 From now on, therefore, we regard no one according to the flesh. Even though we once regarded Christ ac-

*cording to the flesh, we regard him thus no longer. 17 Therefore, if
anyone is in Christ, he is a new creation. The old has passed away;
behold, the new has come.*   —*2 Corinthians 5:6-17*

These verses in Ezekiel comprise a prediction about the restoration of God's people, God's church. During the Babylonian captivity, Ezekiel preached about the destruction of Judah's capital city Jerusalem following the Babylonian siege of Jerusalem, which destroyed Solomon's Temple n 587 B.C. Ezekiel predicted the restoration of the Jewish people to the Land of Israel after the Babylonian captivity. Ezekiel addressed a people who had been forced from their home because they had broken faith with God. As the spokesman for the Lord, Ezekiel defended God's reputation as a holy God. The primary purpose of Ezekiel's message was to restore God's glory to those who had rejected Him. Ezekiel declared judgment on those clinging to false hope, but offered true hope to those who accept God's judgment, God's truth. He linked God's judgment with the hope of a new heart and spirit.

Ezekiel used the image of the cedar tree to represent God's people. Cedar trees are known for their resilience, strength, and beauty. They are a vital part of many ecosystems, providing both shelter and sustenance for wildlife. A notable biblical reference to the cedar tree is found in the Psalms 92:12:

"The righteous flourish like the palm tree and grow like a cedar in Lebanon."

The idea is that those who strive for righteousness will thrive and flourish abundantly, just like the majestic cedar trees.

Calvin said that this prophecy also refers to Christ because, although in some sense God had pity on the people when they returned to Israel under Cyrus and Darius, but the fullness of Ezekiel's prophecy never fully came to be until the reign of Jesus Christ. Ezekiel said that God would take the young branches from the top of the tree, where new growth occurs, suggesting that God was talking about the next generation of His people. God would take those young branches and plant them on a high mountain where they

would get lots of sun and water, where they would grow and produce fruit, and provide shelter for lots of other critters.

This prophecy was given to the Jewish people who had been defeated because they had been unfaithful. It was a perennial promise
to restore God's people, to make of them what God had designed
them to be: strong, healthy, fruitful, and a blessing to the other critters of the world. The image of the cedar provides great significance
and symbolism. Throughout the Bible, this majestic tree is associated
with strength, stability, and the presence of God. The cedar is often
used as a metaphor for spiritual growth, righteousness, and prosperity. Just as the cedar tree stands tall and firm, rooted deeply in the
ground, so should our faith be unwavering and steadfast, and deeply
rooted. And one day God's people will be like the majestic cedar
tree. Jesus Christ brought the dawn of that day.

Paul, also writing about that day, said that God's people "are always of good courage" (v. 6). Like the majestic cedar God's people
are courageous, full of hope and confidence, and are bold in the
Lord. Courage is not a lack of fear, rather it is confidence in spite of
fear. Courage should not be mistaken for foolishness, as in "fools rush
in." The courageous run toward danger, but they don't run foolishly.
The courageous are acquainted with fear. Paul said,

"Therefore, knowing the fear of the Lord, we persuade others" (v.
11).

The courageous are not dissuaded by the fear of the world, but are
encouraged by the fear of the Lord.

What is the fear of the Lord? It is not simply the anticipation or
awareness of danger. It is not simply anxious concern or unpleasant
alarm. Rather, the fear of the Lord is profound reverence and awe toward God. Reverence means to revere and respect, to honor, and to
hold in high regard. Awe is the feeling we get in the presence of
something vast that challenges our understanding of the world, like
looking up at millions of stars in the night sky or marveling at the
birth of a child. Other words for awe are: wonder, amazement, surprise, or transcendence.

Awe reminds us of how small and insignificant we are by showing us how grand God's world really is. God isn't some harsh, mean
tyrant showing off His power to impress us or because He has some
inferiority complex. God, the Great I Am, is all-powerful and
almighty. C.S. Lewis wrote a famous story about God's awe: *The
Lion, the Witch and the Wardrobe:* In the story Aslan represents God.

> "Aslan is a lion—the Lion, the great Lion."
>
> "Ooh!" said Susan. "I'd thought he was a man. Is he quite safe? I shall
> feel rather nervous about meeting a lion"...
>
> "Safe?" said Mr. Beaver. "Who said anything about safe? 'Course he
> isn't safe. But he's good. He's the King, I tell you."

To which we must add that He is also just. God is both merciful and
just.

No one fears mercy, but justice is another matter. People fear
God's justice because they know that they don't want what they deserve. People want mercy, not justice. But God doesn't give one or
the other. God necessarily gives them both.

The people of Nineveh provide the biblical model. They were
wicked and unfaithful so Jonah preached fire and brimstone to them.
And they repented. They changed. They deserved God's justice because they were corrupt. But when they changed, they received
God's mercy—not because they were sorry, but because they actually
changed their ways. That's the way God works.

Paul, writing to the Corinthians about being of good courage,
encouraged them to "walk by faith, not by sight" (v. 7). He was not
encouraging blind faith, rather he was encouraging insightful faith.
Seeing this world as it is, in all of its sin and darkness does not encourage faithfulness. Scaring people with God's damnation of sin
doesn't make people faithful. Seeing the darkness can make people
fearful, but that's not Godly fear, though it is fear of God.

Rather, being faithful, living faithfully, helps people see through
the darkness, to see beyond the sin of the world, and their own sin.
Faith enhances our sight because the light of Christ reveals things
that the darkness hides. So in the light of Christ we need not fear the
darkness. The light of Christ reveals what is in the darkness. The

light of Christ shows us two things: It shows us God's love, and it shows us God's justice.

God's love inspires awe and hope because we see what this world could be. And God's justice inspires fear because we see what this world actually is, what we are apart from God, when we deny God's love and guidance. Justice reveals that we are guilty sinners apart from God. We see that we deserve God's justice. And that produces fear. But God's love shows us how we can live in God's justice. When we live according to Christ's righteousness God's justice is fulfilled. Justice for the righteous is mercy. Justice for the unrighteous is damnation.

Thus, said Paul, "we make it our aim to please him" (v. 9). We please God when we truly want to live in His righteousness. It takes an initial decision and an ongoing commitment to do that. But it takes more than words.

Jesus told a parable about this (Matthew 21:28-32): A man had two sons. One said he would, but didn't. The other said he wouldn't, but did. Both had a change of mind, but one moved away from faithfulness, and the other moved toward faithfulness. Paul said that

> "we must all appear before the judgment seat of Christ, so that each one may receive what is due for what he has done in the body, whether good or evil" (v. 10).

No one escapes God's judgment, God's justice. Faithful people fear the Lord because they know that they will face God's judgment, God's justice. And none of us is perfect, nor will we ever be perfect in this life. And we fear that God expects perfection because He does! So the report that we will give before God's bar of justice will be that we are either increasing in righteousness or decreasing in righteousness. If we are growing in righteousness, we can expect God's mercy. f we are not, we can expect God's justice.

Paul was trying to persuade people to see the truth of God, to see both God's mercy and God's justice. He knew that he was telling the truth about God, and that the dispensation of God's justice was and is inevitable. No one will escape it. God will give mercy to those who deserve it—not the perfect, (because there aren't any) but those who are growing in faithfulness and righteousness. How much growth is required? Not much. It's not the degree, but the desire that God is looking for.

But here's the thing! We can't make it happen. We can't make ourselves righteous. We don't know how, and we don't have the will. So, if it's going to happen, God has to do it for us. And the good news is that He has already done it! God sent Jesus, and Jesus proved Himself worthy, and sent the Holy Spirit to complete the process in us, through us.

When people think that all of this is not true, they are not motivated by it. But when people realize that it really is true, that realization motivates them to believe it and engage it. And because it is true, those who don't believe it are simply deluded. It's not that they don't know the truth already, they do! We all live in a world that has been transformed by Jesus Christ. Of course, the transformation is not complete, but it is well under way. That fact is an historical reality. It's available to everyone. But some people

> "by their unrighteousness suppress the truth. For what can be known about God is plain to them, because God has shown it to them" (Romans 1:18-19).

> "For his invisible attributes, namely, his eternal power and divine nature, have been clearly perceived, ever since the creation of the world, in the things that have been made. So they are without excuse" (Romans 1:20).

This world is already in Christ, but some people don't know it. Some people don't believe it. Nonetheless, Jesus ascended to the throne a long time ago. The world is His. He is the King. That means that the life we are living right now is lived in His Kingdom. Failing to understand or believe this does not make it untrue. It's truth doesn't depend on us understanding or believing it. Consequently, Paul said that we need to treat people accordingly.

> "From now on, therefore, we regard no one according to the flesh. Even though we once regarded Christ according to the flesh, we regard him thus no longer. Therefore, if anyone is in Christ, he is a

new creation. The old has passed away; behold, the new has come"
(vs. 16-17).

Jesus Christ was given all authority a long time ago. We don't
need to help Him get it; He already has it. The world just needs to
get with His program, to realize His truth, to see the truth of the reality in which we already live. People can deny it, but it's like denying the fact that the sun rose this the morning and will rise again
tomorrow.

Paul was saying that such denial is ridiculous. The denial of Jesus
Christ is causing a lot of trouble in this world. It's time to give it up!

WHO AM I?

*Then the Lord answered Job out of the whirlwind and said: 2 "Who
is this that darkens counsel by words without knowledge? 3 Dress for
action like a man; I will question you, and you make it known to
me. 4 "Where were you when I laid the foundation of the earth?
Tell me, if you have understanding. 5 Who determined its measure-
ments—surely you know! Or who stretched the line upon it? 6 On
what were its bases sunk, or who laid its cornerstone, 7 when the
morning stars sang together and all the sons of God shouted for joy?
8 "Or who shut in the sea with doors when it burst out from the
womb, 9 when I made clouds its garment and thick darkness its
swaddling band, 10 and prescribed limits for it and set bars and
doors, 11 and said, 'Thus far shall you come, and no farther, and here
shall your proud waves be stayed'?* —Job 38:1-11*

*Working together with him, then, we appeal to you not to receive the
grace of God in vain. 2 For he says, "In a favorable time I listened to
you, and in a day of salvation I have helped you." Behold, now is the
favorable time; behold, now is the day of salvation. 3 We put no obstacle in anyone's way, so that no fault may be found with our ministry, 4 but as servants of God we commend ourselves in every way:
by great endurance, in afflictions, hardships, calamities, 5 beatings,
imprisonments, riots, labors, sleepless nights, hunger; 6 by purity,
knowledge, patience, kindness, the Holy Spirit, genuine love; 7 by
truthful speech, and the power of God; with the weapons of righteousness for the right hand and for the left; 8 through honor and dis-
honor, through slander and praise. We are treated as impostors, and
yet are true; 9 as unknown, and yet well known; as dying, and behold, we live; as punished, and yet not killed; 10 as sorrowful, yet
always rejoicing; as poor, yet making many rich; as having nothing,
yet possessing everything. 11 We have spoken freely to you,
Corinthians; our heart is wide open. 12 You are not restricted by us,*

*but you are restricted in your own affections. 13 In return (I speak as
to children) widen your hearts also.*   —*2 Corinthians 6:1-13*

Job is one of the most interesting and most difficult books to read
and understand. The language is not difficult. It's poetry, but the
story is pretty straightforward. It's not a complex story, but Job's
friends make it difficult. I suppose what makes it hard is that God
doesn't seem fair. What happened to Job was not fair.

The setup to the story is that Job was a person of superior faith.
And Satan said that the only reason that Job had faith was that God
protected him. Satan said that if God stopped protecting him from
the troubles of this world, Job would lose his faith. God said he
wouldn't; the Devil said he would. So to prove Satan wrong, God
withheld His protection. And Job lost everything: money, family,
health, and friends.

The meat of the story comes from the explanations that Job's
three friends give about Job's loss of fortune. His friends argued that
he lost all of that because he had been unfaithful. But Job argued that
he had not been and was not unfaithful. The crux of the difficulty is
understanding the relationship between faithfulness and the difficulties of life—suffering.

We want to believe that our faithfulness will protect us from
life's difficulties. But that is not Job's story, and Job's friends were intent on mainlining that story, and suggested that Job had lost faith.
Job was insistent that he had not lost faith. But his friends didn't believe it. They were convinced that God would protect faithful people
from difficulties, and the only rational conclusion, therefore, was that
Job had been unfaithful.

Job's friends thought that they understood how God "worked,"
that God rewarded righteousness and punished faithlessness. And
there is much to commend this argument. In fact, this argument is
biblical.

"And if you faithfully obey the voice of the Lord your God, being
careful to do all his commandments that I command you today, the
Lord your God will set you high above all the nations of the earth.

And all these blessings shall come upon you and overtake you."
(Deuteronomy 28:1-2).

"But if you will not obey the voice of the Lord your God or be careful to do all his commandments and his statutes that I command you
today, then all these curses shall come upon you and overtake you.
Cursed shall you be in the city, and cursed shall you be in the field"
(Deuteronomy 28:15-16).

Job's friends were simply arguing what they found in Deuteronomy.
Were they wrong?

Job agreed with the teaching found in God's Word, but also held
on to his faithfulness. It's true that God rewards faithfulness, and
punishes unfaithfulness. But Job maintained that in spite of all of his
losses, he remained faithful, so there must be more to it than that. In
spite of it all, he continued to trust the Lord. His friends accused him
of hypocrisy because they trusted what they thought they knew
about God, and did not trust Job's confession of faith.

The thing that is hard to see is that Job's friends were actually
trusting in themselves, in their own understanding, even their own
understanding of God's Word. But Job was trusting in God, in spite
of what he thought he understood about God, about God's Word.

Our reading is from Job 38; there are 42 chapters of Job. So the
reading comes at the conclusion of the story. What we read is God
questioning Job's friends. God is chastising them for their faithlessness. God is asking them what makes them think that they understand God? God was telling them that they did not understand God,
that they couldn't possibly understand how or why God does what
He does. Job's friends didn't know what they were talking about.

And yet, God was not contradicting His Word. His Word in
Deuteronomy is true. But it's not the whole truth. What God has
told us in Deuteronomy is completely true, but there is more to God
that what we find in the Old Testament. God was saying, *Who do
you think you are!?*

Job's friends were essentially saying that God was the cause of
Job's suffering, and that God was right to make him suffer because
Job had not been faithful. They were accusing God of being the

source of his own pain and suffering in Job's life, and in the world. And Job, in the midst of his pain and suffering, was defending God from such an accusation. God is not the one who brings pain and suffering to the world. Job's friends were relying on their own understanding, and Job was confessing his faith in spite of his lack of understanding.

The Lectionary then sends us to 2 Corinthians 6 where Paul was talking about receiving the grace of God in vain. The connection is that Job's friends were full of vanity, full of themselves because they were trusting in themselves, trusting in what they thought they knew about God. And the difficulty is that they trusted what they thought they knew about God based on a true but limited understanding of God's Word. They understood Deuteronomy correctly. God does reward faithfulness and curse unfaithfulness. What they knew was true, but it was not the *whole* truth.

There is a commonality between the suffering of Job and the suffering of Paul and the apostles. Job was suffering for the sake of the story that was being written about him, the story that God was writing about Job. The lesson that God was teaching was that the world does not revolve around us, that we cannot trust our own thinking, even when our thinking is right! What we think is such a small part of the reality in which we live that it is not trustworthy.

In a similar way the suffering of Paul and the apostles was like the suffering of Job in that it was not about them personally, but was about the story that God was writing about them. Paul was commending the teaching of the apostles in spite of their

"afflictions, hardships, calamities, beatings, imprisonments, riots, labors, sleepless nights, hunger" (vs. 4-5).

The apostles were not suffering because they were faithless. Rather, like Job, they were faithful in spite of their suffering. The whole truth that Job had suffered for was being fully realized through the ministry of Jesus Christ. Job had not suffered at God's whim. God is not whimsical, Job suffered because God was setting up the gospel story for the future, what was future to Job. Paul and the apostles suffered because God was realizing the gospel through the ministry of the resurrected Lord of history, Jesus Christ. Paul and the apostles suffered in order to establish the truth of the gospel. They did not suffer because they were unfaithful. Rather, they were faithful in spite of their suffering.

God was not the cause of their suffering. The sinfulness of the world was the cause of their suffering. But neither would their suffering keep them from being faithful. If they suffered because they had been faithful, then they could end their suffering by ending their faithfulness. But faithlessness does not eliminate suffering. The faithless suffer just as much, if not more, than the faithful. We have limited control over the circumstances of our lives. Sure, we can change jobs, change addresses, even change our friends. But we can't change who we are. Wherever we go, whatever we do, we are who we are.

But here's the thing: we are not who we think we are, anymore than God is who we think He is. Our thinking, our experience of this world, our skills and abilities, our education apart from God's Word is inadequate to rightly understand the world in which we live. We contemporary people have not learned that yet. Our world has made such advances in learning, science, technology, and medicine. And we have! We are way more advanced than any previous generation in history. All of this is true! But it's not the whole truth.

Like Job's friends we still trust in ourselves. We trust in our knowledge, our science, our technology, our medicine because we know that it is right. And it is! It works! But it's not the whole truth! We think we are so smart. Tell me that this world does not trust in itself. It does! We do! What we have learned in terms of science, technology, and medicine is *true*. It works! It's trustworthy. And it's a blessing. Plumbing, sanitation, medicine, advances in farming, electricity—all of these things are blessings. We want them, we trust them, we need them.

Have these things relieved our suffering? They have helped. They make life easier. But is there still suffering in the world? Will plumbing, sanitation, medicine, or electricity end suffering? No! That's what God is showing us right now in 2024. It could be argued that these things have not reduced human suffering, they have only changed it. We still trust ourselves. We trust in politics more than we trust in God's providence. And that means that we have not yet learned the lesson in Job.

The lesson to be learned through the story of Job is still waiting to be learned. And what is that lesson? If I answer that question, does that mean that *you* have learned that lesson? We can only answer that question ourselves. No one else can answer it for us. It's the question of the ages, a perennial question that each and every person needs to answer for themselves.

Who are you? Or perhaps, whose are you? To whom do you belong? Or perhaps, where do you belong? Who do you think you are!

ARK OF HISTORY

2 And it was told King David, "The Lord has blessed the household of Obed-edom and all that belongs to him, because of the ark of God." So David went and brought up the ark of God from the house of Obed-edom to the city of David with rejoicing. 13 And when those who bore the ark of the Lord had gone six steps, he sacrificed an ox and a fattened animal. 14 And David danced before the Lord with all his might. And David was wearing a linen ephod. 15 So David and all the house of Israel brought up the ark of the Lord with shouting and with the sound of the horn. 16 As the ark of the Lord came into the city of David, Michal the daughter of Saul looked out of the window and saw King David leaping and dancing before the Lord, and she despised him in her heart. 17 And they brought in the ark of the Lord and set it in its place, inside the tent that David had pitched for it. And David offered burnt offerings and peace offerings before the Lord. 18 And when David had finished offering the burnt offerings and the peace offerings, he blessed the people in the name of the Lord of hosts 19 and distributed among all the people, the whole multitude of Israel, both men and women, a cake of bread, a portion of meat, and a cake of raisins to each one. Then all the people departed, each to his house. —2 Samuel 6:12-19*

14 King Herod heard of it, for Jesus' name had become known. Some said, "John the Baptist has been raised from the dead. That is why these miraculous powers are at work in him." 15 But others said, "He is Elijah." And others said, "He is a prophet, like one of the prophets of old." 16 But when Herod heard of it, he said, "John, whom I beheaded, has been raised." 17 For it was Herod who had sent and seized John and bound him in prison for the sake of Herodias, his brother Philip's wife, because he had married her. 18 For John had been saying to Herod, "It is not lawful for you to have your brother's wife." 19 And Herodias had a grudge against him and wanted to put him to death. But she could not, 20 for Herod feared John, knowing that he was a righteous and holy man, and he kept him safe. When he heard him, he was greatly perplexed, and yet he heard him gladly. 21 But an opportunity came when Herod on his birthday gave a banquet for his nobles and military commanders and the leading men of Galilee. 22 For when Herodias's daughter came in and danced, she pleased Herod and his guests. And the king said to the girl, "Ask me for whatever you wish, and I will give it to you." 23 And he vowed to her, "Whatever you ask me, I will give you, up to half of my kingdom." 24 And she went out and said to her mother, "For what should I ask?" And she said, "The head of John the Baptist." 25 And she came in immediately with haste to the king and asked, saying, "I want you to give me at once the head of John the Baptist on a platter." 26 And the king was exceedingly sorry, but because of his oaths and his guests he did not want to break his word to her. 27 And immediately the king sent an executioner with orders to bring John's[d] head. He went and beheaded him in the prison 28 and brought his head on a platter and gave it to the girl, and the girl gave it to her mother. 29 When his disciples heard of it, they came and took his body and laid it in a tomb.   —Mark 6:14-29

The reading from 2 Samuel tells of the return of the ark. But to understand the story we need to remember how the ark had been lost, how it got captured. The first thing we need to do is to locate the story of the ark in the larger story of Old Testament Israel. The story begins after the book of Judges.

The story of the judges recounts a four hundred year period of Israel's apostasy. It was a time of relapse into sin and revival that repeated ad nauseam. Israel would fall into faithlessness, and be revived by a charismatic leader, a judge, who would rekindle the faith, rally the troops, win a battle, and save the nation. Only to see it fall into faithlessness again. This pattern continued for four hundred years.

The story in 1 Samuel 4 occurred when Israel was fighting the Philistines at Aphek. Israel lost that battle. As they were analyzing why they lost that battle, they remembered that they were supposed to rely on the Lord to fight their battles. So they brought the ark from Shiloh, where it had been stored and forgotten, and brought it to the battle front. They wanted to use God—the ark—as a shield and a battering ram. Was that what God meant when He said that He would fight their battles? No, we are not to use God, but to rely on God. There's a difference.

When the Philistines learned that the Israelites had brought the ark to the battle they became afraid because the stories of the Hebrew God were powerful. Their fear then made them fight all the harder, and they won the next battle, and captured the ark. Because Israel had fallen into apostasy again Israel deserved to be defeated and carried into exile. But God, represented by the ark, went into captivity instead. The image is that God received the punishment that Israel deserved.

While God was in exile from Israel, the Philistines thought that they had captured the God of the Hebrews, and began to parade the ark all over their country. But everywhere the ark went disease broke out among the people. God was fighting Israel's battles against the Philistines by bringing disease to them.

In Ashdod, the Philistine capital, the Ark was placed in the temple of Dagon. The next morning the statue of Dagon was found prostrate in front of the Ark. After the statue of Dagon was restored to its upright position, the next morning it was again found prostrate, and this time its head and hands had also been broken off. The Philistines decided to try to appease God (the ark) by making gold statues of mice and various sorts of lesions and putting them in the ark. They filled the ark with gold figures. They then gave it two new animals to pull the cart and let it go wherever it would.

It headed straight for Israel. And it is at this point that we pick up the story of David returning the ark to Jerusalem. It is a story of God returning from captivity, reminiscent of Israel escaping from Egypt, and the ten plagues, and of Egypt giving the Israelites gold and valuables as an offering to stop the plagues. The parallels are many and intriguing.

So David brings the ark into Jerusalem with great fanfare. There was music, dancing, and sacrifices galore. This event marks an end to Israel's period of apostasy that we see in the book of Judges, and is the beginning of the kingdom of Israel. The next major phase of Israel's history is the building of the kingdom. The people will call for a king, Samuel will anoint Saul, then David. And a new chapter of Israel's history will begin.

The reading from 2 Samuel today marks the apex between Israel's apostasy and the founding of the nation of Israel under King David. The people wanted a king like the other nations had. God gave them Saul, who was the people's choice. But David was God's choice. That history is long and involved, and very interesting.

The Lectionary then takes us to the death of John the Baptist. But to understand the meaning of John's death, we need to understand the historic context in which John lived because there is a similarity to the time when David brought the ark into Jerusalem. John's context is similar to the time of the Judges, Israel's time of apostasy, when Israel fell into apathy, only to be revived by a charismatic leader who would stir them to recovery and save them from an enemy, only to see them slide into apostasy again … and again … and again. For four hundred years.

John the Baptist was born four hundred years after the closing of the book of the Old Testament. A time when no one had heard a prophet speak in Israel for four hundred years. John came into Jerusalem from the desert proclaiming,

"Repent, for the kingdom of heaven is at hand" (Matthew 3:2).

David had brought the ark into Jerusalem in order to establish the kingdom of Israel, the Kingdom of God in Israel. It was a time between two great historical periods. The ark had come to establish the Old Testament kingdom. John had come into Israel as a precursor of the One who was coming to establish the New Testament Kingdom of God in the world.

John had stirred up the people enough to concern King Herod. John was the talk of the town. Many people, respectable Jews among them, were being baptized by John. And John was proclaiming that a new king was coming. This concerned Herod because it was a challenge to his leadership, his kingship. Herod didn't like it. So he responded in the way that kings always respond to a threat to their power. He put his rival in jail.

Herod needed a pretext in order to arrest John. He needed to justify John's arrest. Herod found John interesting, and dangerous because a lot of people followed him. John was an unpolished preacher of truth from the desert. John was an establishment outsider who didn't respect the power structures of the establishment. And like the prophets of old John didn't care about them, and simply spoke the truth. John was not a delicate preacher who was careful with his words. He just called 'em like he saw 'em. His directness offended those in power.

Herod had put John in prison

> "for the sake of Herodias, his brother Philip's wife, because he had married her" (v. 17).

John the Baptist had rebuked King Herod more than once for divorcing his wife and marrying his niece, Herodias, who had been his brother Philip's wife. He publicly chastised Herodias for an immoral, unbiblical marriage, and she didn't like it. Philip was still alive, and both Philip and Antipas were uncles to Herodias. This meant that Herod's marriage to Herodias was a violation of Leviticus 18:16; 20:21.

> "16 You shall not uncover the nakedness of your brother's wife; it is your brother's nakedness. ... 21 If a man takes his brother's wife, it is impurity. He has uncovered his brother's nakedness; they shall be childless."

Herod was a Jew of sorts. He saw himself as tied to the Jewish religion and tried, to a certain extent, to uphold its laws, even in his own lifestyle. So John felt justified in bringing this infraction to public attention. Herodias seethed with anger toward John because John had made the situation plain—and public.

To appease his wife, Herod had John thrown into prison. Herod could have had John executed, but he knew that John was popular with the people, and much of what John said was true, so he decided not to put him to death. Herod was intrigued by John and liked to hear him speak. But Herodias loathed John and wanted him dead. Her grudge against John resulted in his death.

> "And Herodias had a grudge against him and wanted to put him to death. But she could not, for Herod feared John, knowing that he was a righteous and holy man, and he kept him safe" (v. 19-20).

Herodias sought John's death, but she had to bide her time, and waited for an opportunity. The opportunity came at Herod's birthday party. At the banquet, Herodias's daughter, Salome, performed a provocative dance designed to arouse the audience and Herod himself with lust. Herodias knew that this, along with enough wine, would soften Herod up to suggestion. Salome's performance did please the king and his guests. Herod publicly told her,

> "Ask me for whatever you wish, and I will give it to you ... Whatever you ask me, I will give you, up to half of my kingdom" (vs. 22-23).

The ideas was: *I'll give you what you want, so you will give me what I want.*

Again, King Herod flaunted his generosity and power publicly before his guests. He was king and he wanted everyone to know it. But he would deeply regret this vow.

Salome went to her mother, Herodias, to ask for advice. And Herodias seized the opportunity she had been looking for. Herodias told her to ask for John's head, John's death. Herod was surprised, but complied. Herodias was satisfied. John was dead. People were devastated. But God is sovereign, which means that God controls history.

God used John's death to unite John's disciples with Jesus' disciples in order to slingshot Jesus into greater popularity with the people. Jesus now had no rivals, as God was bringing King Jesus to establish the new kingdom of God on earth. This shows us that God redeems human tragedy. God uses our failures to strengthen us. God uses our mistakes to teach us.

John was beheaded to satisfy Herodias' hatred. Just as Elijah had been hated by Queen Jezebel, so the one who came in the power and spirit of Elijah was hated by Queen Herodias. She used cunning and manipulation that publicly degraded her own daughter to get what she wanted from her husband. She succeeded in silencing John, but God would have the last word. King Herod was so troubled by his guilty conscience that when He heard of Jesus Christ's miracles, he worried that Jesus was actually John the Baptist risen from the dead.

God controls history because it is His story. And His story is not over. He is still writing it. Our job is not to simply read His story; our job is to play the role He gives us in His story. And we all have a role, a purpose. Mostly that role is to simply be faithful where we are, to be faithful among our families and friends.

Let's do that.

Transform, Conform, Reform

"Woe to the shepherds who destroy and scatter the sheep of my pasture!" declares the Lord. 2 Therefore thus says the Lord, the God of Israel, concerning the shepherds who care for my people: You have scattered my flock and have driven them away, and you have not attended to them. Behold, I will attend to you for your evil deeds, declares the Lord. 3 Then I will gather the remnant of my flock out of all the countries where I have driven them, and I will bring them back to their fold, and they shall be fruitful and multiply. 4 I will set shepherds over them who will care for them, and they shall fear no more, nor be dismayed, neither shall any be missing, declares the Lord. 5 Behold, the days are coming, declares the Lord, when I will raise up for David a righteous Branch, and he shall reign as king and deal wisely, and shall execute justice and righteousness in the land. 6 In his days Judah will be saved, and Israel will dwell securely. And this is the name by which he will be called: 'The Lord is our righteousness.'"
                                          —Jeremiah 23:1-6

11 Therefore remember that at one time you Gentiles in the flesh, called "the uncircumcision" by what is called the circumcision, which is made in the flesh by hands—12 remember that you were at that time separated from Christ, alienated from the commonwealth of Israel and strangers to the covenants of promise, having no hope and without God in the world. 13 But now in Christ Jesus you who once were far off have been brought near by the blood of Christ. 14 For he himself is our peace, who has made us both one and has broken down in his flesh the dividing wall of hostility 15 by abolishing the law of commandments expressed in ordinances, that he might create in himself one new man in place of the two, so making peace, 16 and might

*reconcile us both to God in one body through the cross, thereby
killing the hostility. 17 And he came and preached peace to you who
were far off and peace to those who were near. 18 For through him
we both have access in one Spirit to the Father. 19 So then you are
no longer strangers and aliens, but you are fellow citizens with the
saints and members of the household of God, 20 built on the foundation of the apostles and prophets, Christ Jesus himself being the cornerstone, 21 in whom the whole structure, being joined together,
grows into a holy temple in the Lord. 22 In him you also are being
built together into a dwelling place for God by the Spirit.*
—Ephesians 2:11-22

Church problems. Why are the churches so full of problems?
Conflicts, dissension, heresy, apostasy, bickering. Moses com-
plained about it shortly after leaving Egypt.

> "And the people complained in the hearing of the Lord about their
> misfortunes, and when the Lord heard it, his anger was kindled, and
> the fire of the Lord burned among them and consumed some outly-
> ing parts of the camp. Then the people cried out to Moses, and
> Moses prayed to the Lord, and the fire died down. So the name of
> that place was called Taberah, because the fire of the Lord burned
> among them" (Numbers 11:1-3).

In Numbers the people were blamed. In Jeremiah, the Lord was
not blaming the people. He was blaming the shepherds, the leaders.

> "You have scattered my flock and have driven them away, and you
> have not attended to them" (v. 2).

It's bad enough when people complain and bicker, but when the
leaders are causing the problems it's much worse. The leaders can
work with the people to sort out the problems and disagreements.
But when the leaders are the problem, who can step in to solve the
problems? The people can't. Other leaders only add to the problems
because one set of leaders is not likely to take advice from a conflict-
ing set of leaders. You could argue that a bishop or some higher authority could bring peace. But more often than not when hierarchal
authority imposes a solution, the solution is not respected because

imposition, where one person demands something of another, is not a Christian solution. Christianity doesn't work that way. Where problems are caused by leaders, the leaders are usually demanding something of the people in the first place. More demands will not solve a disagreement.

Jeremiah said two things: He said that God would attend to the leaders who were causing the problem; and that He will gather the remnant of His flock Himself, and bring them back to their fold. God Himself would resolve the issues, discipline the leaders, and bring peace. How does God do that? He changes hearts and minds. And how does He do that? He dispatches His Holy Spirit to work on people from the inside. He changes what we value, what we want. He changes our perspective by bringing our thoughts and desires in line with His thoughts and desires.

We might call this process *persuasion*. People are persuaded by interacting with someone who believes differently, someone who is able to articulate their beliefs or their position in a convincing manner. This happens through conversation, and in this case it's a conversation with the Holy Spirit. So how do people have a conversation with the Holy Spirit?

We often think of people having an angel on one shoulder and a devil on the other shoulder, and the person then listens to the advice of each and decides which to believe. In this case we just need to listen to our "better angels." Or conversely, we might say, "The devil made me do it!" But this scenario is wrong on several levels.

First of all, it's just us talking to ourselves. We are simply evaluating the benefits (angel) and liabilities (devil) of some issue. We are simply listening to ourselves because at the end of the day we will decide ourselves to either listen to the angel or the devil. We make the decision ourselves. And people do what they want to do. So in this angel/devil scenario we end up following our own advice. We might attribute it to the Holy Spirit by saying that the voice of the angel is the Holy Spirit. And, well, maybe sometimes it is, but a lot of the time it isn't. And it especially isn't if we have not consulted a trustworthy way of knowing the Holy Spirit.

The only way to really know the Holy Spirit is by reading the Bible, God's Word. If we don't read and understand the Bible, we can't trust our thinking to be Holy Spirit led. And if we do read and understand the Bible, we can trust it to speak God's truth. So, what is the difference between understanding the Bible and not understanding the Bible?

The difference is that those who read the Bible with understanding are transformed by what they read. They are changed by it. Not just changed a little, but transformed. To be transformed is a big deal. It's a big change, a reversal of one's nature, a change of temperament, a new heart, a new character, etc. We might even call it a conversion, where one thing is changed into another thing. Paul said it this way:

> "Do not be conformed to this world, but be transformed by the renewal of your mind, that by testing you may discern what is the will of God, what is good and acceptable and perfect" (Romans 12:2)

Here Paul sets the idea of transformation in terms of not being conformed to the world, not being conformed to the ideas and practices of unbelievers. People are like sheep. We are social beings. Being part of a group is a necessity for our sanity. We come to know ourselves only by socializing with others. We see how other people are, and we find comfort in being with others who are like us. So we self-select into self-similar groups.

The people we know and like are usually people who are like us, people who share our socioeconomic status, our educational or vocational standing, etc., people with whom we have something in common. This is not a bad thing, it's natural. It's tribal, and human tribes are a natural occurrence. It's what social beings naturally do. Of course it can be problematic, which is why Paul counsels Christians to not be conformed to the world. By which he means don't be conformed to sinners. Don't be like sinners. Don't normalize sin. But rather, be transformed, be changed by the renewal of our minds.

The mind is the key to the Christian life. The heart is the key to belief, but the mind is the heart of discipleship. The reason why non-Christians don't respond to Christian truth is that they don't understand spiritual truth. They don't understand it because they don't believe it.

> "The natural person does not accept the things of the Spirit of God, for they are folly to him, and he is not able to understand them because they are spiritually discerned" (1 Corinthians 2:14),

Spiritually discerned means spiritually known. The gospel is a call to repent of sin and trust Christ by faith. Initially we must trust by faith, not by knowledge, because we don't have any initial or automatic knowledge of God. We are not born with knowledge of God. We must learn about God. We do this by trusting that the Bible is true, rather than thinking that it isn't true.

For instance, we read that Jesus walked on water. We need to say, *I wonder how that can be true.* Rather than jumping to a conclusion: *well, that can't be true!* We need to doubt ourselves and trust the Bible, rather than doubting the Bible and trusting ourselves. Our thinking must be changed (transformed) from old, unfaithful ways of thinking into new, faithful ways of thinking.

Our natural human way of thinking is for our hearts to inform our minds. We know that we don't know everything, so we trust how we feel about things because our feeling, our intuition about things is often right. Over time we find that when we don't understand something we trust our feelings, which means that we trust ourselves. But when it comes to God, Isaiah said,

> "'For my thoughts are not your thoughts, neither are your ways my ways,' declares the Lord. 'For as the heavens are higher than the earth, so are my ways higher than your ways and my thoughts than your thoughts'" (Isaiah 55:8-9).

We are limited creatures with limited ability to understand things. God doesn't have our limitations, which means that God understands more than we are able to understand. So we must train ourselves to trust God's Word. And the more we trust God, the more we understand the Bible. Therefore, we must first renew our minds by conforming our beliefs and actions to the Word of God, to the example of Jesus Christ.

The first step is to stop trusting ourselves, our worldly intuitions, our feelings, our fears. We must understand that out thinking is flawed, that we are sinners. When we do that we begin to grow and mature beyond our wildest expectations. It all becomes very worthwhile.

In the Ephesians reading Paul was reminding Christians that they were not born Christians. No one is born a Christian. Being a Christian involves a change of nature, a change of behavior, a change of belief, a change of values and interests. This change is difficult to understand for people who grew up in the church, people who have always known themselves to be Christian. If you were converted as a young child, it's hard to remember when you were not a Christian.

So for those who have grown up in the church and have always considered themselves to be Christians, you might think of the process in terms of growth and maturity. Rather than thinking in terms of believers and unbelievers, or Christians and nonChristians, think of the difference as being baby Christians versus mature Christians.

If you have matured in your faith, you have gone through a process of reevaluation of immature ideas and even changed your mind about some things that you used to believe in your youth, in your immaturity. But if you are someone who grew up in the church and don't know what I'm talking about, you might still have a baby Christian faith. And while that is better than having no faith at all, it is problematic for adults to believe and act as children. There is nothing wrong with children or childishness or immaturity—unless it characterizes an adult.

Here's the thing, the problem: growth is natural, but maturity in Christ is not natural. It's supernatural. No one naturally becomes a Christian as they age. We naturally get old, but we don't naturally become mature Christians. Even if you have been born again, maturity in Christ doesn't happen automatically or naturally. It requires intentionality and effort—discipline, practice, study.

In the long arc of Christian history, over the centuries, Christian evangelism has been quite successful. The Great Awakenings of the

1700s and 1800s brought many people into Christ's fold. In the last century Billy Graham and many others have continued to evangelize the masses. And they have been fairly successful. Most every church has concentrated on outreach programs, evangelistic efforts to bring in new people. And all of that is good. Churches have all sorts of programs for new believers, and that's great!

But what is needed, what has been neglected is the sanctification of believers, growth and maturity in the faith. We tend to think that advanced Bible study or theology is only for pastors or seminary professors, the professional class of Christians. The result of this is that the vast majority of Christians at best know only rudiments of the Bible. People—Christians—for the most part know very little about the Bible or about biblical history. Why is this a problem? Because when people don't know history, they tend to repeat it. When people don't learn from historical errors, those errors tend to be repeated, generation after generation.

The reason that God has provided a written record of His Word is so that people can learn from the errors of others, and not continue to make the same historical errors of judgment over and over. The world today is at an inflection point, a time of significant historical change. These moments tend to last decades because history moves slowly. All of this means that the opportunity to learn God's Word, to learn what God is doing, what God really wants, is upon us. It's actually not difficult to understand, but it takes willing effort, and disciplined practice.

If you want to change the world, read the Bible. To be a change agent you must be a changed agent.

EXPECTATION

42 A man came from Baal-shalishah, bringing the man of God bread of the firstfruits, twenty loaves of barley and fresh ears of grain in his sack. And Elisha said, "Give to the men, that they may eat." 43 But his servant said, "How can I set this before a hundred men?" So he repeated, "Give them to the men, that they may eat, for thus says the Lord, 'They shall eat and have some left.'" 44 So he set it before them. And they ate and had some left, according to the word of the Lord. —2 Kings 4:42-44

After this Jesus went away to the other side of the Sea of Galilee, which is the Sea of Tiberias. 2 And a large crowd was following him, because they saw the signs that he was doing on the sick. 3 Jesus went up on the mountain, and there he sat down with his disciples. 4 Now the Passover, the feast of the Jews, was at hand. 5 Lifting up his eyes, then, and seeing that a large crowd was coming toward him, Jesus said to Philip, "Where are we to buy bread, so that these people may eat?" 6 He said this to test him, for he himself knew what he would do. 7 Philip answered him, "Two hundred denarii worth of bread would not be enough for each of them to get a little." 8 One of his disciples, Andrew, Simon Peter's brother, said to him, 9 "There is a boy here who has five barley loaves and two fish, but what are they for so many?" 10 Jesus said, "Have the people sit down." Now there was much grass in the place. So the men sat down, about five thousand in number. 11 Jesus then took the loaves, and when he had given thanks, he distributed them to those who were seated. So also the fish, as much as they wanted. 12 And when they had eaten their fill, he told his disciples, "Gather up the leftover fragments, that nothing may be lost." 13 So they gathered them up and filled twelve baskets with fragments from the five barley loaves left by those who had eaten. 14 When the people saw the sign that he had done, they said,

"This is indeed the Prophet who is to come into the world!"
                                                    —John 6:1-14

My success as a preacher this morning is dependent upon your expectations. If you get what you expect, I will be successful. If you don't get what you expect, I will not be successful. The success of a church, or any social endeavor, is less dependent upon leadership skills, and more dependent on the expectations of the people involved. How so?

For instance, if your expectations are low, then most any preacher will satisfy you. But if your expectations are high, your satisfaction will require more. Churches with low expectations can be quite successful because a lot of people have low expectations, and they are quite satisfied to have them met. Churches with higher expectations are usually not as popular, and success today is measured by popularity.

Today we are talking about the feeding of the five thousand. In that story Jesus teaches us about our expectations. In one sense a miracle is a violation of our expectations. Miracles are improbable, unexpected. Miracles are disturbing because they don't fit into our understanding. We could say that miracles expand our understanding of the world, or that they violate our understanding of the world. In either case, expanding or violating, miracles stress our understanding of the world because miracles cause us to rethink what we think we understand about the world. And that's a hard thing to do. It takes time and effort.

This story about Elisha in 2 Kings is mostly unknown. Most people are not aware of this story because in the larger flow of the story about Elisha, it plays a minor role. What's the big deal: a guy shows up with some bread and corn in his backpack. Elisha says, *Let's stop and eat.* Someone says, *There's not enough for everyone.* Elisha says, *That's OK. Let's stop and eat anyway.* And everyone eats to their fill, and there is food left over. In an of itself, the story doesn't mean much. Some people had lunch on the road. What's the big deal?

But let's put the story in it's larger context. What else was going on in 2 Kings 4? 2 Kings 4:32-37 is the story of Elisha reviving a boy who was dead. Raising the dead constitutes a serious miracle. 2 Kings 4:38-41 is the story of Elisha purifying a rotten pot of stew with flour. This is very strange, but it constitutes another miracle, a miracle of purification by an ordinary ingredient. Note the conjunction between miracle and something ordinary. 2 Kings 4:42-44, our reading this morning, is this story of a guy with bread and corn, but not enough to feed everyone. And yet everyone is fed with food left over. Another odd miracle. That's three miracles in a row for Elisha. And miracles in the Old Testament establish the credibility of a prophet. Elisha's prophethood is therefore established.

Miracles challenge our expectations. I'm not going to do any miracles this morning. So if you are expecting miracles, you will be disappointed. I'm just going to talk about miracles in an ordinary way.

The second reading this morning is the story of the feeding of the five thousand, which is considered a miracle credited to Jesus. An interesting thing about this miracle is that at the time, in Jesus' day, no one expected Jesus to create food out of thin air. But today Christians do expect this story to be about the miraculous creation of food out of thin air. So I want to look at the story more closely this morning, to help us see the actual miracle because it's not what people expect. And I remind you that theology is just paying closer attention to biblical details than people are used to.

Jesus' public ministry began with His revelation to the Samaritan woman at the well in John 4 that He is the Christ. John 5 is the story of Jesus healing the man at the pool of Bethesda—on the Sabbath. Jesus then announced Himself as Messiah to the Pharisees, who did not receive that news well. So Jesus got out of town, crossed the sea of Galilee, and a large crowd followed Him. That's the set up. Let's look closely at the story. Stories about Jesus' miracles and healings were circulating among the people at the time. People love miracles, everyone needs healing of some sort. People wanted to see a miracle to establish Jesus' spiritual authority, or just to be healed of some malady.

Jesus had a large crowd of people following him, about five thousand. Some commentators say that that figure did not include women and children. Maybe. I don't think it matters. The point is that there were a lot of people. It was Passover, which meant that a lot of people were on the road to the annual festival at Jerusalem. A lot of people came to Jerusalem every year for Passover. This is an important detail. Jesus asked Philip,

> "'Where are we to buy bread, so that these people may eat?' He said this to test him" (vs. 5-6).

Notice two things: 1) Jesus inquired about *buying* bread, and 2) the question was a *test*. A test about what? They were out in the wilderness, but a lot of people were on the road because of Passover. People traveled long distances to get to Jerusalem. And there were no bakeries in the wilderness, no place to buy bread. Jesus was not unaware of this fact. Everyone was aware of that. So the test was about what we might call *reliance on the market*. The market, a human creation, supplies human needs. That's what markets do.

People were out in the desert, without a market to provide for their needs. Jesus knew that there was no place to buy bread. Everyone knew that! The test was for the disciples: what would they do without a market to supply the needs of God's people? They had no idea. And to illustrate the problem to Jesus, Andrew said,

> "There is a boy here who has five barley loaves and two fish, but what are they for so many?" (v. 9).

A boy, not a father, had barley and dried fish. Why would a boy have barley loaves, which is a hard, course grain. Barley was cheap grain, which indicated the poverty of the family. Nonetheless, even this poor waif had barley loaves and dried fish. Whole families went to Jerusalem for Passover. They carried their own provisions for the trip: here was a boy who had barley bread and dried fish. Jesus knew that if a poor child carried his own provision, the people also carried their own provisions for the Passover trip. Most people would spend weeks on the road. The disciples were focused on the market to pro-

vide for God's people. Jesus was about to show them what we call
the doctrine of God's providence.

God provides for His people. Sometimes God uses markets, and
sometimes He doesn't. Jesus told them to sit.

"Now there was much grass in the place" (v. 9).

What an odd detail. Why was it important that grass was available?
Why mention that? We tend to think of grass as mowed lawns, but
this grass was not mowed. We tend to think that grass would be a
nice place to spread a picnic blanket, but that only works on mowed
grass. The point of the grass was that there was provision for their
pack-mules and other animals they were bringing with them to
Jerusalem for Passover sacrifices. God was caring for all of His creatures. The animals could graze.

Jesus then blessed the meal because traditionally Jews always
thanked God for every meal. So, they all ate and twelve baskets of
food were left over. Was the food produced out of thin air? Isn't all
food produced out of thin air? Isn't all food miraculous? Isn't growth
itself miraculous? So, what was the miracle? Jesus demonstrated that
God's people are not dependent upon market economies, that God's
provision is dependable. Is that less of a miracle than producing food
out of thin air? Isn't relying on God's provision for His people more
important, and more real, more dependable, that hoping for bread
from thin air?

What were you expecting? It is the nature of miracles to challenge and contradict our ordinary expectations. For those who cannot think beyond market economies, the feeding of the five
thousand is unexplainable, and is therefore a miracle. There are
many, many people like this. So this is an acceptable understanding
of a miracle that establishes Jesus' credibility. Many of the disciples
were also in this category. For others, Jesus demonstrated that God is
not dependent on market economies to care for His people.

Providence is an older doctrine that has been mostly forgotten in
our modern world. It's called Providence (provide-ence). The doctrine of God's Providence teaches that God is in complete control of
all things. He is sovereign over the universe as a whole (Psalm

103:19), sovereign over the physical world (Matthew 5:45), sovereign over the affairs of nations (Psalm 66:7), over human destiny (Galatians 1:15), over human success and failure (Luke 1:52). God provides for His people (Psalm 4:8). This doctrine stands in direct opposition to the idea that the universe is governed by chance or fate —or politics. God accomplishes His will through His Providence. To ensure that His purposes are fulfilled, God governs human affairs and works through the natural order of things.

The laws of nature are nothing more than God's work in the universe. The laws of nature have no inherent power; rather, they are the principles that God set in place to govern how things normally work. They are "laws" because God decreed them, God established them. God created the world and established how the world functions. God is the power of nature. "Nature" is a substitute word for God's power. God is able to use our free will to accomplish His purposes because He knows us.

The recent assassination attempt of Donald Trump is an example of God's providence: He turned his head at exactly the right moment, in exactly the right amount, which foiled the assassination attempt. We could call it luck, but God doesn't believe in luck. God governs luck. "Luck" is a substitute word for God's providence. Luck excludes God from the world. Are there theological reasons that God would preserve Donald Trump? We don't know yet. The story is not over. Stay tuned. Stay tuned into God's story so that you can play your role.

Don't worry about Trump's role, concern yourself with your role. Your role is more important than you think. The little things in life lay the foundation for the big things. What do you expect? What are you expecting? To whom are you giving *your* attention?

PROVISION

9 Then Moses said to Aaron, "Say to the whole congregation of the people of Israel, 'Come near before the Lord, for he has heard your grumbling.'" 10 And as soon as Aaron spoke to the whole congregation of the people of Israel, they looked toward the wilderness, and behold, the glory of the Lord appeared in the cloud. 11 And the Lord said to Moses, 12 "I have heard the grumbling of the people of Israel. Say to them, 'At twilight you shall eat meat, and in the morning you shall be filled with bread. Then you shall know that I am the Lord your God.'" 13 In the evening quail came up and covered the camp, and in the morning dew lay around the camp. 14 And when the dew had gone up, there was on the face of the wilderness a fine, flake-like thing, fine as frost on the ground. 15 When the people of Israel saw it, they said to one another, "What is it?" For they did not know what it was. And Moses said to them, "It is the bread that the Lord has given you to eat."   —Exodus 16:9-15*

24 So when the crowd saw that Jesus was not there, nor his disciples, they themselves got into the boats and went to Capernaum, seeking Jesus. 25 When they found him on the other side of the sea, they said to him, "Rabbi, when did you come here?" 26 Jesus answered them, "Truly, truly, I say to you, you are seeking me, not because you saw signs, but because you ate your fill of the loaves. 27 Do not work for the food that perishes, but for the food that endures to eternal life, which the Son of Man will give to you. For on him God the Father has set his seal." 28 Then they said to him, "What must we do, to be doing the works of God?" 29 Jesus answered them, "This is the work of God, that you believe in him whom he has sent." 30 So they said to him, "Then what sign do you do, that we may see and believe you? What work do you perform? 31 Our fathers ate the manna in the wilderness; as it is written, 'He gave them bread from heaven to eat.'" 32 Jesus then said to them, "Truly, truly, I say to you, it was

not Moses who gave you the bread from heaven, but my Father gives
you the true bread from heaven. 33 For the bread of God is he who
comes down from heaven and gives life to the world." 34 They said
to him, "Sir, give us this bread always." 35 Jesus said to them, "I am
the bread of life; whoever comes to me shall not hunger, and whoever
believes in me shall never thirst."   *—John 6:24-35*

It's important to see the larger context of the Bible stories that we read together in our worship because there is an always-present-danger of taking things out of context, which leads to false conclusions.

This morning we're reading from Exodus 16. Exodus is the story of Israel's escape from slavery in Egypt. Israel first came into Egypt at the invitation of Joseph in order to escape famine. Egypt was a kind of savior for Israel at that time. But Israel did not blend into Egyptian culture. Israel maintained its own culture in Egypt. Abraham said that God had a special plan for Israel, so Israel set itself apart from the Egyptians, and over time Israel prospered and the Egyptians grew afraid of them because they were different. That fear then led the Egyptians to discriminate against Israel and eventually to oppress them. And in time Moses was chosen to lead Israel out of Egypt. We know the story.

In the book of Exodus Israel has been freed from Egypt and was in the wilderness learning about the new culture that God had for them. The books of Exodus and Numbers tell the stories of God's dramatic and miraculous rescue from Egyptian enslavement, and the early development of the new culture God had for Israel, which would eventually become a culture of faithfulness. In the wilderness they no longer had easy access to food. They were hungry and Moses had nothing to offer them.

So Moses prayed to the Lord for a solution. The Lord sent Mana. Whatever Mana was, it was very delicate and bland. But it was editable. They didn't starve. But they grew tired of it. The point of the story is that the Lord's provision kept them from starving. Nonetheless, the people grew tired of it. It wasn't the first time the people had grumbled, and it wouldn't be the last. As the journey in the wilderness continued, the grumbling increased. Honestly, it's understandable. We would have grumbled too. Life in the wilderness was hard.

By the time the story reaches Numbers there was only one obstacle in Israel's way. It wasn't Pharaoh's army or the entrenched Canaanite forces they encountered in the wilderness. It was their own grumbling hearts. As the Israelite spies returned from Canaan with reports of the strength and size of the Canaanite army, they were met with fear and grumbling:

> "Then all the congregation raised a loud cry, and the people wept that night. And all the people of Israel grumbled against Moses and Aaron. The whole congregation said to them, 'Would that we had died in the land of Egypt! Or would that we had died in this wilderness! Why is the Lord bringing us into this land, to fall by the sword? Our wives and our little ones will become a prey. Would it not be better for us to go back to Egypt?' And they said to one another, 'Let us choose a leader and go back to Egypt'" (Num. 14:1–4).

They were ready to go back to Egypt, back to Egyptian slavery, where at least they had been fed regularly.

When we grumble, we declare our distrust in God's sovereign rule over our lives. We grumble because we are not happy with God's provision. Grumbling issues out of a lack of faith and trust in God's leaders and in God Himself. Grumbling is a mark of faithlessness; gratitude is a mark of faithfulness. Christianity is a journey through grumbling to gratitude.

After the miraculous feeding of the five thousand, Jesus again crossed the sea. And when the crowds found Jesus they asked when He had gotten there. He had walked across the sea? But Jesus didn't answer the question. Rather, He said,

> "Truly, truly, I say to you, you are seeking me, not because you saw signs, but because you ate your fill of the loaves" (v. 26).

He accused them of faithlessness. That doesn't seem very pastoral. It's not something that the leader of a social movement would do. Insulting your followers would seem to be contraindicated. Maybe things were different then, but today insulting people won't garner much of a following. Jesus went on:

> "Do not work for the food that perishes, but for the food that endures to eternal life" (v. 27).

Here Jesus seems to promote works-righteousness, suggesting that we have to work for that which provides eternal life. But He was not saying that salvation can be achieved through works, but that salvation or eternal life should be our highest priority in life. It should be highly valued and desired, above all else. Of course, human effort can never produce salvation. Nonetheless, salvation produces the desire to satisfy God, to be what God wants us to be in Christ, and the interest to work toward that. We know this because He also said that the Son of Man will give us salvation. It is a gift, not a reward.

Jesus Christ has come to provide the way of salvation, to provide the way of eternal life. It is a way of life. God Himself will nourish us in this way of life, this way of living. The Lord Himself is the way of life. Jesus said,

> "I am the way, and the truth, and the life" (John 14:6).

He is the food that endures to eternal life. How do we feed on Jesus? How do we find nourishment in Jesus? How can we be nurtured by Jesus?

God gave Mana to the Israelites in the wilderness. They did nothing to deserve it. They did nothing to produce it. It was pure gift. They got up in the morning and there it was, food for their sustenance. Nonetheless, they still had to collect it, distribute it, and actually eat it. The gift was free. Accessing the gift took individual willingness and effort.

Jesus was disappointed in the response of the people. He accused them of following Him for food and miracles. They didn't want Him personally, they only wanted what He would give them. They didn't want a personal relationship with Jesus Christ, they wanted stuff from Him. It's like a wife saying to her husband: *you don't want to spend time with me, you just want sex. You're not concerned about me, you're concerned about yourself, your own satisfaction.* Are we following Jesus in order to make Him happy? Or are we following Jesus because we want Him to make us happy? It doesn't seem like people understood Jesus that day. They responded, *what do you want us to do? What are we supposed to do?*

At this time in history, the Jewish people had been under the guidance of the Pharisees for hundreds of years. And the Pharisees had been actively teaching works-righteousness because that's what they thought Moses had taught them. So it should come as no surprise that they had no idea what Jesus was talking about. They pressed Him,

> "What must we do, to be doing the works of God?" (v. 28).

He was talking about relationship, they were talking about works. They were stuck in a works-righteousness mindset because that's what they had been taught all their lives. They didn't know anything else. And they were happy to do whatever was necessary for them to achieve salvation. *Tell us what to do, Jesus, and we'll do it! We'll do whatever is necessary to receive eternal life!* And they were serious! They were ready to work for a gift that had already been given. They were mistaking a gift with a reward. It's like the wife says, *I love you.* And the husband says, *I'll do whatever it takes to earn your love.* The problem is that the husband hasn't heard or believed what the wife said. She already loves him. So, Jesus tried to accommodate Himself to them.

> "This is the work of God, that you believe in him whom he has sent" (v. 29).

Jesus was saying, *I love you. I'm with you. I am the gift that God has given to you. I don't need you to do anything. Just believe that what I'm saying is true—because it is true.* But this was not what they expected. They had been nursing the expectations of works-righteousness for hundreds of years. It's actually very difficult to change your expectations because expectations issue from your worldview, your mindset, your values and assumptions about life and reality. To change one's expectations requires first changing one's worldview, one's mindset, one's values and assumptions about life and reality.

We're actually talking about repentance, about rethinking everything that we think we know. That's what repentance actually is. Sure, it's a change of direction, but the direction doesn't actually change until the worldview, the mindset, the values and assumptions are reconfigured.

In our story in John 6, the people still didn't get it.

> "So they said to him, 'Then what sign do you do, that we may see and believe you? What work do you perform?'" (v. 30).

They were still looking for miracles. Jesus previously healed the man at the pool of Bethesda, fed the five thousand, and walked on water. But they were still looking for miracles.

> "Our fathers ate the manna in the wilderness; as it is written, 'He gave them bread from heaven to eat'" (v. 34).

They were caught up in an Old Testament mindset. Rather than seeing the Old Testament through Jesus' eyes, Jesus' point of view, they were seeing Jesus through Old Testament eyes, an Old Testament point of view. Jesus then put it as clearly as He could:

> "Truly, truly, I say to you, it was not Moses who gave you the bread from heaven, but my Father gives you the true bread from heaven. For the bread of God is he who comes down from heaven and gives life to the world" (vs. 32-33).

It's not what Moses had given them back then, it was what God was giving them right now. They were stuck in the past. And Jesus was pointing them to the future. They didn't anticipate the idea that they might be wrong. That thought never entered their consideration. *Okay*, they thought. *It was Mana in the old days, so it might be a different kind of bread today. But whatever it is it will be **bread**.* That seemed like the best they could do. They were locked into the idea of some sort of bread. It was bread in the Old Testament so it must be bread in the New Testament. They couldn't get past the idea that the gift must be some kind of miraculous bread. So

"Jesus said to them, 'I am the bread of life; whoever comes to me shall not hunger, and whoever believes in me shall never thirst'" (v. 35).

Jesus said, *If it's bread that you need, then it is bread that I am.*

Say What?

41 So the Jews grumbled about him, because he said, "I am the bread that came down from heaven." 42 They said, "Is not this Jesus, the son of Joseph, whose father and mother we know? How does he now say, 'I have come down from heaven'?" 43 Jesus answered them, "Do not grumble among yourselves. 44 No one can come to me unless the Father who sent me draws him. And I will raise him up on the last day. 45 It is written in the Prophets, 'And they will all be taught by God.' Everyone who has heard and learned from the Father comes to me— 46 not that anyone has seen the Father except he who is from God; he has seen the Father. 47 Truly, truly, I say to you, whoever believes has eternal life. 48 I am the bread of life. 49 Your fathers ate the manna in the wilderness, and they died. 50 This is the bread that comes down from heaven, so that one may eat of it and not die. 51 I am the living bread that came down from heaven. If anyone eats of this bread, he will live forever. And the bread that I will give for the life of the world is my flesh."   —John 6:41-51*

25 Therefore, having put away falsehood, let each one of you speak the truth with his neighbor, for we are members one of another. 26 Be angry and do not sin; do not let the sun go down on your anger, 27 and give no opportunity to the devil. 28 Let the thief no longer steal, but rather let him labor, doing honest work with his own hands, so that he may have something to share with anyone in need. 29 Let no corrupting talk come out of your mouths, but only such as is good for building up, as fits the occasion, that it may give grace to those who hear. 30 And do not grieve the Holy Spirit of God, by whom you were sealed for the day of redemption. 31 Let all bitterness and wrath and anger and clamor and slander be put away from you, along with all malice. 32 Be kind to one another, tenderhearted, forgiving one another, as God in Christ forgave you. 5:1 Therefore be imitators of God, as beloved children. 2 And walk in love, as Christ

loved us and gave himself up for us, a fragrant offering and sacrifice
to God.   —*Ephesians 4:25-5:2*

In the last chapter we saw that God's people are grumblers. They grumbled in the desert against Moses and God because the journey out of Egypt was difficult. And they grumbled against God's provision of mana because they got tired of it. And here in John 6 we find them grumbling against Jesus because He said that He was the bread of God come down from heaven. Jesus was speaking figuratively, symbolically. But they took His words in their literal meaning.

Jesus was not being mystical, people use figurative or symbolic language all the time. But people also speak literally. Ordinarily, we understand when people are doing one or the another. Misunderstanding comes when literal speech is taken figuratively or symbolically, and when figurative or symbolical language is taken literally. In addition, exaggeration is often used to make a point. We sometimes over state something as a way of emphasizing it. For instance, *I'm so hungry I could eat an elephant!* This is an obvious exaggeration.

If we follow the gospel story of John carefully, we can note that John was establishing a pattern of misunderstanding that had been following Jesus. Nicodemus had misunderstood the idea of being born again in Christ:

> "How can a man be born when he is old? Can he enter a second time into his mother's womb and be born?" (John 3:5).

Earlier the people wanted to make Jesus King, by force if necessary. Yet they failed to treat Him as a king in that they continued to fail to understand His words. The words of a king are law, but the words of Jesus were misunderstood and ignored.

Jesus began by clearly revealing our need of the life He provides:

> "I tell you the truth, unless you eat the flesh of the Son of Man and drink his blood, you have no life in you" (v. 53).

He claimed that the life He was talking about is not merely an optional gift that we can ignore. Apart from life in Christ, we are dead.

Apart from Christ, the world will self-destruct. His claims are stark. Was He exaggerating to make a point? Not really, because what seemed to the people to be an exaggeration, was actually true. Our ignorance and neediness is clearly seen when set against the greatness of the truth He spoke:

> "Whoever eats my flesh and drinks my blood has eternal life, and I will raise him up at the last day" (v. 54).

Jesus promised to provide a higher quality of life now, and resurrection in the future. These are big claims, and can appear to be exaggerations if they are misunderstood. Even if people don't believe that Jesus was speaking literal truth, it's okay to understand Him to be exaggerating in order to emphasize the importance of what He was saying.

Seeing Jesus' statement about eating His literal body and blood as an exaggeration is not an error. It's just inadequate. The historic Christian church understood these words literally, which is not wrong. But it is inadequate to the continuing truth of Christ which has been unfolding over time. The point that Jesus was making was that the physical reality of His church is His actual body. Paul said,

> "Now you are the body of Christ and individually members of it" (1 Corinthians 12:27).

When Christ came into the world, He took on a physical body that was "prepared" for Him (Hebrews 10:5; Philippians 2:7). Through His physical body, Jesus demonstrated the love of God as an actual human being, and especially through His sacrificial death on the cross (Romans 5:8). After His bodily ascension, Christ has continued His work in the world through those He has redeemed. His work continues in the world through the actual bodies of those who believe. Thus, Christ's church functions as the actual Body of Christ, which is present in the world through the spiritual reality of His Holy Spirit who manifests in the lives of believers.

It was hard for those who had known Jesus as a boy to see Him as the long-awaited Messiah of Israel.

"Is not this Jesus, the son of Joseph, whose father and mother we know? How does he now say, 'I have come down from heaven'?" (v. 42).

Were Jesus to manifest in our presence today, we would have the same problem. Jesus understood this issue. He understands this problem. So He told them not to grumble about it. Grumbling is an act of unbelief; it's a failure to trust God's provision. Those who grumble will not be included in the kingdom of God—not because God excludes them, but because they don't believe Jesus.

"No one can come to me unless the Father who sent me draws him. And I will raise him up on the last day" (v. 44).

No one is forced into the kingdom of God. To be drawn in, is to be led or persuaded or convinced. Those who are drawn come willingly. God changes hearts and minds. He changes our thinking. He changes our desires to match His desires for us. The Holy Spirit who inhabits us shows us the reality of God and His kingdom. And once we see it as a reality, it becomes something that we genuinely want. Jesus then made the reality clear:

"Truly, truly, I say to you, whoever believes has eternal life" (v. 47).

"Truly, truly" means that what follows is absolutely true and can be trusted. There is no difference between true belief and eternal life. This is an astonishing statement with far reaching implications. It means that eternal life begins with belief. And belief happens when an opinion is accepted as a fact.

An opinion is an appraisal or evaluation of some idea. We hear about or read about the Holy Spirit, and consider the idea. But when we discover that the Holy Spirit inhabits us, when we see that He has been leading us, His reality in our lives becomes factual. Thus, the reality of the Holy Spirit begins as an opinion. And when we see that He (the Holy Spirit) has been directing our own lives, He is confirmed by whole-hearted belief, and He becomes a fact for the believer.

Jesus, then, who had called Himself *bread* to appease those who had doubted Him, doubled down on the idea because He could see that the Holy Spirit was using the idea of bread to link Him with His believers.

> "I am the bread of life. Your fathers ate the manna in the wilderness, and they died. This is the bread that comes down from heaven, so that one may eat of it and not die. I am the living bread that came down from heaven. If anyone eats of this bread, he will live forever. And the bread that I will give for the life of the world is my flesh" (vs. 48–51).

The Medieval Roman Catholic Church used these verses to develop the doctrine of transubstantiation, the belief that the bread and wine of communion are mystically changed into the actual body and blood of Christ. The Catholic Catechism turns itself inside out to provide an explanation of this reality, which ultimately is claimed to simply be a "mystery." To claim that something is a mystery is to say that it is true, but is beyond explanation.

My simple understanding of this "mystery" is that the symbolical reality of the body and blood of Christ in the bread and wine of communion becomes the actual, physical body of Christ through the miracle of digestion. The molecules of bread and wine become united with the actual bodies of believers, who are the actual body of Christ, the church. It may be an oversimplification, but it makes sense to me. The Catholic error is to think that the change happens to the bread and wine, when the change or the miracle actually happens to the people, who become the body of Christ.

The Lectionary then links all of this to Ephesians 4–5.

> "Therefore, having put away falsehood, let each one of you speak the truth with his neighbor, for we are members one of another" (v. 25).

Paul provided instruction on how to live in the Holy Spirit. And the first thing we need to do is to be honest with one another. We are to speak the truth to each other. This means that we are not to participate in lies, deceptions, or falsehoods that are provided and promoted by unbelievers.

For instance, the idea that males can become females or females can become males is simply not true. What is happening is that males are given estrogen, and females are given testosterone, which then causes some minor bodily anomalies. The changes are drug induced and drug dependent. One's sex does not and cannot be changed because sex is chromosomal. It's in every cell of the body, not just a few external parts. Being male or female is a gift of God, and cannot be changed. It's an assignment.

Paul went on:

> "Be angry and do not sin; do not let the sun go down on your anger, and give no opportunity to the devil" (vs. 26-27).

Anger is not a sin, the sin comes in how we handle our anger. The first thing we must do with our anger is acknowledge it. It's real, it happens, we feel it. Our first response to anger is often revenge. But we must learn not to respond with revenge. And we do that by practicing forgiveness. Forgiveness is the antidote to revenge. However, forgiveness alone is often inadequate.

Paul provided an example: Stealing is wrong, but simple forgiveness is not the complete response to the thief. The thief needs forgiveness, but he also needs to change his behavior. Repentance for the thief is doing honest work. But honest work is not enough either. The thief must also save his own money so that he can provide for others who might be tempted to steal. Thus, the thief becomes a Christian mentor, an example to those who are tempted to steal.

Paul then warned about "corrupting talk." We could also translate this as *grumbling*. Grumbling is corrosive. How so? It's worthless, selfish, cancerous, and destructive. So, when we talk with others our words should not be worthless, selfish, cancerous, or destructive.

Nor are we to grieve the Holy Spirit. The best way to understand this is that we are to please the Holy Spirit. We are to do what the Holy Spirit wants us to do. We are not to make ourselves happy; we are to make the Holy Spirit happy with us. How do we do that?

> "Be kind to one another, tenderhearted, forgiving one another, as God in Christ forgave you" (v. 32).

This is not difficult to understand or to do. We are to simply be the people that God created us to be, to be content with what God has given us, to live our lives as if we are already God's children who live in God's kingdom. "Therefore," said Paul,

> "be imitators of God, as beloved children. And walk in love, as Christ loved us and gave himself up for us, a fragrant offering and sacrifice to God" (v. 5:1).

We are to be like Paul and the Apostles.

What is a Person?

"51 I am the living bread that came down from heaven. If anyone eats of this bread, he will live forever. And the bread that I will give for the life of the world is my flesh." 52 The Jews then disputed among themselves, saying, "How can this man give us his flesh to eat?" 53 So Jesus said to them, "Truly, truly, I say to you, unless you eat the flesh of the Son of Man and drink his blood, you have no life in you. 54 Whoever feeds on my flesh and drinks my blood has eternal life, and I will raise him up on the last day. 55 For my flesh is true food, and my blood is true drink. 56 Whoever feeds on my flesh and drinks my blood abides in me, and I in him. 57 As the living Father sent me, and I live because of the Father, so whoever feeds on me, he also will live because of me. 58 This is the bread that came down from heaven, not like the bread the fathers ate, and died. Whoever feeds on this bread will live forever." —John 6:51-58

15 Look carefully then how you walk, not as unwise but as wise, 16 making the best use of the time, because the days are evil. 17 Therefore do not be foolish, but understand what the will of the Lord is. 18 And do not get drunk with wine, for that is debauchery, but be filled with the Spirit, 19 addressing one another in psalms and hymns and spiritual songs, singing and making melody to the Lord with your heart, 20 giving thanks always and for everything to God the Father in the name of our Lord Jesus Christ. —Ephesians 5:15-20

Jesus continues His conversation about being bread. When He first introduced the idea, He was trying to correct a misunderstanding that people had about God's provision of mana in the desert. The error that people were making was to focus on the gift rather than on the gift Giver, who provides for His people. Focusing on the gift keeps the focus on the problem. The gift is the solution to the problem. So when another problem comes, people focus on another solution to that problem. It keeps us focused on the problem. Whereas if people will focus on the gift Giver, we can trust that He will solve the problem. The one way keeps us focused on the specific solutions to the specific problems, the other way allows us to trust that the Giver will provide what is needed.

Most of the time we don't know how to solve our problems, which makes us worry about them. But if we can simply trust that God will provide what we need, even when we don't know what we need, we can bypass the worry.

Jesus was telling people to feed on Him. But what does it mean, to feed on Jesus?

"the bread that I will give for the life of the world is my flesh" (v. 51).

It is nonsense to think that Jesus was speaking literally here. There are three terms in this sentence that need to be correctly understood: 1) bread, 2) life of the world, and 3) flesh. Jesus was talking about bread in response to His previous discussion of God's provision of mana. In the desert God provided mana. But the people Jesus was talking to were not in the desert anymore. Mana was God's provision in the desert. Bread was God's provision for the five thousand. So when Jesus said "bread" He meant "God's provision." He was talking about God's provision for the life of the world.

For the what? For the "life of the world." By "life of the world" He meant life in this world. He was talking about sustaining a healthy human culture in the world. He was not talking about cannibalism. And yet,

"The Jews then disputed among themselves, saying, 'How can this man give us his flesh to eat?'" (v. 52).

The Jews misunderstood Him, and it seems like they misunderstood Him on purpose. Like they were trying to twist His words into the worst possible construction. Do people do that? *Yes, they do.* We see that in our politics today. Each side tries very hard to misconstrue the words and ideas of the other side, to make opposition to their side seem like nonsense. No one wants to have an intelligent conversation about the real issues, we just want our side to defeat the other side. And people will go to any lengths to do that!

The third term in the sentence under consideration today is *flesh*.

"And the bread that I will give for the life of the world is my flesh" (v. 51).

When Jesus said that would give His flesh, what did He mean? He meant that He would sacrifice His body on the cross for the salvation of the world. He was not talking about what we call a communion service. Rather, He was talking about His service for the communion of the world, His death on the cross. His sacrifice on the cross would produce a sustainable human community. Paul didn't know how that would happen; he just trusted that God would make it happen. God was providing the life of His Son, His body and His blood, as a sacrifice that would establish a new kind of human community.

And at the center of this new way of being human would be a sacrament of bread and wine. Christians understand the sacraments to be visible symbols of the reality of God, as well as channels for God's grace. So, Jesus was referring to what we call a communion service, but the people He was talking to didn't and couldn't know that. All of that was in the future to them, but not to us.

A sacrament is like a rite. A rite is a ceremony or event that leads to a new phase of life, like high school graduation or a bar mitzvah. Rites are rituals. Rituals are prescribed ways of doing things. Rituals are social habits, common ways of community recognition. Marriage is a rite, a ritual, in that there is a common or established way of doing it. Ceremonies, rites, and rituals are ways of creating and maintaining continuity in a community, a culture. Ceremonies feed social norms.

The bottom line is that God wants a personal relationship with His people. He wants that personal relationship to be normal, ordinary, common. Everything we need as human beings will come out of that personal relationship with Jesus Christ. But if we focus on miracles and cures and gifts, we don't get the personal relationship.

So what is a personal relationship? To understand this we need to understand what a person is. And in one sense it sounds like a silly question to ask, because everyone—all persons—should already know. But it's not. In fact, the definition of person may be the most serious issue we currently face. How so? The misunderstanding of "person" is causing two serious social problems right now. The misunderstanding of "person" is at the heart of the abortion issue. And the misunderstanding of "person" is also at the heart of our economic disparity, the lopsidedness of the current economic system.

Let's start with abortion. But the truth is that we can't start with abortion because abortion is not the real problem. Abortion is the result of the problem. Why do women get abortions? Because they have an unwanted pregnancy. An unwanted pregnancy is, for the most part, the result of irresponsible sex. Before I cause undue guilt on the part of women, let me say that I think that irresponsible sex is mostly the fault of men. Not entirely, of course. My mom used to say that it takes two to tango.

There are, however, two other major contributing factors to this problem: the birth control pill, and the idea that sex outside of marriage is okay. We could spend a lot of time analyzing this, but I'm pretty sure that most of us here understand what I'm saying. The pill launched an era of sexual freedom that is still very much a part of the era in which we currently live. The reality of the pill resulted in the separation of sex and marriage, or sex and pregnancy. Without the fear of pregnancy, people were free to experiment with sex outside of marriage. More so than in previous generations. Of course, there have always been birth control measures and methods, but before the pill they weren't reliable and readily available.

No fault divorce also contributed to this problem, and has a long history. In 1757 Frederick the Great in Prussia issued an edict allowing marriages to be dissolved on the ground of serious and continuous hostility between spouses, without pointing to any one guilty party. In 1917 following the October Revolution in Russia the first modern national no-fault divorce law was enacted. Marriage was regarded as a bourgeois institution, and the new government transferred divorce jurisdiction from the Russian Orthodox Church to the state courts, which could grant it on application of either spouse. In

1969 California became the first U.S. state to permit no-fault divorce, and now it is everywhere.

The biblical point to be made is that all sexual activity should happen only within the marriage bond. In today's world of movies, TV, and books sexual activity is never portrayed between husbands and wives, unless it is the cause of problems. When was the last time you saw a movie, or a TV program, or read a book about a married couple who had a healthy marriage and lived happily ever after? It makes for a lousy story, but a great life.

The point is that abortion is not the problem. It's the result of the problem. Our society needs to have a serious conversation about irresponsible sex. But no one wants to hear it! Those who think that abortion is okay don't think that the fetus is a person. They generally think that life begins with the first breath of the child, which is an old Jewish and biblical definition of life. However, current science shows that human life begins at conception. If the fetus is not a person, abortion is okay. If the fetus is a person, it is not.

The second misunderstanding of "person" pertains to corporate personhood, which is legally defined as a juridical person such as a corporation, considered separately from its associated human beings (like owners, managers, or employees). The corporate person has various legal rights and responsibilities enjoyed by natural born persons. In most countries, a corporation has the same rights as a natural person: to hold property, enter into contracts, and to sue or be sued. Why is this a problem? Because corporations are able to amass money and resources that are far greater than any natural born person, who does not incorporate business interests. Why? Because corporations are multi-generational. Corporations don't naturally die.

The current economic disparity in the world is the direct result of the idea that corporations are persons. Corporate persons are abstract ideas, what the Bible calls

"principalities, powers, (and) the rulers of the darkness of this world, against spiritual wickedness in high places" (Ephesians 6;12, KJV).

Corporations have policies, procedures and the power to enforce them. We could call corporations fake persons because they have no real life. The actual personhood of corporations can and should actually belong to only one Person: Jesus Christ.

Because corporate persons have a different status, a different kind of reality, they should be treated differently than ordinary flesh and blood persons, but they are not. The only legitimate corporate person in the world is or should be Jesus Christ, who is Father, Son, and Holy Spirit. And who is being manifested in His church. This is a big idea, and it's not my idea. It's Jesus' idea. How so?

When Jesus was talking about being "bread that came down from heaven" (v. 51), and about feeding on His flesh and drinking His blood, He was talking about His corporate personhood. Feeding on Jesus, eating His flesh and drinking His blood is about digesting Him, His Story, His corporate Story, which is the Bible. When we understand the Story of Jesus in the Bible we assimilate Him. We make His Story part of our story, or we make our story part of His story. We receive His Person into our person. His Story continues in our story. To assimilate means to consume and incorporate nutrients (healthy ideas) into the body. The church is the body of Christ in the world. "Therefore," said Paul,

> "do not be foolish, but understand what the will of the Lord is. And do not get drunk with wine, for that is debauchery, but be filled with the Spirit, addressing one another in psalms and hymns and spiritual songs, singing and making melody to the Lord with your heart, giving thanks always and for everything to God the Father in the name of our Lord Jesus Christ" (vs. 17-20).

Christ is actually present in the life of His church, not just in the communion service, but in everything Christians do in church and out. If you are a Christian, Christ is actually and legally (according to God's law) present in the world through your body.

EMPTY ARMOR

56 "Whoever feeds on my flesh and drinks my blood abides in me, and I in him. 57 As the living Father sent me, and I live because of the Father, so whoever feeds on me, he also will live because of me. 58 This is the bread that came down from heaven, not like the bread the fathers ate, and died. Whoever feeds on this bread will live forever." 59 Jesus said these things in the synagogue, as he taught at Capernaum. 60 When many of his disciples heard it, they said, "This is a hard saying; who can listen to it?" 61 But Jesus, knowing in himself that his disciples were grumbling about this, said to them, "Do you take offense at this? 62 Then what if you were to see the Son of Man ascending to where he was before? 63 It is the Spirit who gives life; the flesh is no help at all. The words that I have spoken to you are spirit and life. 64 But there are some of you who do not believe." (For Jesus knew from the beginning who those were who did not believe, and who it was who would betray him.) 65 And he said, "This is why I told you that no one can come to me unless it is granted him by the Father." 66 After this many of his disciples turned back and no longer walked with him. 67 So Jesus said to the twelve, "Do you want to go away as well?" 68 Simon Peter answered him, "Lord, to whom shall we go? You have the words of eternal life, 69 and we have believed, and have come to know, that you are the Holy One of God."   —John 6:56-69

10 Finally, be strong in the Lord and in the strength of his might. 11 Put on the whole armor of God, that you may be able to stand against the schemes of the devil. 12 For we do not wrestle against flesh and blood, but against the rulers, against the authorities, against the cosmic powers over this present darkness, against the spiritual forces of evil in the heavenly places. 13 Therefore take up the whole armor of God, that you may be able to withstand in the evil day, and having done all, to stand firm. 14 Stand therefore, having fastened on

*the belt of truth, and having put on the breastplate of righteousness,
15 and, as shoes for your feet, having put on the readiness given by
the gospel of peace. 16 In all circumstances take up the shield of faith,
with which you can extinguish all the flaming darts of the evil one;
17 and take the helmet of salvation, and the sword of the Spirit,
which is the word of God, 18 praying at all times in the Spirit, with
all prayer and supplication. To that end, keep alert with all persever-
ance, making supplication for all the saints, 19 and also for me, that
words may be given to me in opening my mouth boldly to proclaim
the mystery of the gospel, 20 for which I am an ambassador in
chains, that I may declare it boldly, as I ought to speak.*
                                            —*Ephesians 6:10-20*

We continue with Jesus' teaching about Him being the bread of heaven. Clearly, this is an important idea because John has spent a lot of time on it. Jesus continued to speak about eating His body and drinking His blood in a physical manner. There can be no doubt that this is what He said, but what does He mean? He was not talking about cannibalism, so we can't take the words literally. Therefore, He was forcing people into a non-literal understanding, forcing people to understand Him in some other way.

Historically, there are four ways to understand Bible stories. The four ways are literal, allegorical, tropological and anagogical. What do these mean? Literal language uses words exactly, according to their direct, straightforward, or conventionally accepted meanings. An allegory is a narrative or story in which a character, place, or event can be interpreted to represent a meaning with moral or politi-cal significance, like fairy tales. Here the point of the story is not in the words or events, but in the lesson to be learned from the story. Tropological understanding refers to cliches or figures of speech, where words carry a meaning other than what they literally signify. An example is: *I have butterflies in my stomach.* We all know what that means, and it has nothing to do with literal butterflies in a literal stomach.

An anagogical interpretation is a mystical understanding of an idea that alludes to a hidden meaning that implies heaven or the afterlife. This involves "reading between the lines" to see various implications or indirect suggestions. For example, take the story of the Prodigal Son. On a literal level, the story is about a young man who squanders his inheritance and returns home to his father. But on an anagogical level, it is a powerful allegory about the grace and forgiveness of God.

The point of all of this is that understanding language and communication is complex. People often speak using unspoken assumptions or implications, and sometimes the words used mean the opposite of their literal definitions. Jesus said that He is the "bread that came down from heaven." But He is "not like the bread the fathers ate, and died" (v. 58). Jesus said these things in the synagogue, where He was teaching, which means that there is a lesson or moral to be gleaned from His words. And those who heard Him said that it was a "hard saying." They were having trouble understanding what He meant.

So, did Jesus then clarify what He meant? *He did not!* He doubled down on His message using the same words. He increased the importance of the correct understanding of His words, but did so without direct explanation of His meaning. It is similar to His parables. As we have seen over the past few weeks, He simply repeated Himself.

But also remember that the Jews seemed to be intent on construing His words in the worst possible manner. He likely knew that no matter how He said it, they would not understand Him because their minds were already made up about who He was. For those who want to understand Him correctly, the message is there. But for those who don't want to understand Him, the message is unavailable. It's not that He is hiding it, but that they didn't want to understand Him. They didn't believe in eternal life. They didn't believe in regeneration. They didn't believe that He was the Messiah, or that He could save them. So they imposed their prior beliefs on His words.

Jesus then asked,

"Then what if you were to see the Son of Man ascending to where he was before?" (v. 62).

He had previously claimed that He had come down from heaven, and here He asked about His going back into heaven. He didn't expect an answer. It was a rhetorical question. He was helping us see that they had no interest in Him, no interest in heaven or salvation. He knew that some of them didn't believe, and wouldn't believe because they didn't want to. The point that He was making was that

"no one can come to me (come to Jesus) unless it is granted him by the Father" (v. 63).

This is a critical point! It means that people don't come to Jesus because they have made a decision to do so. People can only come because God grants them access, because God draws them, because God made the decision for them, because God changed them. So when people "make a decision" to follow Jesus, it's not really a decision. They are just saying "yes" to God's prior decision to bring them in. People have to be willing to come to Jesus. All who come, come willingly. But its more like being drafted than volunteering. And, of course, some draftees are very excited about it, and some are hesitant. But all come willingly. Draft dodgers are in a different category.

Verse 66 is one of the most important verses in the Bible:

"After this many of his disciples turned back and no longer walked with him."

This is a watershed moment in the story of Jesus. The story in John 6 began with five thousand people following Jesus into the wilderness. He fed them loaves and fish, walked on water, told them that He is the "bread of life," and explained the meaning of eternal life.

"After this many of his disciples turned back and no longer walked with him" (v. 66).

Most people walked away when they heard the unvarnished truth. The truth cuts through the lies and falsehoods. The truth has a point. It pricks, and cuts. The truth is like a surgeon's blade that cuts out the cancer to save the patient's life. It's painful and messy, like repentance. Truth is not as sexy as myth. Truth is not fantastic. What is fantastic exists only in fantasy; it is not real. Most people prefer fantasy to reality, and Hollywood provides the proof.

"So Jesus said to the twelve, 'Do you want to go away as well?'" (v. 67).

It almost seems like everyone left except the disciples, but we don't know that for sure. All who remained were disciples, and there were probably more than twelve because all believers are disciples. All believers must become disciples. Believers must take up the disciplines of faithfulness because that's what it means to be a disciple. Peter summed up the response of the disciples:

"Lord, to whom shall we go? You have the words of eternal life" (v. 68)

Jesus is the only option for disciples.

Disciples put away the myths and the fantasies and give themselves to the Truth, to Jesus because He is the Truth. Disciples confess

"we have believed, and have come to know, that you are the Holy One of God" (v. 69).

What exactly is a disciple to do? The Lectionary sends us to Ephesians 6 where Paul talks about the whole armor of God. And the first thing to notice is that it is armor. Armor is a defensive covering that protects the body from the weapons of an enemy. The idea of armor suggests war. To be a disciple is to be involved in a war, a struggle, a conflict between organized groups. The word *war* historically means "to confuse, to perplex, to bring into confusion." The old adage is that truth is the first victim of war. George Washington said,

"To be prepared for war is one of the most effective means of preserving peace."

Newt Gingrich said,

"Politics and war are remarkably similar situations."

Mao Zedong said,

> "Politics is war without bloodshed while war is politics with bloodshed."

Sun Tzu said,

> "The supreme art of war is to subdue the enemy without fighting."

We are American so we'll go with George Washington:

> "To be prepared for war is one of the most effective means of preserving peace."

And how do Christians do that?

> "Finally, be strong in the Lord and in the strength of his might. Put on the whole armor of God, that you may be able to stand against the schemes of the devil" (vs. 10-11).

To win a war it's essential to know who the enemy is. So, Paul identified the enemy for Christians:

> "For we do not wrestle against flesh and blood, but against the rulers, against the authorities, against the cosmic powers over this present darkness, against the spiritual forces of evil in the heavenly places" (v. 12).

God's enemies are not people. God's enemies are all of the things that stand against Truth, against Jesus Christ. Rulers and authorities —ideas—that oppose Truth are enemies of God. But it's not the individuals who hold the offices of rulers and authority, rather it is the policies that oppose God that are the problem. The people can be changed, but the ideas are eternal.

The "cosmic powers over this present darkness" is the history of the world that stands against God. That would be false stories, false ideas, and false Gods that animate the "present darkness." The present darkness suggests worldly ideas that are not exposed to the light of Christ. The gospel of Jesus Christ brings light to the world, and what opposes the light of Christ opposes Truth.

The "spiritual forces of evil" suggest that Satan is real, that there are demonic forces active in the world today—policies, ideas, myths, and what we might call historical momentum. You've heard that ideas have consequences. That's what I mean by historical momentum. Ideas bring policies to life, and policies direct human action. Paul then tells us that the theater of this warfare is "heavenly places," which can also be translated as "high places," places of power and authority.

So what are disciples to do about all of this? We are to put on the whole armor of God. All of it, not some of it, so that we can

"stand firm against evil, against falsehood, lies, and deceit" (v. 13).

There are several pieces of armor to wear: the Belt of Truth, the Breastplate of Righteousness, the Shoes of the Gospel of Peace, Shield of Faith, Helmet of Salvation, and Sword of the Spirit (which is the Word of God). Truth, righteousness, peace, faith, salvation, and God's Word. The first job of a disciple of Christ is to put on the whole armor of God, to practice these things.

I believe that the primary job of disciples is to put on this armor, all of it, and to wear it all of the time, twenty-four-seven. Our job is not to fight, but to wear the whole armor of God. Sun Tzu had it right:

"The supreme art of war is to subdue the enemy without fighting."

Of course Sun Tzu had no idea of what he was talking about, but truth is truth. The biblical war plan is to wear the whole armor of God, period. Because disciples can defeat the enemy by simply wearing the whole armor of God.

All of this armor is defensive except the sword, God's Word. But we don't need to use the sword to kill the enemy. We just need to brandish the sword. To brandish means to wave something around in a defiant, excited way. A synonym is flourish. Wearing the whole armor of God will cause God's people to flourish, to grow, to thrive, to do well and to prosper. And we are to flaunt God's Word because prosperity is attractive.

Christians are not called to fight God's enemies. Christians are called to gird their loins with the whole armor of God and to brandish God's Word. God will do the fighting. Christ's disciples will do the wearing and brandishing. All we have to do is wear the whole armor of God. The armor is no good unless people wear it. We have the tools, but if we don't use them, they are useless.

Church Attendance

And now, O Israel, listen to the statutes and the rules that I am teaching you, and do them, that you may live, and go in and take possession of the land that the Lord, the God of your fathers, is giving you. 2 You shall not add to the word that I command you, nor take from it, that you may keep the commandments of the Lord your God that I command you. —Deuteronomy 4:1-2

22 But be doers of the word, and not hearers only, deceiving yourselves. 23 For if anyone is a hearer of the word and not a doer, he is like a man who looks intently at his natural face in a mirror. 24 For he looks at himself and goes away and at once forgets what he was like. 25 But the one who looks into the perfect law, the law of liberty, and perseveres, being no hearer who forgets but a doer who acts, he will be blessed in his doing. 26 If anyone thinks he is religious and does not bridle his tongue but deceives his heart, this person's religion is worthless. 27 Religion that is pure and undefiled before God the Father is this: to visit orphans and widows in their affliction, and to keep oneself unstained from the world. —James 1:22-27

Where are we in God's story when Moses told Israel to be obedient? Israel has escaped from Egypt, God gave them the Ten Commandments in Exodus 20, and will repeat them in Deuteronomy 5. Moses then instructed the people to do two things: to listen to God's statutes and rules, and to do them. It begins with listening. It sounds pretty simple, but if you have had children you know that teaching people to listen is not as easy as it sounds.

The Ten Commandments begins with what Israel calls the Shema:

"Hear, O Israel: The Lord our God, the Lord is one" (Deuteronomy 6:4).

The very first thing that Israel was commanded to do was to hear, to perceive, to become aware of a God's Word. God speaks, and the only way to know what God speaks is to listen, to hear Him. We can close our eyes and refuse to see something, but we cannot close our ears. Or can we?

In order to listen to someone we must give them our attention. We must attend to them, to pay attention to them. To be faithful, we must pay attention to God. It requires what the psychologists call active listening. In any relationship, attention is essential. It's the glue that keeps two people together and helps them grow closer. Giving someone your undivided attention, especially through one-on-one interactions, requires more than just being physically present. It involves understanding, and truly being present in the moment. When we truly listen to someone we show them that we care about what they have to say, that their thoughts and feelings matter to us.

To accomplish this, it is important to refrain from interrupting or focusing on our own thoughts and ideas about what the other person is saying. There will be a time for interaction, but before we respond to someone we need to be sure that we have accurately heard what they are saying. This is doubly true with God because it is very easy and very common for people hear what they want to hear, rather than to hear what is actually being said.

Listening is an act of reception. We must receive and perceive the message accurately. We do this in our ordinary human relationships by asking questions to make sure that we correctly understand what we are hearing. The same thing goes for God. We need to ask questions. Asking God questions about His message and intent is called prayer. In prayer we enter into a dialog with God. And how do we hear what He has to say? First, we read His Word. We read the Bible because that is the record of His message, His story. We read, and then we think and pray about what we have read. Giving our undivided attention to someone, giving them quality time is one of the most effective ways to make them feel heard and valued.

Quality time is not quantity time, though quality and quantity are related. When you give someone quality time it means that you spend a lot of time with them. But just spending a lot of time with someone does not amount to quality time. Quality time is a function of being genuinely interested in someone. Quality time means being physically present. Sure, we can have a relationship with someone over the phone, or by email, or on social media. But nothing says genuine friendship like physical presence. But how can we be physically present with God? By being physically present with His people. Quality time also means having an emotional connection. An emotional connection means caring about the needs and desires of another.

While God doesn't need anything from us, He desires our faithfulness because our faithfulness means that we value His thoughts. It means that we genuinely want to spend time with Him, with His Word and with His people. Quality time also means good communication. God wants to commune with us, and He wants us to commune with Him.

The word *commune* is both a noun and a verb. The noun puts the accent on the first syllable: *com*mune. Think of a small group of people who live together, like a tribe. The verb puts the accent on the second syllable: com*mune*. To commune with someone is to communicate intimately with them. It's genuine communication. To genuinely commune with someone is to grok them. *Grok* is a verb, to understand profoundly and intuitively. *Grok* was introduced in Robert A. Heinlein's 1961 science fiction novel *Stranger in a Strange Land*. The main character is a Martian-raised human who comes to Earth as an adult, bringing with him words from his native tongue and a unique perspective on the strange ways of earthlings. Grok was adopted by the youth culture of the sixties and has a special meaning for those who grok it. Spending quality time with God allows us to grok God.

The first thing that we are called to do is to listen to God to listen to the statutes and the rules that He is teaching us. The second thing is to do what He says, to be obedient. We can't do what He says without first hearing what He says. But if we truly listen, if we spend quality time with God, we will want to do what He says. Our sinful tendency is to reverse the order of these things: to try to do what God says before we have adequately heard what He says. And we do that by doing what *we* think He said, by doing what *we* think He *ought* to have said, by hearing what *we* want Him to say, and then doing that. It's very easy and very common for people to impose their own understanding on God's Word, to see in God's Word what we want to see, rather than what God wants to show us.

This is often done through a process called equivocation. Equivocation is using a word that has different definitions that are technically equal in order to mask what you really mean. It's a great way to not-quite lie, but still avoid taking the blame for something you did. You may recognize this kind of speech by listening to politicians. I don't mean to pick on politicians and political pontificators, but they do it all the time—all of them. Examples of equivocation include:

- intentional vagueness or ambiguity, also called evasiveness, prevarication;
- falsification by means of vague or ambiguous language;
- making a statement that is not literally false, but that cleverly avoids an unpleasant truth.

I don't mean to pick on politics, but we are inundated with it! We are drowning in equivocation! I bring it up because it is a religious issue, a spiritual concern, and a biblical heresy. James tells us to

"be doers of the word, and not hearers only, deceiving yourselves" (v. 22).

Deceiving yourselves! Self-delusion is real.

The Cleveland Clinic defines "delusional disorder" as a type of mental health condition in which a person can't tell what's real from what's imagined. A delusion is an unshakable belief in something that's not true.

"People with delusional disorder often continue to socialize and function well, apart from the subject of their delusion. Generally, they don't behave in an odd or unusual manner. This is unlike people with other psychotic disorders, who might also have delusions as a symptom. In some cases, however, people with delusional disorder might become so preoccupied with their delusions that their lives are disrupted."

I'm not a doctor or a psychologist or a psychiatrist, I'm just sayin'…. If it looks like a duck and walks like a duck, there's a good chance that it's a duck. The issue here is Truth, knowing the Truth, knowing what is true, what is real, and what is not. For Christians there is nothing more real than God. For unbelievers there is nothing less real than God. For Christians perception is often wrong. For unbelievers perception is reality. For Christians reality is what God says it is. For unbelievers reality is whatever they think it is, whatever they want it to be.

Houston, we have a problem! Apollo 13 had to reconfigure itself in order to make it back to earth. You know the story, if not, see the movie. America has a problem today, and I'm saying that the problem is equivocation. Constant exposure to equivocation produces self-delusion, which produces delusional disorder among the population.

There is a pastoral cure for this problem: church attendance. But I don't simply mean going to some local church every week. Sure, that's part of the cure, but it is not sufficient to cure the spiritual disease. There's more! We must *attend to* God's church. We must give God our attention, pay attention to God, give God's church, God's people quality time. Do we give God the best part of our day? The best part of our lives? Or do we give God leftovers? Squeeze Him in if we have time? Jesus said,

"I am the way, and the truth, and the life. No one comes to the Father except through me" (John 14:6).

To say that Jesus is the only way is a big claim. It is true? Jesus is the Truth, so if we want to know the Truth we need to know Jesus. And if we don't know Jesus, we can't know the Truth. Knowing the difference between what is real and what what is imaginary requires knowing Jesus Christ, and knowing Him intimately. The only way through this muddle that we are in is to know what is true and what is not! The only way is to know Jesus Christ personally!

Bias

2 My brothers, show no partiality as you hold the faith in our Lord Jesus Christ, the Lord of glory. 2 For if a man wearing a gold ring and fine clothing comes into your assembly, and a poor man in shabby clothing also comes in, 3 and if you pay attention to the one who wears the fine clothing and say, "You sit here in a good place," while you say to the poor man, "You stand over there," or, "Sit down at my feet," 4 have you not then made distinctions among yourselves and become judges with evil thoughts? 5 Listen, my beloved brothers, has not God chosen those who are poor in the world to be rich in faith and heirs of the kingdom, which he has promised to those who love him? 6 But you have dishonored the poor man. Are not the rich the ones who oppress you, and the ones who drag you into court? 7 Are they not the ones who blaspheme the honorable name by which you were called? 8 If you really fulfill the royal law according to the Scripture, "You shall love your neighbor as yourself," you are doing well. 9 But if you show partiality, you are committing sin and are convicted by the law as transgressors. 10 For whoever keeps the whole law but fails in one point has become guilty of all of it. 11 For he who said, "Do not commit adultery," also said, "Do not murder." If you do not commit adultery but do murder, you have become a transgressor of the law. 12 So speak and so act as those who are to be judged under the law of liberty. 13 For judgment is without mercy to one who has shown no mercy. Mercy triumphs over judgment.
—James 2:1-10

31 Then he returned from the region of Tyre and went through Sidon to the Sea of Galilee, in the region of the Decapolis. 32 And they brought to him a man who was deaf and had a speech impediment, and they begged him to lay his hand on him. 33 And taking him aside from the crowd privately, he put his fingers into his ears, and after spitting touched his tongue. 34 And looking up to heaven,

he sighed and said to him, "Ephphatha," that is, "Be opened." 35
And his ears were opened, his tongue was released, and he spoke
plainly. 36 And Jesus charged them to tell no one. But the more he
charged them, the more zealously they proclaimed it. 37 And they
were astonished beyond measure, saying, "He has done all things
well. He even makes the deaf hear and the mute speak."
                                                    —*Mark 7:31-37*

James said, "show no partiality (v. 2). But what does that mean? *Partiality* is one of those Bible words that no one uses apart from reading it in the Bible. We are flummoxed to construct a sentence with the world partiality. So we need a word we understand. Partiality is favoritism or bias. Whenever we have a favorite or a bias for or against someone, we are guilty of this sin.

So, why is favoritism a problem, a sin? How does it affect people? A preferred student or child typically receives more presents, clothing, praise, and attention than the others. Being favored shapes lives and legacies. Children who are favored tend to believe in themselves more, and consequently, and they tend to become more successful, probably because they have a positive self-image.

Conversely, unfavored children, those for which we have a negative bias, are inundated with low self-esteem. Feelings of sadness, anger, or depression result as they struggle to cope with unequal treatment. They can begin acting out in rebellion, or engaging in risky behaviors to gain attention. Being unfavored festers an undercurrent of bitterness that's hard to overcome.

Favoritism always has two sides. It always results in winners and losers, the favored and the not-favored. To chose one person or group is not to chose another. This can scar individuals and damage teacher-child, employer-employee, parent-child, and sibling relationships. A sense of ingrained injustice and resentment can persist long into adulthood, affecting how individuals relate to each other and straining one's social relationships for years. Sometimes for a lifetime.

It's easy for me to stand up here and tell you not to play favorites, that we should not be biased. But it's not that simple. So let's look more closely at this issue. James was not talking in general terms, but was talking about how we treat people in church. His instruction and example are simple. We should treat all Christians the same, by which he means that we should not be especially accommodating to the wealthy, nor should we discriminate against the poor. These are the examples James provides. He was responding to a particular problem in the church. The instruction is simple enough, but do we do it? Do Christians and their churches cater to certain kinds of people and tend to ignore other kinds of people? That's the issue.

Of course we do! Every church is guilty of bias because every individual is guilty of bias. We all have our favorites. We are all biased in one way or another. We all like or prefer certain things and dislike or disdain other things. And by "things" I mean certain habits, places, people, styles. We are all full of likes and dislikes, and those likes and dislikes set up particular preferences and biases. It's simply the human condition. And God calls it *sin*.

Our bias, our preferences are determined by our own judgment. We decide what we like, and we decide what we don't like. And we tend to think of ourselves as good and right in our thinking. Everyone does! It's unavoidable. People are naturally attracted to people who are like themselves. We tend to trust people like ourselves because we believe ourselves to be trustworthy.

James was doing two things here: he was dealing with a problem in the church, and he was pointing out the problem of original sin. Original sin is our bias toward sin. What God calls sin seems natural to us. James' conclusion comes in verse 10:

> "For whoever keeps the whole law but fails in one point has become guilty of all of it."

We are called to be sinless, to obey the whole law. And his point is that no one is sinless. We are all guilty of some infraction of God's law. God demands that we all be sinless, but we cannot make that demand of one another. We are not to usurp God's prerogative.

God can make that demand because God provides the solution: Jesus Christ. And Christ's solution comes in the form of mercy and forgiveness. So, in the church—and this is an important condition, in the church we are to be forgiving and merciful. The guilt of having broken God's law falls on those outside of the church. And it is appropriate to present the law to them, to convince them that God's law is good and true, and that they have violated it, and are under God's judgment.

Human sin is the context of the good news of the gospel of Jesus Christ. And apart from that context the gospel is meaningless and toothless. People ignore it because they think that it doesn't apply to them. So the first job of evangelism is to convince people that they are guilty, and stand condemned by God. They are worthy of God's wrath. However, God is not bad or evil because He condemns evil. The fact that God condemns evil proves that God is good. What is evil deserves God's wrath.

Only after agreeing that God is good, that God's law is good, and that "I" have violated God's law and stand condemned by the wrath of God, can the good news of the gospel take affect in my life. Until "I" reach that point of understanding, and acknowledge my own guilt, I don't have any felt need for God's forgiveness. At that point, then, the love and forgiveness of God becomes the most important thing in the world to "me" because it lifts the burden of guilt by giving me a new beginning, a new opportunity to live life in the love and forgiveness of God, among God's people.

So, said James, speaking to the church:

> "speak and so act as those who are to be judged under the law of liberty. For judgment is without mercy to one who has shown no mercy. Mercy triumphs over judgment" (vs. 12-13).

Again, the context is important. There are two pieces of the good news: sin and salvation, wrath and mercy. The order is important because mercy without guilt is meaningless, and guilt without mercy is cruel and hopeless. So mercy triumphs over judgment in the church, for those in the church. And it does so for all who are in the church, regardless of their wealth or status. That is James' point.

This gospel truth is both difficult to rightly hear and difficult to rightly explain because of our sinful bias. It only makes sense to those who have experienced it, those who have acknowledged their own guilt and actually received the forgiveness and mercy of Jesus Christ. Without personal knowledge of these things, they don't make sense.

We see this in the story of the healing of the deaf mute. This story takes place in the region of Tyre, in modern Lebanon. Tyre was a major Phoenician seaport. Jesus mentioned Tyre as an example of an unrepentant city (Matthew 11:21–22; Luke 10:13). So in our scheme of things discussed today, Tyre represents unbelievers, people who have no knowledge or experience of the gospel.

This man had not come to Jesus of his own accord. Rather, the disciples brought him to Jesus, or perhaps other unconverted people brought him. They begged Jesus to lay His hand upon the man, hoping him to be healed. They did it for him because the man couldn't hear and couldn't speak. Or perhaps he couldn't hear or speak very well. And he certainly couldn't hear or speak the gospel.

They expected a miracle, and that's interesting. These unbelievers in Tyre believed that Jesus could perform a miracle, and they begged Jesus to do so. Jesus often used miracles to get people's attention. So Jesus did some miracle stuff: He put His finger in his ear, spit, and touched his tongue.

I hope that you don't expect me to explain any of this. It's in the Book, so it's true that Jesus did these things. But the Book doesn't explain it, and neither do I. Did Jesus' actions cause the miracle? Was it theatrical? I have no idea! Does it matter? If it mattered the Bible would explain it.

Jesus then looked to heaven. This might have spiritual significance, or He might have just rolled His eyes in exasperation. And He sighed. Why do people sigh? Sighing is complex. There can be physical reasons and there can be emotional reasons. Most generally, it's an expression of resignation and frustration. The dictionary defines *sigh* as: To feel longing or grief; to yearn for something. Jesus' sigh could have been an expression of frustration or compassion. We don't know. All we know is that He sighed.

And He spoke in Aramaic. Why is that important? Aramaic was an international language that had a long history among the Phoenicians, and Tyre was Phoenician. So, it is likely that Aramaic would have been a known language in Tyre. Jesus may have determined that Aramaic was the native language of those who brought this deaf mute to Him. Thus, He spoke in a language that they could understand. And He said one word; *be opened*. And suddenly, the man could hear and speak.

The wider implication of this miracle is that the previously deaf mute could now hear the voice or message of Jesus. He could hear because the man had a personal experience with Jesus. Whatever else happened, the man could now hear Jesus in his native language. We are all in the condition of the deaf mute prior to experiencing Jesus. We are all unable to hear or speak the gospel rightly. But when we hear Jesus in our native tongue, we are then able to hear and speak God's truth rightly. Thus, the story has universal application.

The gospel message of Jesus Christ reached this deaf mute's soul and he could hear Jesus. And because he could hear Jesus, he could also speak the gospel. The healing of the deaf mute is a story about his conversion.

THE RIGHT STORY

3 Not many of you should become teachers, my brothers, for you know that we who teach will be judged with greater strictness. 2 For we all stumble in many ways. And if anyone does not stumble in what he says, he is a perfect man, able also to bridle his whole body. 3 If we put bits into the mouths of horses so that they obey us, we guide their whole bodies as well. 4 Look at the ships also: though they are so large and are driven by strong winds, they are guided by a very small rudder wherever the will of the pilot directs. 5 So also the tongue is a small member, yet it boasts of great things. How great a forest is set ablaze by such a small fire! 6 And the tongue is a fire, a world of unrighteousness. The tongue is set among our members, staining the whole body, setting on fire the entire course of life, and set on fire by hell. 7 For every kind of beast and bird, of reptile and sea creature, can be tamed and has been tamed by mankind, 8 but no human being can tame the tongue. It is a restless evil, full of deadly poison. 9 With it we bless our Lord and Father, and with it we curse people who are made in the likeness of God. 10 From the same mouth come blessing and cursing. My brothers, these things ought not to be so. 11 Does a spring pour forth from the same opening both fresh and salt water? 12 Can a fig tree, my brothers, bear olives, or a grapevine produce figs? Neither can a salt pond yield fresh water.
—James 3:1-12

27 And Jesus went on with his disciples to the villages of Caesarea Philippi. And on the way he asked his disciples, "Who do people say that I am?" 28 And they told him, "John the Baptist; and others say, Elijah; and others, one of the prophets." 29 And he asked them, "But who do you say that I am?" Peter answered him, "You are the Christ." 30 And he strictly charged them to tell no one about him. 31 And he began to teach them that the Son of Man must suffer many things and be rejected by the elders and the chief priests and the scribes and be killed, and after three days rise again. 32 And he said this plainly. And Peter took him aside and began to rebuke him. 33 But turning and seeing his disciples, he rebuked Peter and said, "Get behind me, Satan! For you are not setting your mind on the things of God, but on the things of man." 34 And calling the crowd to him with his disciples, he said to them, "If anyone would come after me, let him deny himself and take up his cross and follow me. 35 For whoever would save his life will lose it, but whoever loses his life for my sake and the gospel's will save it. 36 For what does it profit a man to gain the whole world and forfeit his soul? 37 For what can a man give in return for his soul? 38 For whoever is ashamed of me and of my words in this adulterous and sinful generation, of him will the Son of Man also be ashamed when he comes in the glory of his Father with the holy angels."   —*Mark 8:27-38*

In the last chapter we talked about Jesus healing a deaf mute in Tyre. In essence, an unbeliever engaged Jesus personally and was then able to hear Jesus and to speak. I suggested that this healing story was essentially the story of a man who came to faith through a personal encounter with Jesus, who could then hear the gospel, and because he could hear it, he could speak it.

This week the Lectionary provides a caution aimed at new believers learning to speak the gospel. New believers are often the most adamant about wanting to tell others about salvation in Jesus Christ. Because the faith is new to them, and because they have genuinely discovered its truth and it has changed their lives, they are eager to share their story with other unbelievers. It's all quite natural, and it's a good thing, to a certain extent. But there is a caveat, a caution:

"Not many of you should become teachers, my brothers, for you know that we who teach will be judged with greater strictness" (v. 3).

New believers have a passion to share what has completely changed them and brought them a perspective that has changed everything for them. The desire to share what they know fuels genuine evangelism. Yet the caution is important: New Christians are baby

Christians. What they know is true and valuable, and their desire to share what they know is genuine. It is jet fuel for evangelism. So they should be encouraged to share what they know about Jesus. But the truth is that they don't actually know very much. And there is a natural tendency for people to want to appear to be knowledgeable, so the temptation is say more than what they actually know.

In today's world there are so many different and competing ideas about Jesus in the public domain that it is difficult to know which are true and which are not. Sorting through the volumes of information about Jesus Christ generated by the various denominations over the last couple thousands years requires determination and patience. Paul knew the difficulties of knowing God's truth because he had been a life-long Pharisee before his conversion on the Damascus Road. The result of his conversion was the complete reversal of everything that he thought he knew. And he thought he knew a lot.

So, following his conversion Paul went into the desert for three years in order to sort things out. Then he spent the rest of his life distinguishing the differences between what is true about Jesus and what is not. He did that by writing letters to various churches to help them in their quest for the truth about Jesus.

Apparently James had a similar experience and was describing it in this letter. Sharing what we know about Jesus is good, but James cautioned new believers because they don't actually know much. As new believers share what they know with other unbelievers, some of those unbelievers push back and challenge what these new believers think they know. Arguments easily ensue, and in the midst of defense new believers are tempted to say more than they know, to fill in the the gaps of their knowledge with their own best guesses. Or to repeat something that they heard from others. In today's world we could say that they would repeat what they read on the Internet, things that seem right to them.

James talks about the necessity to tame the tongue. His discussion about the tongue is both convicting and illuminating. This chapter reveals various things about the tongue:

- it is a small part of the body, but it makes great boasts (verse 5);

- it is a fire and a world of evil that defiles the whole person (verse 6);
- it is set on fire by hell (verse 6); and
- it is full of deadly poison (verse 7).

Is it any wonder, then, that God declares that taming the tongue is impossible?

"but no human being can tame the tongue. It is a restless evil, full of deadly poison" (v. 8).

James' conclusion is quite damning. But the situation is not hopeless. He says,

"From the same mouth come blessing and cursing" (v. 10).

It's not all cursing. It's not all evil. Good can come from our words. We can use our words to bless as well as to curse.

When we look at the changes in people as they come into personal contact with Jesus and become believers we see a process of transition. First they are unbelievers, then they become new believers, and over time they become mature believers. When we map the ideas of blessing and cursing on this process we see that unbelievers are full of cursing, new believers can both bless and curse, and mature believers are full of blessing.

James was talking to new believers, explaining that they needed to be particularly careful because they were capable of both blessing and cursing. New believers need to be particularly careful about what they say about Jesus, and about others, because they don't actually know very much. His concluding thoughts in this section provide important advice:

"Does a spring pour forth from the same opening both fresh and salt water? Can a fig tree, my brothers, bear olives, or a grapevine produce figs? Neither can a salt pond yield fresh water" (vs. 11-12).

What he is driving at is that new believers need to complete the process of their conversion in order to keep from saying things that are not true. New believers must know for sure that they are saved.

Many Christians throughout history have written about their struggles regarding being assured of their salvation. The problem is that many followers of Jesus Christ look for the assurance of salvation in the wrong places. People tend to seek assurance of salvation in the things that God is doing in their lives, in their spiritual growth, and in their good works and obedience to God's Word. People tend to look for the assurance of their salvation in their own behavior, in themselves, in their own faithfulness.

While these things can be evidence of salvation, they are not what we should base the assurance of our salvation on. Rather, the assurance of our salvation is found in the objective truth of God's Word. The assurance of our salvation is confident trust that we are saved because of the promises God has declared, not because of our subjective experiences, not because of our efforts to be faithful. If our assurance depends on *us* being faithful, it has become works-righteousness. We can think that we have been saved by the grace of God alone, and think that remaining faithful depends on us.

Am I saying: *once saved, always saved?* Yes and no. There is a sense in which this is true, and there is a sense in which it is not true. The difference is a matter of self-delusion. People can think that they are saved when they are not. The proof of this comes in Matthew 7:21-23.

> "Not everyone who says to me, 'Lord, Lord,' will enter the kingdom of heaven, but the one who does the will of my Father who is in heaven. On that day many will say to me, 'Lord, Lord, did we not prophesy in your name, and cast out demons in your name, and do many mighty works in your name?' And then will I declare to them, 'I never knew you; depart from me, you workers of lawlessness.'

Here we have people who were prophesying, doing miracles, and casting out demons in the name of Jesus Christ. They would be considered by most people to be faithful Christians doing real ministry. But were they? They seemed to be doing the things that Jesus did. But there was a problem: they *thought* that they knew Jesus, but Jesus said that *He* didn't know them.

The assurance of salvation requires both truly knowing Jesus and being truly known by Jesus. There are two sides to the relationship, and both are necessary. It's like being in love. If a man loves a woman, but the woman doesn't love the man (or visa versa), it doesn't work. True love requires mutuality.

The key issue here is how salvation begins, how our relationship with Jesus Christ begins. Faithfulness is a dance, and when we start on the wrong foot, it doesn't work. So how does it start? Do we begin by letting Jesus into our hearts? Do we begin by giving our lives to Jesus, and then walking in faith? Is that where the gospel story begins? Where in the world does the gospel story begin?

Most people are tempted to think that it begins with "me," that my salvation begins with *my* acknowledgment of the Lordship of Jesus Christ. But if it begins with me, then it depends on me. In truth the gospel began in the mind of God.

> "Blessed be the God and Father of our Lord Jesus Christ, who has blessed us in Christ with every spiritual blessing in the heavenly places, even as he chose us in him before the foundation of the world, that we should be holy and blameless before him. In love he predestined us for adoption to himself as sons through Jesus Christ, according to the purpose of his will, to the praise of his glorious grace, with which he has blessed us in the Beloved" (Ephesians 1:3-6).

Our salvation is not *our* story about God. Our salvation is *God's* story about *us*, not God's story about *me*, but God's story about *us*. The story begins with God. God calls, and we respond.

After Peter confessed that Jesus was the Christ, Jesus began telling them His story. It was a story that they didn't like,

> "that the Son of Man must suffer many things and be rejected by the elders and the chief priests and the scribes and be killed, and after three days rise again" (v. 31).

He said it plainly, clearly! And Peter, who had just made a genuine confession that Jesus was the Christ of God, then rebuked Jesus! Peter didn't like the story that Jesus told him, and he rebuked Jesus for it. Peter thought that he knew better than Jesus. And there it is: original sin coming out of the mouth of a new believer.

Immediately Jesus recognized the words coming out of Peter's mouth as satanic. Satan was speaking through Peter! What was Peter's problem? Jesus said,

> "For you are not setting your mind on the things of God, but on the things of man (v. 33)."

Peter had the gospel bass-ackwards.

And calling the crowd to him with his disciples, he said to them,

> "If anyone would come after me, let him deny himself and take up his cross and follow me. For whoever would save his life will lose it, but whoever loses his life for my sake and the gospel's will save it'" (vs. 34-35).

Is it possible to get the gospel story wrong? Absolutely! In fact, people get it wrong more often than they get it right. We—Christians—need to be more careful with the gospel story. We need to get it right before we try to get it out. We need to be sure that we are drawing from fresh water, not salt water. We need to know the difference between good news and fake news.

STOP THAT, DO THIS!

38 John said to him, "Teacher, we saw someone casting out demons in your name, and we tried to stop him, because he was not following us." 39 But Jesus said, "Do not stop him, for no one who does a mighty work in my name will be able soon afterward to speak evil of me. 40 For the one who is not against us is for us. 41 For truly, I say to you, whoever gives you a cup of water to drink because you belong to Christ will by no means lose his reward. 42 Whoever causes one of these little ones who believe in me to sin, it would be better for him if a great millstone were hung around his neck and he were thrown into the sea. 43 And if your hand causes you to sin, cut it off. It is better for you to enter life crippled than with two hands to go to hell, to the unquenchable fire. 45 And if your foot causes you to sin, cut it off. It is better for you to enter life lame than with two feet to be thrown into hell. 47 And if your eye causes you to sin, tear it out. It is better for you to enter the kingdom of God with one eye than with two eyes to be thrown into hell, 48 'where their worm does not die and the fire is not quenched.' 49 For everyone will be salted with fire. 50 Salt is good, but if the salt has lost its saltiness, how will you make it salty again? Have salt in yourselves, and be at peace with one another."   —Mark 9:38–50

13 Is anyone among you suffering? Let him pray. Is anyone cheerful? Let him sing praise. 14 Is anyone among you sick? Let him call for the elders of the church, and let them pray over him, anointing him with oil in the name of the Lord. 15 And the prayer of faith will save the one who is sick, and the Lord will raise him up. And if he has committed sins, he will be forgiven. 16 Therefore, confess your sins to one another and pray for one another, that you may be healed. The prayer of a righteous person has great power as it is working. 17 Elijah was a man with a nature like ours, and he prayed fervently that it might not rain, and for three years and six months it did not

rain on the earth. 18 Then he prayed again, and heaven gave rain,
and the earth bore its fruit. 19 My brothers, if anyone among you
wanders from the truth and someone brings him back, 20 let him
know that whoever brings back a sinner from his wandering will save
his soul from death and will cover a multitude of sins.

—James 5:13-20

Here we find someone casting out demons in Jesus' name, and was not part of the group of disciples, and Jesus has a completely different response than He did in Matthew 7 when He said:.

> "Lord, Lord, did we not prophesy in your name and in your name drive out demons and in your name perform many miracles?' Then I will tell them plainly, 'I never knew you. Away from me, you evildoers!'" (Matthew 7:22-23).

Here He said that no one can work in His name without eventually becoming faithful.

If we are looking for a principle that can discern between true believers and false believers that can be universally applied, we will come up short because these two stories oppose the idea that there is a universal principle to perfectly determine faithfulness. The only conclusion that can be drawn from these contrasting stories is that they describe different situations, and that Jesus alone is able to determine true faithfulness.

In the one case those who were casting out demons were not faithful; in the other case, they were faithful. And in both cases it is Jesus who makes that determination of their faithfulness. The point is that we are not able to apply a universal principle of faithfulness because making that determination is the prerogative of Jesus, not us. And to drive this point home Jesus discusses the cause of sin. The lesson here is that whatever causes sin must be eliminated.

If you cause a little one to sin, then you must be eliminated, drowned in the sea. Whatever causes sin must be eliminated. If your hand causes sin, cut it off. If your foot causes sin, cut it off. If your eye causes sin, tear it out. This is pretty stark—shocking even. If we fail to understand it correctly the result will be pretty nasty. Is Jesus recommending self-mutilation? Of course not! So how should we understand this?

These are "if, then" statements. *If this, then that.* And we tend to focus on the conclusion because it is so dramatic. But the secret to understanding these statements is found in the "if" clause. The conclusion is valid only when the "if" clause is true. The theme of each of these statements is the cause of sin. What is the cause of sin? Is it the hand or foot or eye? Each of these may be involved in sin, but none of them in and of themselves cause sin. But if they did, it would make sense then to eliminate them in order to eliminate sin.

But cutting off your hand or your foot or gouging out your eye will not eliminate sin. You would simply become a one-armed, one-legged, half-blind sinner. The body is not the cause of sin, though it is involved in sin. Jesus then added two ideas that will help us understand what He means. He describe hell as a place

"'where their worm does not die and the fire is not quenched.' For everyone will be salted with fire" (vs. 48-49).

What?! Let's start with the worm. He is quoting from Isaiah 66:24:

"They will go out and look on the dead bodies of those who rebelled against me; the worms that eat them will not die, the fire that burns them will not be quenched, and they will be loathsome to all mankind."

Isaiah was talking about the consequences for those who rebel against God—sinners. And he was pointing out the eternal nature of hell, that hell is an eternal reality in that it always stands as a consequence of faithlessness. It's not simply that hell is place of eternal damnation, punishment, and pain, but that hell is an eternal, everlasing threat to sin. He was indicating that, just as hell threatened people in the Old Testament, that same threat is always present. The fact of God's grace and forgiveness does not negate the reality of hell, the reality that the consequence of sin is always damnation. Hell is an eternal reality, an ever-present option, and a very real possibility.

We need to eliminate those things that result in the death and destruction characterized by hell. And it is not hands and feet or eyes. It is desires and temptations. It is fear and distrust. It is faithlessness. These are the things that need to be eliminated. The consequence of not understanding Jesus correctly is serious. That's the point.

What does it mean that

"everyone will be salted with fire" (v. 49)?

First note that it will happen to everyone, not just unbelievers. He was referring to Leviticus 2:13:

"Season all your grain offerings with salt. Do not leave the salt of your covenant of your God out of your grain offerings, add salt to your offerings."

Paul was talking about this issue when he said:

"Therefore, I urge you, brothers and sisters, in view of God's mercy, to offer your bodies as a living sacrifice, holy and pleasing to God— this is your true and proper worship" (Romans 12;1).

There are two elements here: salt and fire. Salt is both a preservative and a flavor additive. It both preserves and makes food taste better. It is pleasing to the senses. Regarding worship, we need to preserve the truth, and to do what we can to make God's truth pleasing to people. It needs to be inspiring, thoughtful, and meaningful.

Fire is purging, destructive. To purge means to clear of guilt or to free from moral or ceremonial defilement. Fire is used to purify metals. When gold or silver are melted the impurities of the metal float to the top and can be eliminated, which then increases the purity of the metal. Here fire is used for purification. Again, the application is to purify worship, but not simply Sunday morning worship services. True worship is much more than an hour on Sunday mornings. True worship is what you do with your life. True worship is the integration of Jesus Christ into your life. True worship is living for Christ 24/7. But fire also brings warmth and light, and these make it attractive. Worship should be attractive. It should draw people into the consideration of Jesus Christ as Lord and Savior.

We are to persevere, to preserve what is true and good and honorable, and be at peace with one another. So, how do we do that? The Lectionary sends us to James 5. Here we see that prayer is the antidote for suffering. Does prayer eliminate pain? No. What it does is make suffering meaningful, which makes suffering transformative.

Think of surgery as a kind of purging. The surgery is necessary to remove or repair some malady, which causes more pain, but the pain is endured because the surgery brings healing and a better life. Think of prayer as consultation with the surgeon. The surgeon has a plan that will bring healing and a better life.

Then Paul suggests singing praise as the best way to express cheerfulness. Again, the context here is worship, what we do with our lives. Cheerfulness apart from Christ is temporary. But when we channel our cheerfulness into songs of praise, we lift up and experience a taste of heaven. In Christ there is eternal joy! Singing on Sunday mornings is good, but Paul has more in mind. Singing is emotionally satisfying, it builds community and cooperation, and should be integrated into all of our lives.

So we see that worship is for those who are suffering, and for those who are cheerful. But it's also for those who are sick. The Greek word for sick doesn't just mean illness. It means to be weak, or feeble, to be without strength, powerless, needy, poor. Here James was saying that worship will strengthen your resolve. It will increase your strength, your passion for life.

He was encouraging people to be anointed with oil in the name of the Lord. Being anointed goes back to the Old Testament. It was a ceremonial calling to service in that kings and priests were anointed with oil. Anointing was a kind of investment with power and authority to serve the Lord. James said that

> "the prayer of faith will save the one who is sick, and the Lord will raise him up" (v. 15).

The prayer of faith can also be translated as faithful prayer. Faithful prayer will save the weak and feeble. Those without strength and power will receive strength and power through faithful prayer. In addition, forgiveness comes through faithful prayer. And we can help each other find new strength and power in Christ by confessing our sins to one another, which will lead to the forgiveness of those sins by one another. And the more we do this, the more healing will come to the body of Christ. The church, the people of God, will be strengthened by two things: the elimination of the causes of sin, and the engagement of faithful prayer. Elijah provides an example of this. The idea is that we can do what Elijah did because

"Elijah was a man with a nature like ours" (v. 17).

Then James tells us that spiritual growth is uneven, two steps forward and one back. There are times of growth and there are times of back-sliding. And we can help one another by praying, by praying alone and praying together. The prayer of faith or faithful prayer will save those who are weak and wandering in the church, in the body of Christ. We can help one another in all sorts of ways by praying for one another.

Faithfulness begins in prayer, so be sure you are speaking to the Lord regularly.

HARD TRUTH, GREATER GRACE

18 Then the Lord God said, "It is not good that the man should be alone; I will make him a helper fit for him." 19 Now out of the ground the Lord God had formed every beast of the field and every bird of the heavens and brought them to the man to see what he would call them. And whatever the man called every living creature, that was its name. 20 The man gave names to all livestock and to the birds of the heavens and to every beast of the field. But for Adam there was not found a helper fit for him. 21 So the Lord God caused a deep sleep to fall upon the man, and while he slept took one of his ribs and closed up its place with flesh. 22 And the rib that the Lord God had taken from the man he made into a woman and brought her to the man. 23 Then the man said, "This at last is bone of my bones and flesh of my flesh; she shall be called Woman, because she was taken out of Man." 24 Therefore a man shall leave his father and his mother and hold fast to his wife, and they shall become one flesh.
—Genesis 2:18-24

2 And Pharisees came up and in order to test him asked, "Is it lawful for a man to divorce his wife?" 3 He answered them, "What did Moses command you?" 4 They said, "Moses allowed a man to write a certificate of divorce and to send her away." 5 And Jesus said to them, "Because of your hardness of heart he wrote you this commandment. 6 But from the beginning of creation, 'God made them male and female.' 7 'Therefore a man shall leave his father and mother and hold fast to his wife, 8 and the two shall become one flesh.' So they are no longer two but one flesh. 9 What therefore God has joined together, let not man separate." 10 And in the house the disciples asked him again about this matter. 11 And he said to them,

"Whoever divorces his wife and marries another commits adultery against her, 12 and if she divorces her husband and marries another, she commits adultery." 13 And they were bringing children to him that he might touch them, and the disciples rebuked them. 14 But when Jesus saw it, he was indignant and said to them, "Let the children come to me; do not hinder them, for to such belongs the kingdom of God. 15 Truly, I say to you, whoever does not receive the kingdom of God like a child shall not enter it." 16 And he took them in his arms and blessed them, laying his hands on them.

—Mark 10:2-16

W omen! God love them, and He does! God made them. God took a rib from Adam to make Eve, but this removal of a rib from Adam did not result in men having one less rib. Why not? Is an interesting question.

> "The Lord God formed a man from the dust of the ground and breathed into his nostrils the breath of life, and the man became a living being" (Genesis 2:7).

Man here is a generic term. It does not mean male; it means human. The design of the human body is amazing, in part because we are created in the image of God (Genesis 1:27). God created Adam and gave him a job before He gave him a wife. His job was to name the animals. Adam was a taxonomist. Taxonomy is the science of classification. Taxonomists name things and group them into classifications. Taxonomy is the first science. Adam's job was taking an inventory of the earth's animals. He named them according to their function or character. Adam's job then revealed to him that, while all of the other animals had mates, he was without a mate.

> "For Adam no suitable helper was found" (Genesis 2:20).

All of the other animals could reproduce through male/female paring. Prior to Eve, Adam could not.

There are two creation stories: Genesis 1, then Genesis 2 repeats the creation story, adding additional detail. The creation of Eve tells us that the original creation of humanity (Adam) was different from the ongoing reproduction of humanity. The ongoing method of reproduction involves the paring of male and female to produce a child. But the original creation by God was different. Think of a factory that produces widgets. The first or prototype widget is not produced in the same way that the factory replicates widgets. The first one, the model, involves creativity and a different process. The others are replicas of the prototype. This is the point of the story of the creation of Eve.

How God created the woman is significant. In Genesis 2:21–22, after causing Adam to fall into a deep sleep, God took a rib out of the man and used it to form the woman. So Adam and Eve were of the same substance and were connected biologically. All people are from Adam, including Eve. Of course Eve involved a modification of the prototype that would allow for self-reproduction or self-replication.

When God brought the woman to the man, Adam said,

"This is now bone of my bones and flesh of my flesh; she shall be called 'woman,' for she was taken out of man" (Genesis 2:23).

He named her according to her function: *womb man*. Why did God use a rib? God made a chromosomal change in Eve. Every human child has the DNA encoding that produces twelve pairs of ribs. Adam's sons and daughters all have the same number of ribs that Adam originally had. Similarly, the son or daughter of a kidney donor will have two kidneys, and the daughter or son of an amputee will not be born missing a limb.

But there is another interesting fact about ribs: Ribs regenerate. All bones in the human body are able to mend themselves, but rib bone is unique in that it can regenerate. When a surgeon performs a costectomy (the removal of part or all of a rib), he will be careful to leave the perichondrium (the membrane surrounding the rib). The rib taken can then be used for bone grafts elsewhere in the body, and a new rib will regrow in the spot of the missing rib within one or two months. Consequently Adam lived out the rest of his days with the same number of ribs that he had been created with. And Eve was created from the part of Adam that is able to regenerate.

"Therefore a man shall leave his father and his mother and hold fast to his wife, and they shall become one flesh" (v. 24).

One flesh echoes the language of the preceding verse where Adam exclaims,

"This one is bone of my bone, and flesh of my flesh!" (v. 23).

Marriage is not mentioned, but this is all about marriage. Adam and Eve then unite; two whole and individual people become one in a new, God-designed and God-purposed life together. Adam and Eve are then the first unit of humanity that God created.

God was creating more than individuals. Humanity is more than individuals. An individual is not sustainable. An individual cannot reproduce. Reproduction requires a male/female bonding. This bonded unit, this family, this male/female bond is the creation of God. It is of God and for God and serves God's purpose. The family is God's primary building block of human society, human culture.

So when God created Adam (mankind, humanity), He created more than an individual or two. He primarily created the self-reproducing biological family unit. The purpose of the family is more than the reproduction of individuals. The purpose of the family is the maturity and replication of families. The family is the foundational replicator of Godly human culture.

Thus, the family structure is essential for human culture, human society. And sin is the enemy of God's family structure, which we see almost immediately, when Cain killed Abel. The first son killed the second son. The result of that murder was a division of God's family structure. Abel was dead, and Cain was banished from the family. How important is God's family structure to the sustainability and longevity of human culture, human society? It is absolutely fundamental. So marriage and divorce are very important to God.

When the Pharisees asked Jesus about divorce, they were in a hostile mood. They weren't asking in order to get clarity. They were trying to catch Jesus in a "gotcha" moment. Moses had already ruled on the issue, as the Pharisees indicated.

"When a man takes a wife and marries her, and it happens that she finds no favor in his eyes because he has found some uncleanness in her, and he writes her a certificate of divorce, puts it in her hand, and sends her out of his house, when she has departed from his house, and goes and becomes another man's wife, if the latter husband detests her and writes her a certificate of divorce, puts it in her hand, and sends her out of his house, or if the latter husband dies who took her as his wife, then her former husband who divorced her must not take her back to be his wife after she has been defiled; for that is an abomination before the LORD, and you shall not bring sin on the land which the LORD your God is giving you as an inheritance" (Deuteronomy 24:1-4).

Jesus discounted the passage by offering a rebuttal.

"Because of your hardness of heart he wrote you this commandment. But from the beginning of creation, 'God made them male and female. Therefore a man shall leave his father and mother and hold fast to his wife, and the two shall become one flesh.' So they are no longer two but one flesh. What therefore God has joined together, let not man separate" (vs. 5-9).

Deuteronomy put all of the blame for divorce on the woman. If her husband was not pleased with her, he could get rid of her. The only good thing that Moses did was to require the husband to write out a certificate of divorce and submit it to the elders. The husband had to explain himself to the elders. This was an improvement from previous pagan practice. Nonetheless, it was a reflection of the hard hearts of the Israelites that existed at the time, which Jesus noted.

Jesus then pivoted to the Genesis explanation of marriage, God's original plan. In that plan the two became one. They were to function as a unit. They became two halves of a single being. God had joined them together, and what God joined should remain joined. That was the end of the matter for Jesus. And with that He had answered the question. But the disciples had more questions. We don't know what the disciples asked. Their questions are not in the text. All we have is Jesus' answer to them.

It is important to notice that Jesus' answer was for the disciples. It probably should apply to all people, but the text tells us that His answer was for the disciples. Why is that important? Because the disciples had faith in Christ. But not everyone had such faith, especially at that moment in history. His answer accused disciples who divorced of adultery, both husband and wife would be guilty of adultery regardless of who was at fault. Jesus' answer then applies to believers. Believers who marry believers should not get divorced, period. And believers should only marry other believers. Why? Because God is working on sanctifying believers. God is actively working on believers, and believers should know that, and respond appropriately.

The appropriate response to suffering, assuming that marital difficulties cause suffering (and they do), is to persevere because God is using that suffering to bring greater sanctification, greater growth and maturity in Christ to the individuals in the marriage. God knows that divorce will happen because people are sinful. Even believers are sinful. So divorce will happen even among believers. But believers have a greater responsibility to not sin, and when they do, they are to make every effort to reconcile, not to succumb to the sin, but to use the sin, the problem, for their sanctification. When people are quick to divorce at the first sign of trouble, they cut themselves off from God's process of sanctification. They do not learn from their mistakes.

But when they learn from their mistakes, when they persevere in spite of their mistakes, they find that God not only heals the original problem, but God uses the process of reconciliation to fuse a stronger, better marriage bond. When we persevere in Christ through marital difficulties—and difficulties always come—we grow closer to Christ, and closer to our mate. When we persevere through the bad times the good times become much sweeter.

Finally then, children are the fruit of marriage, so the Lectionary closes with a story about Jesus and children. Parents were bringing children to Jesus with the hope that He would bless them. But the disciples rebuked the parents, thinking that Jesus' gospel was for adults, not children. Jesus disagreed, and rebuked the disciples, saying that the kingdom of God belongs to God's children. Jesus then received the children, held them, hugged them, and blessed them.

This story is used to defend infant baptism, even though the idea of baptism is nowhere to be found. Why do they do that? Because baptism is the beginning of a personal relationship with Jesus Christ. And the children in this story are actively involved in the beginning of a personal relationship with Jesus Christ.

The greater concern here is not the procedure of baptism, but the result or fruit of baptism. Baptism is not about immersion, sprinkling, or pouring. Nor is it about the age of those who are baptized. Baptism is about the beginning of a personal relationship with Jesus Christ. The purpose of baptism is the fruit of that relationship, not distinguishing between the different processes of the ceremony. We don't know the ages of these children, nor does it matter. Jesus doesn't get hung up with procedure; Jesus is interested in results.

The focus on procedure tends to bind the Holy Spirit. But the Holy Spirit is not bound by our ceremonies and procedures. The Holy Spirit is free to produce results however He wants. And that's what He does! He dispenses God's grace without concern for our ceremonies and procedures. That was Jesus' message to the Pharisees of the Old Testament, and that is Jesus' message to the church today.

POSSESSED

They hate him who reproves in the gate, and they abhor him who speaks the truth. 11 Therefore because you trample on the poor and you exact taxes of grain from him, you have built houses of hewn stone, but you shall not dwell in them; you have planted pleasant vineyards, but you shall not drink their wine. 12 For I know how many are your transgressions and how great are your sins—you who afflict the righteous, who take a bribe, and turn aside the needy in the gate. 13 Therefore he who is prudent will keep silent in such a time, for it is an evil time. 14 Seek good, and not evil, that you may live; and so the Lord, the God of hosts, will be with you, as you have said. 15 Hate evil, and love good, and establish justice in the gate; it may be that the Lord, the God of hosts, will be gracious to the remnant of Joseph. —Amos 5:10-15

17 And as he was setting out on his journey, a man ran up and knelt before him and asked him, "Good Teacher, what must I do to inherit eternal life?" 18 And Jesus said to him, "Why do you call me good? No one is good except God alone. 19 You know the commandments: 'Do not murder, Do not commit adultery, Do not steal, Do not bear false witness, Do not defraud, Honor your father and mother.'" 20 And he said to him, "Teacher, all these I have kept from my youth." 21 And Jesus, looking at him, loved him, and said to him, "You lack one thing: go, sell all that you have and give to the poor, and you will have treasure in heaven; and come, follow me." 22 Disheartened by the saying, he went away sorrowful, for he had great possessions. 23 And Jesus looked around and said to his disciples, "How difficult it will be for those who have wealth to enter the kingdom of God!" 24 And the disciples were amazed at his words. But Jesus said to them again, "Children, how difficult it is to enter the kingdom of God! 25 It is easier for a camel to go through the eye of a needle than for a rich person to enter the kingdom of God." 26 And they

were exceedingly astonished, and said to him, "Then who can be saved?" 27 Jesus looked at them and said, "With man it is impossible, but not with God. For all things are possible with God." 28 Peter began to say to him, "See, we have left everything and followed you." 29 Jesus said, "Truly, I say to you, there is no one who has left house or brothers or sisters or mother or father or children or lands, for my sake and for the gospel, 30 who will not receive a hundredfold now in this time, houses and brothers and sisters and mothers and children and lands, with persecutions, and in the age to come eternal life. 31 But many who are first will be last, and the last first."
—Mark 10:17-31

Amos lived in the eighth century B.C. He was a contemporary of Isaiah and Hosea. All three of them were prophets. Prophets prophesied, that is, they spoke and wrote the Word of God. As such, they were motivated and inhabited by the Holy Spirit, and they all had a similar theme to their messages. They all were concerned about the faithlessness of Israel, and they blamed the Temple priests for the faithlessness of the people. Isaiah was a Temple priest, Amos and Hosea were not. This suggests that God could and did use anybody to convey His message.

The prophets were critical of the established Temple leaders. The job of the prophets was to point out social problems, and social problems always had religious roots, religious origins. In order to solve a problem, the first order of business is to correctly diagnose the problem. A wrong diagnosis will result in an ineffective and potentially dangerous cure. When a doctor misdiagnoses a patient, the patient will receive the wrong medicine. And the problem will persist, maybe even get worse. Correct diagnosis is the foundation of healing, or problem solving.

Healing and problem solving begin with the realization that there is a problem. Too often, people deny problems, and refuse to even acknowledge them until they grow much larger. The art of problem solving, and of prophesying, is early detection. Small problems are easier to solve than large problems.

Amos said that people who were in the midst of problems in his day didn't want to hear the truth. This is a result of the denial of the problem. People who are caught up in denial have difficulty hearing the truth. They don't like it, they don't want it, and they don't believe it. The reason that problems are denied is that problems usually require a change of behavior. The problem indicates that something is wrong, and the root of the problem is usually some wrong idea, belief, or behavior that feeds the problem.

Amos said that

"They hate him who reproves in the gate" (v. 10).

Doing so in the gate means doing it publicly. The gate was the place of public business. So who are the "they" that hate public reproval, public disapproval, public criticism. Of course no one likes public criticism because it exposes their faults, their short-comings, their errors of judgment. But those who dislike public criticism the most are those who are responsible for public policies.

Amos' accusation was that "they … trample on the poor" (v. 11). Who tramples on the poor? Not the poor! They don't trample on themselves. It is the not-poor who trample on the poor. In other words, Amos was blaming society, the social structures, the normal way of business, the corruption of social institutions. He blamed the leaders of the society, the leaders of the Temple because they were the ones who set the social habits, structures, and procedures of society. These are the "they" who "hate him who reproves in the gate … who speak the truth" (v. 1) publicly. In essence, Amos was saying that the general or overall structure of society was causing too much poverty.

Jesus said that we would always have the poor (Matthew 26:11). Poverty cannot be eliminated, but it can be reduced. And it gets reduced by expanding the middle class.

The causes of poverty are seen in verse 12. The leaders of society

"afflict the righteous … take a bribe, and turn aside the needy in the gate."

What does it mean to afflict the righteous? Who are the righteous? They are those who practice righteousness, God's righteousness because there isn't any other. The righteous do what is right. The righteous are people who practice and promote honesty, integrity, and industry. Honest people speak the truth (v. 10). People with integrity strive to adhere to a moral or ethical code. And the only moral code that is worth a hoot is found in the Bible. Think of the Ten Commandments, or the fruits of the spirit:

> "love, joy, peace, forbearance, kindness, goodness, faithfulness, gentleness and self-control" (Galatians 5:22-23).

Industrious people work hard.

Amos was speaking about a society in which the leaders disapproved of these things. And apparently it was a problem in Amos' day. It's a problem whenever and wherever it occurs. When the leaders of a society fail to promote honesty, integrity, and industry poverty increases. It's not rocket science! Amos called it an "evil time" (v. 13). Amos then provided a solution:

> "Seek good, and not evil, that you may live; and so the Lord, the God of hosts, will be with you … Hate evil, and love good, and establish justice in the gate" (vs. 14-15).

Note that the solution to the problems of poverty is to promote the ideas, values, and practices of the Bible. When people lack honesty, integrity, and industry poverty increases. When society promotes these things poverty decreases. The middle class increases. In order for this to happen, the leaders of society must believe the truth of the Bible enough that they promote it. They must understand the Bible to be valuable.

Who are the leaders of society? The wealthy, the rich. So the Lectionary takes us to a story about a rich young man. This particular man came to Jesus with a question.

> "Good Teacher, what must I do to inherit eternal life?" (v. 18).

The very first thing that Jesus tells him is that he had made a wrong assumption, and that this assumption had produced a wrong understanding of humanity. That wrong assumption caused this rich young man to have a faulty worldview that affected himself and his view of others.

He called Jesus "good." At this point this young man had no idea of Jesus' divinity. He simply thought of Jesus as a religious teacher, like other religious teachers. In essence this young man thought either that people are good natured, or that some people (religious teachers) are good natured. What's the problem with that? It is a denial of sin, a denial of the extent, the degree, or the consequences of sin.

When Adam sinned in the Garden, the result was the Fall of humanity. Why did Adam's sin have such a grand effect? Because Adam was not an ordinary person. Adam was a human prototype, after which all other human beings would be modeled. We talked about how the prototype model is different from the production units in the previous chapter. The sin of Adam was part of the prototype, and all human beings are reproductions of Adam. If I have a document, a prototype document, and want to make copies of it. I run it through the copier. But if that original document, the prototype, has a flaw, that flaw will be reproduced on all of the copies.

All of this is to say that the rich young man was in denial of sin. So, Jesus used him to make a point. Jesus turned him to the Ten Commandments, which were thought to provide a cure for sin. That was the general idea taught by the Pharisees. They taught that obedience to the Ten Commandments, which included all of the Temple sacrifices, would or could eliminate sin. We know that that didn't work. But that young man didn't know what we know. Jesus then summed up the Commandments:

> "Do not murder, Do not commit adultery, Do not steal, Do not bear false witness, Do not defraud, Honor your father and mother" (v. 19).

Murder, adultery, theft, gossip, deceit, and disrespect. Don't do these things. The young man then testified that he hadn't done any of these things. Really? That would be unlikely. This young man was living in denial. Jesus knew him to be a sinner because Jesus knew that God had sent Him to rescue sinful humanity. Jesus would provide the cure for human sin, but that cure was not yet completed. The cross and resurrection hadn't happened yet. So, Jesus' cure wasn't available yet. Nor had Jesus performed a miracle on this young man.

So Jesus told him that he lacked one thing. Something had blinded this young man to the truth of his situation. He had not seen the reality of the human predicament. He was in denial of the extent, the degree, or the consequences of sin. Something kept him from seeing this truth. And it was his wealth. This young man was blinded by his wealth. He didn't possess the wealth, his wealth possessed him. He was captivated by his wealth. He spent the bulk of his time thinking about money and possessions.

The young man left disheartened. We don't know what happened to him after that, but a seed was planted in his life. Maybe it took root, maybe it didn't. We don't know. But the conversation about wealth continued among His disciples. Jesus illustrated His point with the camel through the eye of a needle story. There are many explanations and interpretations of this story.

One suggested that Jesus was referring to a small, low gate in the Jerusalem wall, the Needle Gate. The camel would have to get on its knees to pass through. But there is no proof that such a gate existed. Another suggested that the word for camel should be translated as rope, and we have the difficulty of getting a rope though the eye of a needle. But the most likely explanation is that Jesus was using hyperbole, a figure of speech that exaggerates for emphasis. Jesus used this technique at other times, referring to a "plank" in one's eye (Matthew 7:3-5) and swallowing a camel (Matthew 23:24).

Nonetheless, Jesus' message is clear—it is impossible for anyone to be saved on his own merits, by himself, with his wealth. Because wealth was seen as proof of God's approval, it was commonly taught by the rabbis that rich people were blessed by God and were, therefore, the most likely candidates for heaven. But Jesus destroyed that idea again and again, no one can earn eternal life.

The disciples then asked, "Who then can be saved?" (v. 26). If the wealthy among them, which included the super-spiritual Pharisees and scribes, were unworthy of heaven, what hope was there for a poor man? Jesus taught that on the basis of merit, there is no hope. But with God all things are possible.

At that point Peter began to defend himself and the disciples, saying that they had left everything and followed Jesus. With the implication being that surely *they* were worthy of heaven. Jesus then pointed out that the disciples, those who had or would give up everything and follow Jesus, would receive back everything that they had given up—a hundred fold—including *persecutions*! They would get it all back, but persecutions would be added to their return. Yet in the age to come they would find themselves in eternal life.

It was like Jesus was saying, *Yeah, yeah, that's all good. Don't worry about what you give up. You'll get it all back. But you will also experience a lot of persecution in the process. But don't worry about that either, because those who persist will make it to heaven.*

And He ends with *the first will be last and last will be first* puzzle. This concluding idea tells us that in the kingdom of God there will be a reversal. The blind will see, and the sighted will be blind. The poor in spirit will be in heaven. The meek will inherit the earth. Etc. The greatest reversal will be that God's curse will become a great blessing.

It was a curse to be hung on a tree. Jesus was hung on a cross, made from a tree. And Jesus has become the world's greatest blessing. The bottom line: *wealth is a gift, but it can be misleading.* It's better to just trust Jesus, and that trust begins with believing Him.

OUT OF ORDER

Surely he has borne our griefs and carried our sorrows; yet we esteemed him stricken, smitten by God, and afflicted. 5 But he was pierced for our transgressions; he was crushed for our iniquities; upon him was the chastisement that brought us peace, and with his wounds we are healed. 6 All we like sheep have gone astray; we have turned —every one—to his own way; and the Lord has laid on him the iniquity of us all. 7 He was oppressed, and he was afflicted, yet he opened not his mouth; like a lamb that is led to the slaughter, and like a sheep that before its shearers is silent, so he opened not his mouth. 8 By oppression and judgment he was taken away; and as for his generation, who considered that he was cut off out of the land of the living, stricken for the transgression of my people? 9 And they made his grave with the wicked and with a rich man in his death, although he had done no violence, and there was no deceit in his mouth. 10 Yet it was the will of the Lord to crush him; he has put him to grief; when his soul makes an offering for guilt, he shall see his offspring; he shall prolong his days; the will of the Lord shall prosper in his hand. 11 Out of the anguish of his soul he shall see and be satisfied; by his knowledge shall the righteous one, my servant, make many to be accounted righteous, and he shall bear their iniquities. 12 Therefore I will divide him a portion with the many, and he shall divide the spoil with the strong, because he poured out his soul to death and was numbered with the transgressors; yet he bore the sin of many, and makes intercession for the transgressors.
—Isaiah 53:4-12

5 For every high priest chosen from among men is appointed to act on behalf of men in relation to God, to offer gifts and sacrifices for sins. 2 He can deal gently with the ignorant and wayward, since he himself is beset with weakness. 3 Because of this he is obligated to offer sacrifice for his own sins just as he does for those of the people.

239

4 And no one takes this honor for himself, but only when called by God, just as Aaron was. 5 So also Christ did not exalt himself to be made a high priest, but was appointed by him who said to him, "You are my Son, today I have begotten you"; 6 as he says also in another place, "You are a priest forever, after the order of Melchizedek." 7 In the days of his flesh, Jesus offered up prayers and supplications, with loud cries and tears, to him who was able to save him from death, and he was heard because of his reverence. 8 Although he was a son, he learned obedience through what he suffered. 9 And being made perfect, he became the source of eternal salvation to all who obey him, 10 being designated by God a high priest after the order of Melchizedek. —Hebrews 5:1-10

Isaiah wrote 700 years before Christ. At that early date Isaiah knew the mission of Jesus Christ in the world. Isaiah's insight is nothing less than miraculous. We know Isaiah now because his work has been part of the Bible since forever. But at the time that Isaiah was writing, Isaiah was an outlier. He offered a different view from the rest of the Temple priests. Isaiah was protesting against the establishment view of things.

Isaiah knew that the Messiah would not be what Israel expected. The Messiah would be what God needed Him to be. And how could it be otherwise? People still don't know what they need. They just know what they want.

The Messiah is God's "arm" (God's work or tool) whom Isaiah spoke about (Isaiah 53:1), but who was rejected by many. The Messiah grew up like any young person does, there was nothing abnormal or majestic about His human appearance or experience. He was a man of sorrows and greatly despised, and people did not recognize or esteem Him (Isaiah 53:3a).

Isaiah tells us that Jesus the Messiah, the Christ, was pierced for our transgressions and crushed for our iniquities (Isaiah 53:5a). He was afflicted not because of any deficiency of His own, but He took on our transgressions and iniquities and paid the price that you and I owed to God. Romans 6:23 says that the wages of sin is death. Paul explains there that the consequence of Adam's sin is death (Romans 5:12), or eternal separation from God.

Since the Fall of Adam and Eve, humanity has lived in a lost state —being dead in sin, separated from God because of sin (Ephesians 2:1–3). But even as God pronounced judgment on humanity after the Fall, He promised that there would be redemption that would be accomplished by one specific Person (Genesis 3:15; Isaiah 53).

And this is how Jesus has borne our griefs. Paul explains that, while we were still sinners and totally helpless, Christ was born, lived, and died for us (Romans 5:8) because we have all sinned and fallen short of God's glory (Romans 3:23). We have all gone astray like wayward sheep. We have all gone our own way, done our own thing, become our own person (Isaiah 53:6a). Yet God allowed the eternal penalty for our sins to be paid by Jesus. The Lord caused our iniquity to fall upon Him (Isaiah 53:6b). He died *for* our sin, *because of* our sin, as a *result of* our sin.

> "He was oppressed, and he was afflicted, yet he opened not his mouth; like a lamb that is led to the slaughter, and like a sheep that before its shearers is silent, so he opened not his mouth" (v.7).

What does it mean that He didn't open His mouth? He said nothing about His afflictions or oppression. He didn't complain. He didn't accuse. He didn't get angry or frustrated. He was silent before Pilate who accused Him. He didn't mount a defense. Why not? Because He knew what must happen. His response was simple silence, patience, and acceptance. God needed to use Him, and He cooperated with God, knowing that His cooperation would lead to a painful death.

> "Yet it was the will of the Lord to crush him; he has put him to grief; when his soul makes an offering for guilt, he shall see his offspring; he shall prolong his days; the will of the Lord shall prosper in his hand" (v. 10).

It was God's will to crush Him! But why? In the long history of this world God was in the process of changing the religion of humanity, changing the worship practices of the ancient world. That story began a very long time ago. Abraham grew up in Ur, an important Sumerian city-state in ancient Mesopotamia. The city's patron deity was *Nanna* (in Akkadian, *Sin*), the Sumerian and Akkadian moon god. The two names, *Nanna* and *Sin*, came from different languages, but they both named the same god. There is evidence that human sacrifice was practiced in Ur as part of the religious rituals of *Sin* or *Nanna*.

Abraham's father, Terah, was the son of Nahor and the father of the patriarch Abraham. Genesis 11:31 reads,

> "Terah took Abram his son and Lot the son of Haran, his grandson, and Sarai his daughter-in-law, his son Abram's wife, and they went forth together from Ur of the Chaldeans to go into the land of Canaan, but when they came to Haran, they settled there."

This means that Abraham went with his father, Terah, to Canaan, but Terah died on the way. It was then that God had told Abram to leave his country and kindred and go to a land that he would show him, and promised to make of him a great nation, bless him, make his name great, bless them that bless him, and curse them who curse him.

Abraham was either born in Ur or born on Terah's journey to Canaan. So, when God called Abraham to leave his country and kindred, God was calling Abraham to leave his family's religion, the human sacrificing religion of Ur, the religion of *Sin* or *Nanna*. So, later when God told Abraham to sacrifice his son, Isaac, Abraham had little compunction about such sacrifice because he was familiar with it. He had grown up in a human sacrificing religion. God then stopped Abraham before the sacrifice of Isaac, and provided a substitute, a goat or lamb.

And long before this happened Abraham met Melchizedek. Lot, Abraham's nephew had gotten into trouble and had been captured by an enemy. Abraham gathered an army and rescued Lot, and following that rescue Abraham found himself in the area where the city of Jerusalem would be. And the king or prince or ruler of that area, Melchizedek, met with Abraham to seal a peace treaty that included Lot's rescue. At the conclusion of that treaty Abraham and Melchizedek shared bread and wine to seal the deal. And as part of that deal Abraham tithed to Melchizedek from his war booty. Abraham then gave all of the booty back. He refused to keep any of it because it might cause a conflict later. This is the only encounter with Melchizedek in the Bible. Psalm 110 praises Melchizedek, and the book of Hebrews then identifies Melchizedek as belonging to an entirely different order of priests; and said that Jesus belongs to that order.

The significance of this cannot be over stated. So, what does it mean? The entire Old Testament temple culture was built on the priesthood of Aaron and Levi. Aaron was the elder brother of Moses, and served as Moses' spokesman as Moses negotiated with Pharaoh for the release of the Israelites from Egypt. Part of the Law given to Moses at Sinai gave Aaron the priesthood for himself and his descendants, and Aaron became the first High Priest of the Israelites. Levitical priests were also required to be descendants of Aaron.

Over time the duties of the priesthood were divided. The Aaronites tended the temple worship, and the Levites managed the building and the accrued wealth. This division has persisted through the Old and New Testaments, and has come to be known as Elders and Deacons. But the point is that the priesthood of Aaron was the priesthood of the Old Testament. The Old Testament is the story about the priesthood of Aaron and the Temple at Jerusalem.

In Christian theology much is made of similarities between Jesus Christ and the Old Testament Temple. And it is very interesting and significant. We learn a lot about Jesus by comparing and associating Him with the Old Testament Temple. We do this because Jesus said that He is the Temple.

Jews understood that any changes made to the Temple required divine authority as mediated through the High Priest of Israel. In other words, the ancient Jews believed that only the High Priest or the Messiah could do something like that which Jesus did when He cleansed the temple of animal sellers and moneychangers (John 2:13–17). This was why the Jews responded by asking Him for a sign. They wanted proof that Jesus had the messianic authority to remove the merchants from the temple.

But Jesus did not give them a sign right away; instead, He said that "this temple" would be destroyed and in three days He would raise it up. No one understood what Jesus was talking about. Even the disciples did not understand it until His resurrection. The Jews thought Jesus was talking about the physical temple in Jerusalem. John then inserted an explanatory comment in John 2:21, saying that the temple was Jesus' body. Thus, the Lord identified Himself as the new and true temple.

The old covenant sanctuary was being superseded by a new temple: Jesus Himself, in whom His people are being knit together as the true sanctuary of God (1 Peter 2:4–5). If Jesus Himself is the new temple, that means that the people of Christ themselves are the new temple. Jesus mentioned this in John 17:21. Paul discussed this extensively in Romans 12, 1 Corinthians 12, Galatians 3:28, and Ephesians 4:4. The church is not the buildings in which we meet, but the believers who meet together.

> "Now you are the body of Christ and individually members of it" (1 Corinthians 12:27).

This means that all of the theological insights that come from a Christian analysis of the Old Testament Temple apply to Jesus Himself, and by extension, to the people of Christ. Not to the buildings in which we meet. It means that the focus of Christian development, Christian sanctification, and maturity, should be on the flesh and blood of the people of Christ. Not on the bricks and mortar of the buildings in which Christians meet. This is not an argument against having nice buildings in which to meet. It's an argument about the primary focus and purpose of the institution of Christianity.

> "So also Christ did not exalt himself to be made a high priest, but was appointed by him who said to him, 'You are my Son, today I have begotten you'; as he says also in another place, 'You are a priest forever, after the order of Melchizedek'" (vs. 5-6).

God Himself said this. Christ was appointed a high priest by God Himself, not by a council of human beings. And the priesthood of Jesus Christ is not like the priesthood of the Old Testament Temple, though much can be learned about the character of Jesus Christ by studying the various details of the Temple.

While we don't know much about Melchizedek, we do know a lot about Jesus Christ. And we can extrapolate backwards from Jesus to Melchizedek to learn about Melchizedek because what is true about Jesus is also true about Melchizedek. We don't learn about Jesus by studying Melchizedek; rather, we learn about Melchizedek by studying Jesus because Jesus, being a High Priest in the order of Melchizedek, is equivalent to Melchizedek.

Melchizedek (*malkī-ṣeḏeq*) means king of righteousness, or my king is righteousness. Melchizedek was the king of Salem at that time. *Salem* means *peace*, and the area of Salem would become the site of Jerusalem, the city of peace. All of this means that the key to world peace, to human peace, is *righteousness*. And righteousness means right living or living rightly, living correctly, living morally in the light of Christ.

Right living means living into the fruit of the Spirit: love, joy, peace, patience, kindness, goodness, faithfulness, gentleness and self-control (Galatians 5:22-23). And from other lists we can add: modesty, chastity, continence, honesty, integrity, and industry. Christian righteousness means living for Christ because Christ lives for you. It means living in Christ because Christ lives in you, but not just in you. Christ lives in us, in His body, the church, who are the people of God.

Christ's church is the people who genuinely imitate the character of Jesus Christ. There is no such thing as a Christian who is not part of Christ's church. There is no such thing as a Christian who does not genuinely imitate the character of Jesus Christ.

So, let's do this. If we imitate Christ, we won't be out of order. But who can to this perfectly or adequately? No one. So we rely of the power and presence of the Holy Spirit to guide us. Amen!

PRIORITY

"Now this is the commandment—the statutes and the rules—that the Lord your God commanded me to teach you, that you may do them in the land to which you are going over, to possess it, 2 that you may fear the Lord your God, you and your son and your son's son, by keeping all his statutes and his commandments, which I command you, all the days of your life, and that your days may be long. 3 Hear therefore, O Israel, and be careful to do them, that it may go well with you, and that you may multiply greatly, as the Lord, the God of your fathers, has promised you, in a land flowing with milk and honey. 4 "Hear, O Israel: The Lord our God, the Lord is one. 5 You shall love the Lord your God with all your heart and with all your soul and with all your might. 6 And these words that I command you today shall be on your heart. 7 You shall teach them diligently to your children, and shall talk of them when you sit in your house, and when you walk by the way, and when you lie down, and when you rise. 8 You shall bind them as a sign on your hand, and they shall be as frontlets between your eyes. 9 You shall write them on the doorposts of your house and on your gates.

—Deuteronomy 6:1-9

28 And one of the scribes came up and heard them disputing with one another, and seeing that he answered them well, asked him, "Which commandment is the most important of all?" 29 Jesus answered, "The most important is, 'Hear, O Israel: The Lord our God, the Lord is one. 30 And you shall love the Lord your God with all your heart and with all your soul and with all your mind and with all your strength.' 31 The second is this: 'You shall love your neighbor as yourself.' There is no other commandment greater than these." 32 And the scribe said to him, "You are right, Teacher. You have truly said that he is one, and there is no other besides him. 33 And to love him with all the heart and with all the understanding and with

all the strength, and to love one's neighbor as oneself, is much more
than all whole burnt offerings and sacrifices." 34 And when Jesus saw
that he answered wisely, he said to him, "You are not far from the
kingdom of God." And after that no one dared to ask him any more
questions.   —*Mark 12:28-34*

The Ten Commandments are given twice in the Bible: Exodus 20 and Deuteronomy 5. So our reading in Deuteronomy 6 comes right after the giving of the Ten Commandments. Here Moses tells Israel to obey the commandments " that you may fear the Lord your God" (v. 2). The motivation for action is fear.

Believers and unbelievers understand the world very differently. For the unbeliever, the fear of God is the fear of the judgment of God and the punishment for sin, which is eternal separation from God (Luke 12:5; Hebrews 10:31). But for the believer, the fear of God is something much different. The believer's fear is understood as reverence of God. Hebrews 12:28-29 is a good description of this:

> "Therefore, since we are receiving a kingdom that cannot be shaken, let us be thankful, and so worship God acceptably with reverence and awe, for our 'God is a consuming fire.'"

Reverence and awe are what the fear of God means for Christians. Reverence, to revere means to honor with profound respect. Awe is the feeling we get in the presence of something vast, something that challenges our understanding of the world, like looking up at millions of stars in the desert sky or marveling at the birth of a child. Other words that describe awe are: wonder, amazement, surprise, and transcendence.

Then Moses said, "Hear therefore, O Israel" (v. 3). Moses commanded the people to hear what he was saying. Can hearing be commanded? I can tell you to listen, but I can't make you hear. It's a bit like commanding love. Love given in response to a command is not reciprocal love.

When our children were small we would sometimes say, *Did you hear what I said?* It was more of a statement than a question. It means: *do you understand what I mean?* Similarly, to hear God is not so much a mystical voice as it is an understanding of intent. To hear God is to understand what He means, to understand His Word, the Bible.

God's instruction to Israel as they were entering the land He promised to give them was to pay attention to and actually obey the rules He was establishing for them, so that things would go well for them in the new land. If they listened to God, if they heard the Lord of life, and were diligent to actually obey God's rules, things would go well for them. If they didn't, things wouldn't go well.

The Jewish prayer known as the *Shema* serves as a centerpiece of the morning and evening Jewish prayer services. Its first verse encapsulates the monotheistic essence of Judaism:

"Hear, O Israel: The Lord our God, the Lord is one" (v. 4).

To say that God is "one" means two things: 1) that there is only one God, and 2) that God is first. One meaning has to do with quantity, the other has to do with order.

Let me provide a brief sidebar into number theory because it is interesting and it points to some interesting theological suggestions. There are several different kinds of numbers, but we want to consider only *cardinal* and *ordinal* numbers. We begin with cardinal numbers or counting numbers (1, 2, 3, etc.).

The number 1 is unique because it is the multiplicative identity. It is the only number for which these special facts are true:
- Any number multiplied by 1 equals itself.
- Any number divided by 1 equals itself.
- Any number except 0, divided by itself equals 1.

The number 1 cannot be divided by any other number larger than itself so that the result is a whole number because it results in a fraction. Theologically, then, we can say that God cannot be multiplied; because there is actually only one God. God cannot be divided; God is whole, a unity, one essence. God has no parts.

Ordinal numbers are defined differently than cardinal numbers. Ordinal numbers refer to order rather than quantity: first, second, third, etc. The theological significance of this is that it means that God is first, first among all others.

So, from number theory we see that the *Shema* means that there is only one real, actual God; and that God is to be our first priority, above all other priorities. This means that there was to be nothing more important than God for the ancient Israelites. God should always be our first consideration.

Moses continued,

> "You shall love the Lord your God with all your heart and with all your soul and with all your might" (v. 5).

Israel's love of God was *commanded*! But love cannot be commanded. We can't command anyone to love, but apparently God can. There is an important related issue here: can love be learned? It's an interesting and important question. Both psychology and science tell us that love can be learned.

Consider a new born infant born out of wedlock and given up for adoption by its mother, who does not, cannot, and/or will not love the child. It's an unfortunate reality in the world. Such a child is deprived of the natural love that parents usually have for their children. Can such a child learn to love? Maybe. But without a doubt, he begins life with a disadvantage.

We modern Americans are inundated with the idea of romantic love, the idea that love is a feeling that people fall into, a feeling that comes upon us. It is suggested that this kind of love is beyond our control. It just happens, or it doesn't. We don't nurture it, we *fall* into it and then respond to it.

In the church this is similar to the idea of God's grace, freely given, and once we become aware of this grace we are compelled to respond with love and appreciation. Being saved is like falling in love with God, with Jesus, who first loved us. The problem with all of this is that it puts our love of God outside of our control. It just happens, or it doesn't.

But come back to the question: *can love be learned?* Can people learn to love God? It is possible for people who don't love God to change their minds and love God? And if it is possible to learn love, how does it happen? Can we nurture the love of God in others? To help us better understand this let us think about the object of God's love. Exactly who is it that God loves so much

"that he gave his only Son, that whoever believes in him should not perish but have eternal life" (John 3:16).

John said that God so loved the *world*, defined as the inhabitants of the earth, the human family, the ungodly multitude; the whole mass of people alienated from God, and who are therefore hostile to the cause of Christ. God loves both believers and unbelievers. Notice that God's love is not directed at specific individuals, but at humanity as a whole, as a species. He loves the world. God loves everyone, even the unlovable, even those who hate Him. According to John, God's love for the world is not directed at specific individuals; and that runs counter to a lot of contemporary ideas. But John said it so it must be true, and it is true.

God's first love is His love of humanity as a species. But when people—individuals—respond to God's love, our love for God becomes personal. We experience God's love in individual, personal ways and we respond to God in individual, personal ways. So our love for God is not *humanity's* love for God because you and I don't represent all of humanity. So only when each and every human individual loves God will God's love for humanity be reciprocated.

However, when we personally respond to God's love, everything in our lives changes. When we love someone who doesn't love us in return, we call it *unrequited love*, and it is often painfully tragic. But when we love someone who loves us in return, we call it love fulfilled, and it is joyfully idyllic. The same is true for God. He loves everyone, but He holds those who love Him in return in a special relationship, a closer relationship. When you are trying to have a conversation with someone and they don't respond, it falls flat. But when people respond in kind the relationship grows and develops into something special.

So we come back to the question: *can love be learned?* Can individuals learn to love? Can people learn to be loving? Of course, we can! So how does that happen? Can love be taught?

The Lectionary takes us to Mark 12 for the answer. There Jesus answered the question about which commandment is the most important. The first is the *Shema*:

> "'you shall love the Lord your God with all your heart and with all your soul and with all your mind and with all your strength.' The second is this: 'You shall love your neighbor as yourself'" (vs. 30-31).

Love God and love your neighbor.

> "And the scribe said to him, 'You are right, Teacher'" (v. 32).

The scribe called Jesus *Teacher*, which suggests that these things can be taught and learned. So love can be learned and it can be taught. But we can't teach what we don't know, nor can we give what we don't have. And this means that in order to teach love one must first learn it. Therefore, love—real love, God's love, love of God—doesn't just happen.

God has already given His love to humanity, to all. But only when that love is reciprocated, given back, does it blossom. Being loved is easy, giving love is a discipline, a practice, an art. So, what exactly is love? For a biblical definition we turn to 1 Corinthians 13: 4-13:

> "Love is patient and kind; love does not envy or boast; it is not arrogant or rude. It does not insist on its own way; it is not irritable or resentful; it does not rejoice at wrongdoing, but rejoices with the truth. Love bears all things, believes all things, hopes all things, endures all things. Love never ends. As for prophecies, they will pass away; as for tongues, they will cease; as for knowledge, it will pass away. For we know in part and we prophesy in part, but when the perfect comes, the partial will pass away. When I was a child, I spoke like a child, I thought like a child, I reasoned like a child. When I became a man, I gave up childish ways. For now we see in a mirror dimly, but then face to face. Now I know in part; then I shall know fully, even as I have been fully known. So now faith, hope, and love abide, these three; but the greatest of these is love."

It turns out that people learn to love by practicing love; and people can teach others to love by practicing loving them. We learn by teaching, and we teach by learning, and the method is practice. We learn by imitating. If you want God to love you, you're in luck because God already loves humanity as a species, and you are one! God already loves you.

But that's not really the issue. The problem is not that God doesn't love us. The real issue is whether we love God. If you aren't sure, waiting for a bolt of lighting to strike you in confirmation is a bad idea because what you are waiting for has already been given. You're just ignoring it.

You can be assured of God's love only by loving Him in return. Don't wait for some mystical feeling to overpower you. Just practice the definition of love given in 1 Corinthians 13 and see what happens. You have nothing to lose and everything to gain.

GOD'S PRESENCE

8 Then the word of the Lord came to him, 9 "Arise, go to Zarephath, which belongs to Sidon, and dwell there. Behold, I have commanded a widow there to feed you." 10 So he arose and went to Zarephath. And when he came to the gate of the city, behold, a widow was there gathering sticks. And he called to her and said, "Bring me a little water in a vessel, that I may drink." 11 And as she was going to bring it, he called to her and said, "Bring me a morsel of bread in your hand." 12 And she said, "As the Lord your God lives, I have nothing baked, only a handful of flour in a jar and a little oil in a jug. And now I am gathering a couple of sticks that I may go in and prepare it for myself and my son, that we may eat it and die." 13 And Elijah said to her, "Do not fear; go and do as you have said. But first make me a little cake of it and bring it to me, and afterward make something for yourself and your son. 14 For thus says the Lord, the God of Israel, 'The jar of flour shall not be spent, and the jug of oil shall not be empty, until the day that the Lord sends rain upon the earth.'" 15 And she went and did as Elijah said. And she and he and her household ate for many days. 16 The jar of flour was not spent, neither did the jug of oil become empty, according to the word of the Lord that he spoke by Elijah. —1 Kings 17:8-16

24 For Christ has entered, not into holy places made with hands, which are copies of the true things, but into heaven itself, now to appear in the presence of God on our behalf. 25 Nor was it to offer himself repeatedly, as the high priest enters the holy places every year with blood not his own, 26 for then he would have had to suffer repeatedly since the foundation of the world. But as it is, he has appeared once for all at the end of the ages to put away sin by the sacrifice of himself. 27 And just as it is appointed for man to die once, and after that comes judgment, 28 so Christ, having been offered once to bear the sins of many, will appear a second time, not to deal with

sin but to save those who are eagerly waiting for him.
                                                —*Hebrews 9:24-28*

The story of the widow of Zarephath stands as a challenge to our faith. The first question that people need to deal with is whether or not the story is true. Clearly, the story at face value violates our understanding of reality. Flour and oil do not normally appear out of nothing. If our concern is how such a thing is possible, we will be left in doubt because we don't know. As far as we know, such a thing is not physically possible.

If we dismiss the story at this point because we don't understand how it could actually happen, we will miss the opportunity to learn anything from it. If, on the other hand, we want to learn something from the story, we need to ask the question in a different way.

There are two elements of truth: facts, and the interpretation of facts. A fact is defined as something that is known to have happened or to exist, especially something for which proof exists, or about which there is information.

The story of the widow of Zerephath constitutes a fact because it is purported to have happened and there is information about it. But the only information we have about it is the biblical story. We don't have any information about whether the events of the story actually happened. All we have is the story. Nor is is possible to have that kind of information. All we know is the biblical report of the story. How we understand the facts of the story depends on our interpretation of the facts.

All facts require interpretation, and differences of opinion come from different interpretations of the same facts. When differences of opinion arise, it is often that the disagreement is not about the facts; the disagreement is about the interpretation of the facts. In the case of this particular story all we can do is to investigate the integrity of the source of the story, the integrity of the Bible. If the source of the story has integrity, then we can apply that integrity to the story. The integrity of the Bible is well-documented, so we can trust the factuality of the story itself. The integrity of the Bible applies to its various stories.

If we don't assume the factuality of the story, or don't trust the integrity of the Bible, we turn it into a myth or fiction, and will dismiss it without further consideration. But just because something is fictional doesn't mean that it doesn't convey important truth. Imaginary scenarios can describe and convey important truths that are deeper and more complex that ordinary facts. So it doesn't really matter whether or not the story of the widow of Zerephath actually happened. That's not what the story is about. Whether it did or not cannot be established. All we have is the story. In order to evaluate the story we must take it at face value.

And the integrity of the Bible suggests that the story is worth our consideration. If we dismiss the story because we think it didn't actually happen, we cannot learn anything from it. And because it is in the Bible, we must assume there is something important to learn from it.

The story of Elijah and the widow at Zarephath is a story of faith, obedience, and generosity. It has three important lessons that teach us: to trust God, to faithfully manage what little we have, and to help others in need. Elijah obeyed God and went to Sidon. He left Israel and went to this Gentile Phoenician town. Israel was not a dependable resource during the drought, so Elijah found help outside of Israel, in a Gentile nation. This in itself is an important insight. The faith of the Israelites was not reliable.

Elijah was not sent to trust or rely on the Phoenician government of Sidon, but to rely on a widow there. There was a faithful widow in this Gentile town, which suggests that faithfulness could not be found in Israel, but could be found outside of Israel.

Elijah went and found her and asked her for help, for food and water. She was very poor, and was at the end of her tether. She didn't have enough for herself and her son, not to mention a guest. Elijah told her not to worry, but to make a small offering to a man of God, to him, and then to tend to her own needs. Give to God first from what you have, then tend to your own needs. And by putting God first, she would be blessed because putting God first is an act of faithfulness. God rewards faithfulness, even when you have very little to share. It is important to help others because you you might be contributing to God's mission.

So, is this story true? Did it actually happen? Was Elijah saved from the famine? Did he actually heal the widow's son? Did any of this help God's mission? Did anyone learn anything important? Did *you* learn anything? Was your faith strengthened?

The truth of this story is not found in the facts of the story. The truth of this story is found in our response to it. If you are encouraged by it, then God's truth is established. Sometimes the lessons of a story are truer, more important, than the simple facts of the story.

The ninth chapter of Hebrews deals with a much larger story in the history of Israel. Hebrews discusses the change of administration from the Old Testament sacrifices to the New Testament reality. Is this story in Hebrews true?

The purpose and practice of Temple sacrifices is described and discussed. We are reminded of the substitutionary element of the Temple sacrifices, that the death of the animal represents the death of sin, that the blood of the sacrifice represents the blood of the sinner. And that the death of the animal represents the payment of the penalty for sin, and that the payment of the penalty represents the redemption of the sinner, who offered the animal as a payment for sin. *So*, says Hebrews, *the death of Jesus Christ on the cross qualifies as an actual offering to God for the sin of the world, following the pattern of the Old Testament sacrifices.*

But while the Old Testament sacrifices had to be offered over and over, year after year, the sacrifice of Jesus Christ on the cross was "once for all" (v. 26). It was one and done, not to be repeated. The sacrifice of Jesus Christ on the cross was the culmination of the Old Testament sacrificial practices. Jesus Christ was the final and last sacrifice, which meant that the administration of the Old Testament was finished, completed. No more blood sacrifices were needed.

The old religion of blood sacrifice, the ancient religion of Abraham's childhood, was finished. God's mission to end the old religions of human sacrifice and vengeance was accomplished. A new day had begun, a new religious administration had been founded by Jesus

Christ. It was the administration of grace, mercy, love, and forgiveness. Jesus Christ had come to live and die "to put away sin by the sacrifice of himself" (v. 26). The purpose of Christ's death was to "put away sin" (v. 26). The power of sin has been defeated by the death of Christ. The moon god of Ur was finished—banished.

Is this true? Is it a fact? Again a fact is defined as something that is known to have happened or to exist, especially something for which proof exists, or about which there is information. This story of Jesus is known to have happened, and there is information about it. And that information is as reliable as the Bible. It is as reliable as the story of the widow of Zerephath. Does this story help God's mission? Did anyone learn anything important? Did *you* learn anything? Was your faith strengthened?

The truth of this story is not found in the facts of the story. The truth of this story is found in our response to it. If you are encouraged by it, then God's truth is enhanced. But this story is not over.

> "Christ, having been offered once to bear the sins of many, will appear a second time, not to deal with sin but to save those who are eagerly waiting for him" (v. 28).

The story of Christ's life, death, and resurrection has already happened, a long time ago. That story about the end of the Old Testament administration is over. And a new story has begun. The new story is not about sin. Sin has been dealt with on a global scale by Christ's death. The death of Jesus Christ on the cross is sufficient for the forgiveness of the sin of the whole world. The new story is about God saving "those who are eagerly waiting for him" (v. 28). The old story was about the death of sin through the death of Christ. The new story is about the life of faithfulness through the resurrection of Jesus Christ, who lives eternally in His church, in His people. The new story is the Evangelical story of Jesus Christ, the good news of new life in Christ. The new story is *our* story. Is it true? Is this new story story true? Is *your* story true? Is there new life in Christ? Are you eagerly waiting for Him, waiting upon Him?

The world is dying to hear your answer.

KING OF WHAT?

Now these are the last words of David: The oracle of David, the son of Jesse, the oracle of the man who was raised on high, the anointed of the God of Jacob, the sweet psalmist of Israel: 2 "The Spirit of the Lord speaks by me; his word is on my tongue. 3 The God of Israel has spoken; the Rock of Israel has said to me: When one rules justly over men, ruling in the fear of God, 4 he dawns on them like the morning light, like the sun shining forth on a cloudless morning, like rain that makes grass to sprout from the earth. 5 For does not my house stand so with God? For he has made with me an everlasting covenant, ordered in all things and secure. For will he not cause to prosper all my help and my desire? 6 But worthless men are all like thorns that are thrown away, for they cannot be taken with the hand; 7 but the man who touches them arms himself with iron and the shaft of a spear, and they are utterly consumed with fire."

—2 Samuel 23:1-7

33 So Pilate entered his headquarters again and called Jesus and said to him, "Are you the King of the Jews?" 34 Jesus answered, "Do you say this of your own accord, or did others say it to you about me?" 35 Pilate answered, "Am I a Jew? Your own nation and the chief priests have delivered you over to me. What have you done?" 36 Jesus answered, "My kingdom is not of this world. If my kingdom were of this world, my servants would have been fighting, that I might not be delivered over to the Jews. But my kingdom is not from the world." 37 Then Pilate said to him, "So you are a king?" Jesus answered, "You say that I am a king. For this purpose I was born and for this purpose I have come into the world—to bear witness to the truth. Everyone who is of the truth listens to my voice."

—John 18:33-37

David was an unlikely king. The story of how he became king is filled with unexpected twists and turns. Israel first wanted a king in order to be like the other pagan nations. Israel had been in the Promised Land for more than four hundred years without a king. But they had not conquered the other nations because they had not obeyed God. Their disobedience manifested at many levels, but militarily they failed to totally eradicate the previous inhabitants as God had directed.

We still flinch at the horror of such a command. Nonetheless, that is what God said. And Israel's failure has led to the history of conflict in the world ever since. Israel wanted a king in order to compete with the other pagan nations. They determined that they needed a national king to organize them for defense from the other nations, and to eventually conquer them militarily.

So the people asked Saul to appoint a king for them. Saul thought it was a bad idea, but asked the Lord about it. And the Lord thought it was a bad idea, too. But because the people wanted a king, God would give them a king.

God chose David to be king, but the people wanted Saul. Saul was a bad choice. Saul was a Benjaminite, the worst, most unfaithful of the tribes. The Benjamites were ambidextrous warriors who could whiled swords with both hands. They were the most immoral and unfaithful of the Israelites. But Saul was a head taller than everyone else, and was well-sculpted. He was handsome and strong. Saul looked good!

So God gave the people what they wanted, but told them that they would be sorry because things would not work out for them. God's choice was David, who was still a boy at the time. David was completely insignificant at that time. He tended his family's sheep, and played the lyre, a small, stringed harp. David got a job in Saul's court because Saul liked his music. And that job gave David a ring-side seat in which he learned how not to be a king. He learned from watching Saul's mistakes. As he grew, David advanced in Saul's army and made a name for himself, which made Saul jealous.

Over time Saul began to hate David, and pursued him as an enemy. David became a felon in Israel as the king sought to kill him.

And David found refuge among the people. Long story short: David was popular among the people and when Saul was killed, David became king.

There are many lessons in the story of David's rise to power and his kingship. Underlying this story is the Hand of God, who brought David to power. And David was aware that God was guiding him because David prayed and listened to God—most of the time. Not always, but most of the time. And so David became the mouth of God in Israel. God spoke through David, both guiding him and correcting them when David went wrong, which he did on many occasions.

The story of David and Bathsheba revealed David to be a philanderer and a murder. David's sins were many, but when he realized them he repented and asked for forgiveness. And that is why David was the apple of God's eye; because David repented and asked for forgiveness. David then became the model king for Israel, not because he was sinless, but because he was able to repent and ask for forgiveness.

So God made an eternal covenant with David, promising that David's example of repentance and forgiveness would guide the throne of Israel forever. David's last words are a testament to this fact:

> "The God of Israel has spoken; the Rock of Israel has said to me: When one rules justly over men, ruling in the fear of God, he dawns on them like the morning light, like the sun shining forth on a cloudless morning, like rain that makes grass to sprout from the earth" (vs. 3-4).

Kings must listen to the Word of God and rule with justice, God's justice; and when they do, things will go well for the nation. God's Justice was to be the hallmark of national authority for Israel, and for all nations. God used Israel as a case study and model for the world. Justice is another word for righteousness. Without righteousness at the top levels of government and throughout the society, justice is not possible. And when I say *righteousness* I mean God's definition of righteousness because there is no other. The lesson here is that if you want justice in society, you must pursue righteousness in your own life. There are no shortcuts, nor magic bullets.

The Lectionary then connects David's kingship with Jesus, who described His Kingship when Pilate asked Jesus about His Kingdom. Jesus answered,

> "My kingdom is not of this world" (v. 36).

Jesus did not say what His Kingdom is, He said what it is not. So, what is Jesus' Kingdom? To say that it is not of this world does not mean that it has no effect on this world. It just means that it operates at a different level. His kingdom is not about law, or social rules of behavior because these things must be imposed upon people. Laws and social rules of behavior work by imposition. They are imposed on people from the outside, from the culture or from the law. People conform to laws because laws are enforced. To break a law will bring unpleasant consequences by force if necessary. To violate a social norm will bring social ostracising.

God's Kingdom is not and cannot be imposed on people. People must voluntarily submit to God's Kingdom by practicing God's righteousness, God's definition of righteous. No one can be forced into God's Kingdom against their will. And any effort to do so will not and cannot work. Though government can impede God's Kingdom, it cannot bring it about. Thus John Adams said,

> "Our Constitution was made only for a moral and religious people. It is wholly inadequate to the government of any other."

And by moral and religious he meant *Christian*. He didn't specifically say *Christian* because at the time he and most Americans understood Christianity to be the ultimate religion of the world. He assumed it and assumptions are rarely stated.

Adams and the founders designed the American Constitution to apply to people who generally shared the values and beliefs of Christianity. And apart from those shared values and beliefs, the Constitution won't work, because people who do not share the values and beliefs of Christianity will simply ignore the guidance of the Constitution. People who do not share the values and beliefs of Christianity do not abide or respect Christian norms, Christian values.

What norms and values in particular? People who do not share the values and beliefs of Christianity do not value or practice the "fruits of the Spirit" as given in biblical examples. People who do not share the values and beliefs of Christianity do not define love as Christians do. They do not define *joy* or *peace* as Christians do. They have a different understanding of goodness and faithfulness than Christians have.

The problem is that communication between people who hold different values and beliefs is difficult, if it happens at all. Such people will often use the same words, but will define those words differently, and will not understand or misunderstand one another. And because people naturally believe themselves to be right, they will think that those who disagree with them are wrong, or are liars. And here we are! We are living in such a world of diverse values and beliefs, a world of competing truths, competing worldviews.

No society can continue to exist without common values and beliefs because competition in values and beliefs leads to confusion, competition, and destruction. Modern society absolutely requires cooperation, and cooperation requires common values and beliefs, common definitions and norms. Jesus knew this, and said as much:

> "For this purpose I was born and for this purpose I have come into the world—to bear witness to the truth" (v. 37).

The truth that Jesus bears witness to is God's truth, also known as absolute truth, or common truth, even shared truth. But this truth cannot be imposed, except by God.

God can and does impose His truth through what the Bible calls His judgment. God imposes His judgment on individuals through regeneration and damnation. He dispatches the Holy Spirit to convince people that His judgment is good and right, so that they willingly conform to it. God is very patient and merciful, but when things get too far out of whack, He will impose His judgment on a society through some sort of crisis for the sake of the survival of humanity. But God doesn't like doing that because He wants people to prosper on their own.

Just as we want our children to be self-sufficient, God wants His children to accept their place in the world, to love and enjoy the world as God has made it, because no other kind of world is actually sustainable. This truth is universal, the world over. And so Jesus said,

"Everyone who is of the truth listens to my voice" (v. 37).

We can conform to God's judgment about how to live in this world, or we can experience a crisis of correction. Such a crisis is not a punishment, but an opportunity to learn. If you understand what I'm talking about, engage the Lord with all of your might. If you don't, buckle up. You're in for a painful lesson.

CHRISTIAN IMAGERY: HEADS UP

14 *"Behold, the days are coming, declares the Lord, when I will ful-*
fill the promise I made to the house of Israel and the house of Judah.
15 In those days and at that time I will cause a righteous Branch to
spring up for David, and he shall execute justice and righteousness in
the land. 16 In those days Judah will be saved, and Jerusalem will
dwell securely. And this is the name by which it will be called: 'The
Lord is our righteousness.'" —Jeremiah 33:14-16

25 *"And there will be signs in sun and moon and stars, and on the*
earth distress of nations in perplexity because of the roaring of the sea
and the waves, 26 people fainting with fear and with foreboding of
what is coming on the world. For the powers of the heavens will be
shaken. 27 And then they will see the Son of Man coming in a cloud
with power and great glory. 28 Now when these things begin to take
place, straighten up and raise your heads, because your redemption is
drawing near." 29 And he told them a parable: "Look at the fig tree,
and all the trees. 30 As soon as they come out in leaf, you see for
yourselves and know that the summer is already near. 31 So also,
when you see these things taking place, you know that the kingdom
of God is near. 32 Truly, I say to you, this generation will not pass
away until all has taken place. 33 Heaven and earth will pass away,
but my words will not pass away. 34 "But watch yourselves lest your
hearts be weighed down with dissipation and drunkenness and cares
of this life, and that day come upon you suddenly like a trap. 35 For
it will come upon all who dwell on the face of the whole earth. 36
But stay awake at all times, praying that you may have strength to
escape all these things that are going to take place, and to stand be-
fore the Son of Man." —Luke 21:25-36

Advent is a time in the church calendar that anticipates the birth of Christ. The anticipation of the birth of Christ is as important as the birth itself because without the anticipation, the historical context that gives meaning to the birth, Christ's birth would be meaningless. However, our anticipation of Christ's birth is imaginary because we live two thousand years after Christ's birth. So we have to imagine what the original anticipation was like, because we do not live during the historical time of that anticipation. It is impossible to anticipate something that happened long ago. The best that we can do is to imagine it, to think of it in terms of images or symbols.

Our theme for this year's Advent season is Christian Imagery. Imagery is defined as a set of mental pictures or images that use vivid or figurative language to represent objects, actions, or ideas. Imagery is a literary technique that employs expressive or evocative images, exaggerated ideas or symbols that convey something exceptional.

Our concern as Christians is whether imagery is real or true. Is it a reliable source of God's truth, biblical truth? Is it factual? And by *factual* people usually mean *literal*. Is imagery factual? It's a hard question because the definition of imagery is the opposite of the definition of factual. Imagery is defined as vivid or figurative language used to represent things; it employs expressive or evocative images. Imagery employs exaggeration, metaphor, and embellishment. And literal is defined as simple, nonfigurative, ordinary definitions. What is literal avoids exaggeration, metaphor and embellishment.

So why is imagery used in the Bible? By using descriptive language and figures of speech effectively, story tellers appeal to our senses as well as personal emotion and feelings. Imagery attempts to recreate a story or occurrence in a way that can be experienced as it was experienced when it first happened. Facts tend to be dry and sterile, so in order to communicate the factual truth of a story or situation that is super-important, the story teller tries to emulate the original feeling and passion that the story first evoked with thoughts and ideas that are fantastic. Imagery is an attempt to make a story or event feel real, to make it seem super-important.

The fact of the matter is that the baby Jesus was born. But babies are born all the time. So another birth is not a big deal. But the birth of Christ is a big deal. So, to better communicate the importance of His birth, the story teller uses imagery to enhance the story with images that suggest additional importance and meaning. The images of a story are not always factual, but neither are they untrue. The imagery is not "the truth," but it represents "the truth," a truth that is greater than the mere factuality of the story they tell. In other words, the birth of Jesus is about more than the birth of a baby. The birth of Jesus in Nazareth was an historical event of unparalleled proportion. It was a very BIG DEAL! Something that must never be forgotten. So it is described with exaggerated elements, but the fact of the matter is not an exaggeration.

Jeremiah anticipated the birth of Jesus, the coming of the Messiah who would save the world. Jeremiah provides the historical context for the Messiah by relating the anticipated Messiah to King David, who was Israel's greatest king. David was the greatest king because he upheld the righteousness of God. He didn't always conform to God's righteousness, but he recognized it by repenting and asking for forgiveness when he realized his own failure to live it. David made an effort to live righteously according to God's definition. And he failed often and profoundly. But he recognized his own failures and confessed them. He didn't try to hide them, to cover them up. He faced them and admitted his failings. So Jeremiah said that David's reign provided a beginning for righteousness to manifest in the halls of government.

The first step toward righteous living in this sinful world is the recognition of one's own failures to live righteously. The first step toward the solution of a problem is to recognize that there is a problem. The second step is to correctly diagnose the problem. A faulty diagnosis will produce a faulty prescription, a wrong solution.

David began his righteous kingship in Israel, and Jeremiah anticipated that God would continue that process, that kind of king, that kind of government, by causing a Righteous branch to spring up following David. What is a "Righteous branch"?

A branch is part of a tree, and in this case Jeremiah meant a family tree. The "house" of David ruled Israel when David was King. The world "house" can also be translated as "household." In those days it was common for sons to go into the same business as their father. Thus, kingship was often passed from father to son, not always, but regularly. So did Jeremiah mean that David's literal or actual, biological sons would inherit the throne? Yes, because Solomon did so. But no, because Jeremiah was also aware of the corruption of Israel's kings.

Jeremiah, who lived long after David, was well-aware of Israel's civil war that had been raging for centuries, and the many evil kings in both Israel and Judah. So by using the term "Righteous branch" Jeremiah was not defining a family relationship biologically. He was defining David's family spiritually. David's sons were those who were like David, able to recognize God's righteousness and to repent when they failed to live up to it. Jeremiah said that the family of David would represent God's righteousness as the foundation of government: "The Lord is our righteousness" (v. 16).

Luke tells a story in anticipation of the coming of the Son of Man. Jesus is referred to as the "Son of Man" eighty-two times in the New Testament. It's the primary title Jesus used when referring to Himself. Stephen spoke of the Son of Man when he was being martyred (Acts 7:56). The title, "Son of God," is an overt reference to His deity, while "Son of Man" focuses on the humanity of Christ. The prophet Ezekiel is referred to as "son of man" ninety-three times, emphasizing Ezekiel's humanity. Jesus Christ was fully human. He came "in the flesh" (1 John 4:2). That's the point.

The use of this title in the New Testament suggests a fulfillment of prophecy. Jesus Christ is pure righteousness. And to make this point in a way that people will understand the full, historical significance of Jesus' birth Luke used literary imagery. The birth of Jesus was a world-sized event, not a local event, and to make that point Luke employs world-sized imagery. He wrote of sun and stars and the earthly distress of nations. He was noting and predicting world changes that could only be described as historical and global.

To say that "the powers of the heavens will be shaken" (v. 26) points to cataclysmic world events. At the time that Luke wrote no one could know exactly what changes Jesus would bring. All he knew was that Christ would change the world in in ways that no one could expect or predict. And such changes have already happened. It began a long time ago, and continues today. And as with all such historic, cataclysmic, global changes, creative destruction would be involved.

The "new" would come to replace the "old." This means that the "old" would have to be removed, ignored, or destroyed in order to make way for the "new." And it was! That creative destruction manifested in Jerusalem in A.D. 70 when Rome sacked Jerusalem and destroyed the Temple, which ended the period of Second Temple Judaism. But at the time that Jesus spoke, these events had not yet happened. Jesus was anticipating them. The creative destruction of Second Temple Judaism was a future event for Jesus when He told a parable about it. He knew it was coming. But He didn't know all the details, yet He knew that the fulfillment of the law was a big deal.

> "Look at the fig tree, and all the trees. As soon as they come out in leaf, you see for yourselves and know that the summer is already near. So also, when you see these things taking place, you know that the kingdom of God is near. Truly, I say to you, this generation will not pass away until all has taken place. Heaven and earth will pass away, but my words will not pass away" (vs. 29–33).

This prophecy was fulfilled in A.D. 70 with the destruction of the Temple. The destruction of Jerusalem was a local event, but it had world-wide implications. This event marked the end of the "old" world and the beginning of the "new" world. Did they actually see

> "the Son of Man coming in a cloud with power and great glory" (v. 27)?

Do we understand this literally? Or metaphorically? The destruction of Jerusalem and the Temple did actually happen. The historian Josephus wrote about it and called it the greatest cataclysm the world had ever seen. Did Josephus actually see

> "the Son of Man coming in a cloud with power and great glory" (v. 27)?

The birth of Christ marked the beginning of the greatest change that has ever happened to the earth, to humanity. Hearts were changed. Minds were changed. History was changed. The world was changed forever for the better! Is this story true? Or is it imaginary? It is imagery! But it is also true! History testifies to it. The church testifies to it. Christians everywhere are a testimony to the truth of it. Do you testify to it? Has the birth of Christ rocked your world?

The interesting thing about the birth of Christ is that it began a long time ago, but it's not over. Christ continues to be reborn in His people. This world-shaking, historical change has begun, but it is not finished. It is in process. The "old" world is still passing away, and the "new" world is still coming into existence.

God's truth is true whether people believe it or not. So whether you believe it or not, heads up! Keep your eyes open! Watch your six! God is still on the move. He began way back when, and He ain't done!

CHRISTIAN IMAGERY: COMING

Behold, I send my messenger, and he will prepare the way before me. And the Lord whom you seek will suddenly come to his temple; and the messenger of the covenant in whom you delight, behold, he is coming, says the Lord of hosts. 2 But who can endure the day of his coming, and who can stand when he appears? For he is like a refiner's fire and like fullers' soap. 3 He will sit as a refiner and purifier of silver, and he will purify the sons of Levi and refine them like gold and silver, and they will bring offerings in righteousness to the Lord. 4 Then the offering of Judah and Jerusalem will be pleasing to the Lord as in the days of old and as in former years. —Malachi 3:1-4

In the fifteenth year of the reign of Tiberius Caesar, Pontius Pilate being governor of Judea, and Herod being tetrarch of Galilee, and his brother Philip tetrarch of the region of Ituraea and Trachonitis, and Lysanias tetrarch of Abilene, 2 during the high priesthood of Annas and Caiaphas, the word of God came to John the son of Zechariah in the wilderness. 3 And he went into all the region around the Jordan, proclaiming a baptism of repentance for the forgiveness of sins. 4 As it is written in the book of the words of Isaiah the prophet, "The voice of one crying in the wilderness: 'Prepare the way of the Lord, make his paths straight. 5 Every valley shall be filled, and every mountain and hill shall be made low, and the crooked shall become straight, and the rough places shall become level ways, 6 and all flesh shall see the salvation of God.'" —Luke 3:1-6

Malachi is the last book of the Old Testament. Malachi prophesied after the reconstruction and dedication of the Second Temple in 516 B.C. He lived during the times of Ezra and Nehemiah, the rebuilding of the Temple following Israel's Babylonian captivity. The abuses that Malachi mentions are the same as those Nehemiah found on his second visit to Jerusalem in 432 B.C. So it seems reasonably certain that he prophesied concurrently with Nehemiah or shortly after. Malachi describes a lazy and corrupted priesthood, an underfunded, rebuilt Temple that was without the support of the people, and rampant divorce and disregard of traditional marriage.

Sound familiar? The Bible continues to call people to the Old Paths, the old ways because people continue in the old sins. This is why the words of Malachi sound so contemporary, so applicable today. We live in the same patterns of unfaithfulness as Israel did 2500 years ago. That's amazing! The world has made so much progress in so many ways, yet the character of our sin remains the same.

Malachi was written 500 years before Jesus, which means that the anticipation of the Old Testament Jews simmered for 500 years prior to the arrival of Jesus. It is interesting to note how Malachi's hope for a resolution to the problem of sin fits the character of Jesus. The Hebrew word *malachi* means messenger. And scholars believe that the book title is not the name of an individual, but is the job description of the people at large.

> "he will purify the sons of Levi and refine them like gold and silver,
> and they will bring offerings in righteousness to the Lord" (v. 3).

Malachi's message was for the priests, the leaders of Israel. Malachi believed that the Temple establishment was responsible for the character of the people. The idea of representative government would wait thousands of years to occur to people. At the time that Malachi wrote it was not believed that the leaders should represent the people or to do what the people wanted them to do. Rather, the people were called to imitate the leaders. So Malachi aimed his message at the leaders, the priests. And his solution to the problem of faithlessness was personal and social righteousness.

It's the same solution that we saw last week in Jeremiah's call for the growth of the branch of David, who was lauded for his righteousness. Again, David was lauded because he recognized God's righteousness, not because he consistently lived it himself. When David became aware of his own unrighteousness, he consistently repented and asked for God's forgiveness. David recognized God's righteousness, which caused him to see his own unrighteousness—and to admit it, and to seek forgiveness and correction.

Malachi calls for the priests, the leaders, to

"bring offerings in righteousness to the Lord" (v. 3).

This is an allusion to the sacrificial practices—offerings—of the Temple. But the offering of righteousness is a different kind of sacrifice. To put this in contemporary gospel format we would say that the old, sinful lives of the priests were to be drowned in the waters of baptism so that their new lives in Christ could be born, because new life in Christ reflects the righteousness of God.

Luke's story of John the Baptist begins by providing an historical date. Establishing a real date is important because the story is about something that actually happened. It's not an imaginary story. To do that Luke named Tiberius Caesar and Pontius Pilate, the emperor of Rome and the governor of Judea. To confirm the authentication of the story, he also mentioned Herod's brother, Philip, who was

"tetrach of Ituraea and Trachonitis, and Lysanias tetrarch of Abilene, during the high priesthood of Annas and Caiaphas" (vs. 1-2).

The dating of the story is very specific, which indicates its reality. Thus, we can conclude that John the Baptist was a real person who lived at a specific time and proclaimed a specific message. He proclaimed a baptism of repentance for the forgiveness of sins.

Jewish tradition mentioned six options for baptism or bathing, starting with using natural pits or cisterns of standing water, which were acceptable but least desirable, moving up to pits that are re-freshed by rainwater, which were slightly more desirable, then the custom-built ritual baths, then fountains, then flowing or living waters. "Living waters" (as found in natural lakes and rivers) were con-sidered to be the best possible option for baptism/bathing. There is also biblical reference for Old Testament baptism:

"The Lord said to Moses, 'You shall also make a basin of bronze, with its stand of bronze, for washing. You shall put it between the tent of meeting and the altar, and you shall put water in it, with which Aaron and his sons shall wash their hands and their feet. When they go into the tent of meeting, or when they come near the altar to minister, to burn a food offering to the Lord, they shall wash with water, so that they may not die. They shall wash their hands and their feet, so that they may not die. It shall be a statute forever to them, even to him and to his offspring throughout their generations'" (Exodus 30:17-21).

Actual bathing represented ritual purity or cleanliness. Remember that the priests were slaughtering animals and ritually handling blood, so bathing was important. Baptism or bathing provided a measure of sanitation, and represented ritual purity or cleanliness. So each time baptism was engaged it was for sanitation and ritual purity. Each bath was a renewal of ritual purity.

And this is the idea that John the Baptist used in his call for a baptism of repentance.[1] John took the idea out of the Temple and offered it to the people. John was offering and providing a sacred Temple practice to the common people. And it was an affront to the Temple priests, who would have thought that John was offering pearls before swine. The Temple establishment thought of themselves as a completely different class than the common people.

The Temple establishment was practicing what is called classism. Classism is a form of personal bias or prejudice or a pattern of institutional discrimination based on social class and typically directed against individuals or groups of a lower socioeconomic status. It differentiates rich and poor or educated and ignorant or the cool people from the nerds. The term can be used to characterize the attitudes and behavior of individuals toward others or the structure and systemic practices of institutions or whole societies. It is a form of discrimination similar to racism and sexism.

The important thing here is to see that John the Baptist, and Jesus, opposed these kinds of social divisions. At the time that John the Baptist came, Israel was not unified. We have talked about how the Jews had taken the gospel of Abraham, who promised blessing for the whole world, and applied it to themselves exclusively. This is

1 *Evangelical Essentials: Holy Baptism,* T. R. Hendershot, Createspace, 2017.

where the idea of racial purity comes from. Originally the Jews applied it to themselves by distinguishing between Jews and Gentiles. And Jesus came to destroy that idea.

But at the time that John and Jesus lived, the Jews were divided against themselves! The Temple establishment thought of the common people of Israel as *hoi polloi*, the dregs of society. The leaders looked down on the common people; thought them to be ignorant and unworthy. Sound familiar? Its an old problem that Jesus came to correct.

John, repeating the words of Isaiah said that

"all flesh shall see the salvation of God" (v. 6).

God's intention is to save all people, not just some people. But there is a problem because God will not and cannot save unrepentant sinners. Unrepentant sinners will bring their sin with them into the kingdom of God. And God cannot allow that because sin will destroy the kingdom of God. So the God of the Old Testament was conflicted: He wanted to save all people, but people were sinners. Sin would have to be eliminated in order for people to be saved.

To solve this dilemma God dispatched Jesus to overcome sin. But because people love their sin and willingly choose to engage it, it would take more than the law to keep people from their sin. The solution was for Jesus to change hearts and minds so that people would not want sin. But sin is a habit and habits cannot simply be eliminated. Bad habits must be replaced with good habits. Habits are hard to break, and new habits are hard to form.

So Jesus would pour His infinite love upon all people, and we call that love: grace. Jesus genuinely loves humanity, all individuals are included in the love of Jesus. And that love has already been freely given. Love, true love, then elicits a response. When someone genuinely loves us, we are compelled to return that love. If that love is not returned, it is not true. Nothing changes human behavior like falling in love. When the love is real, the changes in behavior are real. And that's how we know when we are loved. When we find our actions and desires changing to accommodate the person we love, then we know that our love is real. We feel it because it changes us.

God's love works the same way. When our behaviors and desires change to accommodate a personal relationship with Jesus Christ, God knows that our love is real. And forgiveness, which was freely given at the outset, is then acknowledged by both parties, and mutual love is confirmed. A love union is forged.

This is what Malachi and Isaiah and Jeremiah and John were waiting for. They were waiting for God to show His perfect love, which He did through Jesus Christ. And God is now waiting for people to confirm their mutual love for God. That confirmation begins the process of engagement and relationship. This is the anticipation of the coming Messiah, who has already come, who is still coming today, and who will come again. God is waiting for our confirmation of His love. The ball is in your court.

Praise be to God!

CHRISTIAN IMAGERY: TRUTH TELLING

"Behold, God is my salvation; I will trust, and will not be afraid; for the Lord God is my strength and my song, and he has become my salvation." 3 With joy you will draw water from the wells of salvation. 4 And you will say in that day: "Give thanks to the Lord, call upon his name, make known his deeds among the peoples, proclaim that his name is exalted. 5 "Sing praises to the Lord, for he has done gloriously; let this be made known in all the earth. 6 Shout, and sing for joy, O inhabitant of Zion, for great in your midst is the Holy One of Israel."
               —Isaiah 12:2-6

7 He said therefore to the crowds that came out to be baptized by him, "You brood of vipers! Who warned you to flee from the wrath to come? 8 Bear fruits in keeping with repentance. And do not begin to say to yourselves, 'We have Abraham as our father.' For I tell you, God is able from these stones to raise up children for Abraham. 9 Even now the axe is laid to the root of the trees. Every tree therefore that does not bear good fruit is cut down and thrown into the fire." 10 And the crowds asked him, "What then shall we do?" 11 And he answered them, "Whoever has two tunics is to share with him who has none, and whoever has food is to do likewise." 12 Tax collectors also came to be baptized and said to him, "Teacher, what shall we do?" 13 And he said to them, "Collect no more than you are authorized to do." 14 Soldiers also asked him, "And we, what shall we do?" And he said to them, "Do not extort money from anyone by threats or by false accusation, and be content with your wages." 15 As the people were in expectation, and all were questioning in their hearts concerning John, whether he might be the Christ, 16 John answered them all, saying, "I baptize you with water, but he

who is mightier than I is coming, the strap of whose sandals I am not
worthy to untie. He will baptize you with the Holy Spirit and fire.
17 His winnowing fork is in his hand, to clear his threshing floor and
to gather the wheat into his barn, but the chaff he will burn with un-
quenchable fire."18 So with many other exhortations he preached
good news to the people.   *—Luke 3:7-18*

In order to understand this prophecy by Isaiah we need to put it in
historical context. Isaiah preached during a time of decay, idolatry,
and a pro-Assyria foreign policy. Ahaz, king of Judah in the south,
met with a coalition formed by northern Israel and Damascus. These
kings wanted him to join them in opposing the Assyrians, who were
preparing to attack Israel. Isaiah counseled Ahaz to trust in God
rather than foreign alliances, and told him to ask for a sign to confirm that Isaiah was speaking a true prophecy (verse 7:11).

But Ahaz refused, saying he would not test God (7:12). Isaiah
replied that Ahaz would have a sign whether he asked for it or not.
And the sign would be the birth of a child who would be called Immanuel, meaning "God-with-us" (7:13–14).

Ahaz was an evil king who offered his own son as a burnt offering to Molech, a Canaanite god. Ahaz set up high places and offered
sacrifices to false deities (2 Kings 16). Ahaz's idol worship was abom-
inable. Then Ahaz saw a pagan idol and told Uriah, the priest, to
build a replica of it, which he did, and placed it in the temple. During this time of conflict Judah lost many captives to Syria.

This was also the time when Rezin, the king of Syria, and Pekah,
the king of Israel, warred against Jerusalem in Judah. They didn't
conquer her (Is 7:11), but they did a lot of damage. Syria and Israel
would have captured Jerusalem except that Ahaz, the wicked king of
Judah, asked the pagan Assyrians to help him defend Jerusalem. This
is the background of Isaiah's prophecy.

Jerusalem was battle weary, dead bodies were strewn about,
death and destruction dominated Jerusalem. And the king was apos-
tate! It was a very dark day in Jerusalem. But Isaiah looked to the future. He had no idea how far into the future his vision would
manifest. Nonetheless he saw it as a certainty.

"Behold, God is my salvation; I will trust, and will not be afraid; for the Lord God is my strength and my song, and he has become my salvation" (v. 2).

The people who received this Word, those who had survived the decimation and near defeat of Jerusalem, were broken, dispirited, and depressed. Their city, though not defeated, was on the brink of starvation and collapse when Isaiah said:

"Give thanks to the Lord, call upon his name, make known his deeds among the peoples, proclaim that his name is exalted" (v. 3).

Sometimes we think that we have it bad today, that our lives are hard, that our struggles are overwhelming, and our hope is gone. Isaiah prophesied to a truly broken people:

"Sing praises to the Lord, for he has done gloriously; let this be made known in all the earth. Shout, and sing for joy, O inhabitant of Zion, for great in your midst is the Holy One of Israel" (vs. 5-6).

Jerusalem was exhausted and war-torn, and the king worshiped false gods. But Isaiah said to the people: take heart! God is not finished with you. He has great plans for your great, great, great, great, etc. grandchildren.

As we know, Jesus then came some 700 years later. That's a long time to maintain hope. But hope was maintained! By everyone? No! But by a few. It's always been that way. Holding on to hope in the face of disaster is not easy. But it is possible because—Immanuel, God is with those whose hope is true.

Luke 3 is a story about John the Baptist, who anticipated Jesus. John was a popular preacher. The establishment didn't like him, but the people did. John told the people to repent and be baptized, to change their ways, change their thinking, and to cleanse their lives of their various idolatries, their false beliefs and ideas. Some of those in the crowd were Pharisees, or were people who believed as the Pharisees taught.

John called them mean names: "You brood of vipers!" (v. 7). By referring to them as snakes he was accusing them of lying. It is a reference to the snake in the Garden, who was Satan, the father of lies.

John's initial response was pretty confrontive. Many people would consider it to be unChristian, but it's not. Jesus did the same thing. Five times Jesus said,

> "Woe to you, scribes and Pharisees, hypocrites!" (Matthew 23).

He called them "blind fools," "blind guides," "whitewashed tombs." Was Jesus being unkind? Or was He being honest? It is not kind to treat people dishonestly.

Sometimes people think that being kind means shielding people from the harsh realities of truth. But is it really? If you hide the truth from those you love, when they learn the truth they will realize that you were being dishonest with them.

> "Faithful are the wounds of a friend; profuse are the kisses of an enemy" (Proverbs 27:6).

Friends don't hide the truth from each other.

John said to them,

> "And do not begin to say to yourselves, 'We have Abraham as our father.' For I tell you, God is able from these stones to raise up children for Abraham. Even now the axe is laid to the root of the tree. Every tree therefore that does not bear good fruit is cut down and thrown into the fire" (vs. 8–9).

This means that people are not faithful because their parents were faithful. Faithfulness is not an inherited quality. The rewards of faithfulness are inherited, but not faithfulness itself. Grace is a free gift, but faithfulness is our obligation, our duty. Faithfulness must be intentionally practiced.

Many people responded to John faithfully, and submitted to John's baptism. And after they were baptized they had questions.

> "What then shall we do?" (v. 10).

They wanted to be faithful, but didn't know how. They didn't know because faithfulness is more than an attitude; it's a behavior. It's more than a decision, it's a way of life. Faithfulness calls people to action, and action is more than assent. Action is more than agreement. Faithfulness begins with agreement, but if it doesn't move to action, it is stillborn. Faithfulness involves more than thinking about being faithful. Faithfulness requires that we put skin in the game, that we put our lives on the line, that we step up and stand out.

So how did John respond to the question? He said: s*hare what you have.* To the tax collectors he said: *don't pad your bills.* To the soldiers, those who had authority, he said: *be honest; don't practice extortion or false accusation, and be happy with what you have*—which means: *don't be greedy.* Those with authority are under a higher burden, a higher responsibility. Those who have authority are tempted to coerce and intimidate people, and to falsely accuse others in order to take advantage their authority.

We say that power corrupts, which means taking advantage of one's authority for one's own social, monitory, or political advantage. Corruption is evident when that happens. As people listened to John, they began to see how compromised they were. The acknowledgment of sin is not when you see how sinful someone else is, of how sinful the world is. The acknowledgment of sin is seeing how sinful *you* are.

Pointing out the sins of other people doesn't help very much. Most people don't like it; they don't respond well to those who point out their sins. Most people get defensive, some will deny the accusations, others get angry. A few people appreciate it, but that's a small group. John had his supporters, but a lot of people got defensive and angry. The people John accused were people with authority, the Scribes and Pharisees, the power brokers, the establishment.

So, should we not tell people the truth because they might get angry at us? Or should we be honest and truthful with our friends? Truth always comes with a cost. Grace is free, truth is costly. We are easily tempted to distort the cost of truth. That cost can be distorted in two ways: The first is by deflation: by lowering the cost of truth by downplaying its demands. With the motivation to win people over to the truth, we are often tempted to speak in ways that promise ease and comfort for believing the truth. But Scripture explicitly promises the opposite.

"all who desire to live a godly life in Christ Jesus will be persecuted (2 Timothy 3:12).

False promises scatter seed upon rocky soil. And when such people come to see the real price of truth, they fall away (Matthew 10:20-21).

The second way to distort truth is through inflation. This happens when the already-high cost of truth-telling is done by being unnecessarily offensive. We live in a world with people who love darkness rather than light (John 3:19). Consequently, to shine the light of truth offends many people. But there's a difference between speaking an offensive truth and speaking the truth offensively.

Our words must always reflect the grace and truth that Jesus spoke to the world around Him, and our firmness of belief must not be mistaken for hardness of heart towards others who bear God's image. Truth always comes with a cost in this world, but it is a price worth paying. Whether that cost is being slandered or losing a job, a relationship, or like Stephen, who was stoned to death, even losing our lives. The cost of not telling God's truth out weighs the cost of speaking God's truth.

And what is the truth that we are called to speak? Jesus said,

"I Am the Way, and the Truth, and the Life" (John 14:1).

God's truth is a Person, not an idea. But we can't say what we don't know. So to speak God's truth we must first know Jesus. And knowing Him means hearing his accusation against us. Jesus doesn't divulge the sins of others; He shows us our own sin. Faced with the undeniable reality of our own sin, we can get defensive, or we can go into denial, or we can get angry. Usually people do all of the above before they get to acceptance of God's truth. The acceptance of the reality of our own sin then throws us into the loving arms of Jesus' forgiveness. Only then do we begin to realize the immensity of God's love, only when it becomes personal.

And when people see us do that, see us confront and accept our own sin, even when it is personally painful and embarrassing—especially when it's personally painful and embarrassing, then they see the light of Christ in us. This, then, is called *witnessing*, and God uses it for evangelism because when people see it, they are moved. It touches people emotionally. At that point people can see God's presence; people feel it.

This is the true Spirit of Christmas.

CHRISTIAN IMAGERY: MARY'S CHRISTMAS

But you, O Bethlehem Ephrathah, who are too little to be among the clans of Judah, from you shall come forth for me one who is to be ruler in Israel, whose coming forth is from of old, from ancient days. 3 Therefore he shall give them up until the time when she who is in labor has given birth; then the rest of his brothers shall return to the people of Israel. 4 And he shall stand and shepherd his flock in the strength of the Lord, in the majesty of the name of the Lord his God. And they shall dwell secure, for now he shall be great to the ends of the earth. 5 And he shall be their peace. When the Assyrian comes into our land and treads in our palaces, then we will raise against him seven shepherds and eight princes of men;   —*Micah 5:2-5*

39 In those days Mary arose and went with haste into the hill country, to a town in Judah, 40 and she entered the house of Zechariah and greeted Elizabeth. 41 And when Elizabeth heard the greeting of Mary, the baby leaped in her womb. And Elizabeth was filled with the Holy Spirit, 42 and she exclaimed with a loud cry, "Blessed are you among women, and blessed is the fruit of your womb! 43 And why is this granted to me that the mother of my Lord should come to me? 44 For behold, when the sound of your greeting came to my ears, the baby in my womb leaped for joy. 45 And blessed is she who believed that there would be a fulfillment of what was spoken to her from the Lord."   —*Luke 1:39-45*

I hesitate to discuss Mary, but will do so anyway because Mary is an important person—topic—that has provided a lot of confusion and misunderstanding for a very long time. Who am I to weigh in on such an important topic? Just a small town country preacher on the edge of civilization. Then again, how can I not speak about such an important topic? But where to start?

The story begins in the Old Testament with expectation. We read about Micah's prediction of a "ruler in Israel" (v. 2) who would one day be born. And the fact that this ruler would be born involves a woman who would give birth to Him. Micah doesn't refer to the pregnancy of a virgin, but Isaiah does.

Isaiah's reference gets picked up in the gospels. And the virginal aspect of Mary's pregnancy has led to much confusion. The word translated *virgin* in both Hebrew and Greek simply means an unmarried woman. The original, historical understanding of the word meant that the woman was unmarried and had, therefore, not yet engaged in sex. Sex was strictly reserved for marriage in those days.

Mary's case is clearly provided by Luke. The angel Gabriel was sent to Mary, who was

"a virgin betrothed to...Joseph" (Luke 1:20).

Mary was engaged, but not married. Nor had she and Joseph been fooling around, which means that she had not engaged in sex. This is important!

Mary was troubled by Gabriel's message that she would would bear a son who would be given the throne of "his father David" (Luke 1:32). David was long dead, and Mary didn't understand how David, who was long dead, could sire a son through her, especially since she was still a virgin, and engaged to Joseph. The idea troubled her. So the angel answered her,

"The Holy Spirit will come upon you, and the power of the Most High will overshadow you" (Luke 1:35).

There's the answer, but what does it mean? Well, no one actually knows, but the literal sense is that the Holy Spirit will obscure the pregnancy process. Literally, *overshadow* means to cast a shadow over something, to darken or obscure something. The bottom line is that Mary had a baby and the Father was the Holy Spirit. How is that possible? That information is classified. It's not available. We don't

know. We can't know because we can't understand it. Not even if
we try. Nor is it necessary for us to understand the process.

The traditional understanding is that the birth of Jesus Christ
was a miracle. God accomplished the impossible. And that's the
point! We are not allowed to understand it, to rationalize it, because
if we understood it, it would not be considered to be a miracle. We
can only accept it by faith, or not. If we don't accept it by faith, we
turn it into a myth, a fairy story that isn't literally true. And we dismiss it. But if we do accept it, that story becomes the foundation of
the divinity of Jesus Christ. How so?

Israel had been freed from Egypt long ago through the leadership of Moses. And Moses took Israel into the wilderness for forty
years to cure the people of their habit of slavery. Becoming indepen-
dent and self-reliant is not easy. It takes discipline and practice. New
life habits need to form. It takes time. Israel was freed from Egypt,
but getting free from sin proved to be much more difficult.

The story of Israel from the wilderness to the time of Jesus is the
story of their struggle with sin. They were not able to conquer sin.
The story is long ane messy. The bottom line was that they were not
able to extract themselves from sin. God's law and institutions were
helpful, but inadequate. So the prophets said that God would have to
send someone who could rescue them because they could not do it
themselves. And their history proved that to be true. So they waited
for a Savior, a leader to show them the way.

And Gabriel then told Mary that she would give birth to *that*
Savior. And suddenly Mary was pregnant. Our scientific minds want
to know *how* that was possible. But "how?" is the wrong question.
We don't need to know how.

We all rode in an automobile to get to church this morning. Do
you understand how an automobile works? I turned on the lights in
the sanctuary. Is it necessary to understand how electricity works to
turn on the lights? Of course not. "How?" is the wrong question.

So what does it mean that the Father of Jesus is the Holy Spirit
and the mother of Jesus is Mary? It means that Jesus has two natures;
He is both fully divine and fully human at the same time and without
confusion. The nature of the Father and the nature of the mother are

joined in Him. Jesus has a human mother and a divine Father. And this is the most important truth about Jesus because it is the foundation of the doctrine of the Trinity, which is the most unique thing about the Christian religion. The Person Jesus Christ is both divine and human. He is both fully God incarnate and an ordinary bloke at the same time. This dual nature is Jesus' super power! It's important!

So what about Mary? Most Protestant Christians believe that God chose Mary to fulfill His purpose, but that Mary was a sinner like everyone else.

> "For all have sinned, and come short of the glory of God" (Rom. 3:23).

But the Roman Catholic Church teaches the doctrine of the Immaculate Conception of Mary, that she was free from sin which makes her like Jesus. Jesus is the only mediator between God and man; so for the Catholics Mary becomes mediatrix.[2] Protestants reject the idea of Mary as a "mediator" or intercessor. That's Jesus' job based on 1 Tim. 2:5:

> "For there is one God, and one mediator between God and men, the man Christ Jesus."

Roman Catholics and Orthodox Catholics give Mary the title: *Mother of God.* That title is not biblical, but that doesn't mean that it isn't true. Clearly Mary gave birth to Jesus, so she is His mother. And He is both fully God and fully human.

There is much confusion about the Catholic position, and the various arguments are long and torturous. Lord, help us understand your Word.

2   Mary's title of mediatrix arises from her cooperation in the Incarnation and in the Redemption of mankind. Through her "yes" (Lk 1:38), she became the Theotokos (God-bearer), and, as the "New Eve," she is "the Mother of all living." … Thus the graces that come through Jesus may be said to come to us, in a secondary way, via Mary—not as the origin of the graces, but as a conduit. The Catholic Church always has taught that Jesus Christ alone redeemed mankind (neither Mary nor any other creature had the power to do so), and ultimately only through him are salvation and grace obtained (from *Catholic Answers*).

The doctrine of the Immaculate Conception was not defined as an official church dogma of the Roman Catholic Church until 1854 when Pope Pius IX issued the papal bull (ruling) *Ineffabilis Deus*. The Immaculate Conception is the belief that Mary was free of original sin from the moment of her conception with Jesus to Mary's death—and beyond, of course.

Here's the problem with that: if Mary was free from sin then she was more like Jesus than like the rest of us. Their argument is that what is sinful cannot produce what is sinless—Jesus. Therefore, Mary must have been sinless. But Mary then becomes divine like Jesus. All human beings have always been sinners, except Jesus who took sin upon Himself. So the idea that Mary was sinless contradicts the Bible and messes with Jesus' dual nature because Mary then becomes like Jesus—divine. It destroys the idea of Jesus' humanity. In addition, if that is true, then she is an entirely unique person who does not share our common human nature.

The issue here is how sin became attached to human nature. When God first created Adam and Eve, He created them "very good" (Genesis 1), which means without sin. Sin came into the picture later through the Serpent. We know the story. God created Adam and Eve without sex; Adam from dirt, and Eve from Adam's rib. And every human being following this original creation is both created through sex and born a sinner. We call this the doctrine of original sin.

The issue here is whether sin is a function of biology or of morality. The long and short of this is that the traditional Catholic teaching focuses on biology, and the traditional Protestant teaching focuses on morality. This misunderstanding by the Catholics has played itself out over eons of history in the Catholic understanding of sex (coitus) as being morbid, which means characterized by unwholesome thoughts and feelings. While this may not be the current teaching of the Catholic Church, it is the historic understanding of the people in the pews.

The Catholic idea is that sin is a function of birth; it's biological. Avoidance of sin is good because sin is bad. Therefore, sex—the agent or cause of sin—should be avoided as much as possible. The evidence of this is the requirement of celibacy for Roman Catholic Priests and Nuns.

Again (or still) we find ourselves deep into the weeds, which is unfortunate because clarification requires discussion. The traditional Protestant teaching of original sin emphasizes that sin is a function of morality rather than biology. The Protestant understanding is that people choose sin because they prefer it, because they like it. Here sin is a function of selfishness or self-centeredness and it becomes a life habit. Here, people are natural sinners because people naturally choose sin. People could overcome sin by choosing otherwise, but they/we don't.

Sinners naturally choose sin because they are not aware that it's a problem or that there is a viable alternative. If you don't know about something, you can't choose it or not choose it. Again, sinners are not able to choose not to sin until they become aware of the problem and a viable alternative. In order to become aware of something people must be told about it, or come to realize that it exists.

But people must also believe that an alternative to sin is viable, that it is real, that it works! There must be a change of mind, or a new insight, or a realization of something that they hadn't previously considered. New thinking, a new worldview is required.

Paul said that the law revealed the sinfulness of humanity, that prior to the law people had no idea of sin. The law of Moses then gave Israel a choice. If you are going seventy when the speed limit is fifty, and there are no speed limit signs, you don't know you are speeding. The awareness of your infraction comes only with seeing the sign, or being told by an officer. But if you don't care about the law, or think that you can get away with speeding, you won't slow down even if you see the sign. You will ignore the officer.

Morality is about right and wrong, about doing the right thing because it's right, and not doing the wrong thing because it's wrong. Morality is caring about the difference between right and wrong, between good and evil. Morality begins with knowing that some things are wrong.

Mary wasn't thinking about any of this when she was called into Christian service by the Angel's announcement. It was not an invitation. She wasn't asked, she was told. Gabriel said, *God has a plan for your life*. And Mary said, *OK*. This simple response made Mary the ideal Christian and worthy of great honor. And we can all be like Mary because she was not unique, not exceptional, not sinless. She was just an ordinary, uneducated, country girl who was not sinless. But who chose to do what the Lord asked her to do long before she understood any of it.

The lesson in all of is is: *Be like Mary and God will eventually answer all your questions and quell all your fears*. Just trust God and avoid a lot of difficulties. It sounds simple, but it's not as easy as it sounds. Nonetheless, Christ's presence, Christ's reality in your life is the most important gift you will ever receive. And Christmas is about the gift of Christ's presence.

CHRISTMAS REUNION

11 For this is the message that you have heard from the beginning, that we should love one another. 12 We should not be like Cain, who was of the evil one and murdered his brother. And why did he murder him? Because his own deeds were evil and his brother's right-eous. 13 Do not be surprised, brothers that the world hates you. 14 We know that we have passed out of death into life, because we love the brothers. Whoever does not love abides in death. 15 Everyone who hates his brother is a murderer, and you know that no murderer has eternal life abiding in him. —1 John 3:11-15

Christmas is a *kiros* moment. There are two kinds of time: *chronos* and *kiros*. Chronos time is measured by our clocks and calendars. *Chronos* time moves forward in equally long segments: seconds, minutes, hours, days, months, years. *Kiros* time is more flexible. It moves forward in unequally long segments of expectation. When it is dinner time *chronos* time looks at the clock, but *kiros* time looks at the kitchen because dinner isn't served until it's ready. *Kiros* time is expectant time and it doesn't come until whatever is expected is ready.

Christmas is driven by the calendar. It comes on December 25, come rain or shine, sleet or snow. But Advent is a celebration of a *kiros* moment in history. Advent is the anticipation of the birth of Christ, and like all births, the baby comes on his or her schedule, not ours. Mary anticipated a baby. That Baby anticipated a Kingdom. Mary delivered a baby who delivered God's people.

Though we all know the story, it is remarkable that God was fully manifest in human form, in Jesus Christ, who began life like all of us: naked, cold, and terrified. Jesus Christ was an actual human being. Jesus was like us so that we could be like Him. Not that we can ever be God, we can't! But God created human beings in His own likeness, which means that we can live like Jesus lived: full of God's grace.

So our celebration of Jesus' birth is also a celebration of the the birth of the children of God, who anticipate the Kingdom of God. The children of God are people who have been born into this world as human beings, *and* who have been born again into the likeness of Jesus Christ. Being children of God means we have been born into God's family. It means that we learn our manners and customs from our Father, who art in heaven. We become God's children through faith in Jesus Christ through our personal spiritual rebirth:

> "But to all who believed him and accepted him, he gave the right to become children of God. They are reborn—not with a physical birth resulting from human passion or plan, but a birth that comes from God" (John 1:12–13, NLT).

Like physical birth, we are born as individuals. Each one of us is absolutely unique. We all have our own personalities, with our own individual strengths and weaknesses. But like physical birth, we are also born into families. Families are composed of people who have a common parent, or who have been legally adopted.

The Christian family is no different. We all have a common Father, who art in heaven—not by blood, but by adoption. The first time adoption is mentioned directly in the Bible is in Exodus 2. Moses, who brought Israel out of captivity and into the Promised Land, was adopted. Before Moses was born, Pharaoh decreed that all Jewish male infants should be killed. Moses was born into a world where being a baby was a dangerous thing.

God's alternative to the killing of babies has always been adoption. Moses was hidden in a river, and could have died. But Moses was found by Pharaoh's daughter. She asked her handmaiden, Moses' birth mother, to retrieve the infant, and Moses was brought to live in Pharaohs' palace. Moses, a Jew by birth, was an adopted Egyptian.

We are all spiritual orphans at our physical birth because we are all estranged from God from birth. The Holy Spirit is the Father of Jesus because the Holy Spirit caused Jesus to be born. He overshadowed Mary, who gave birth to Jesus. And the Holy Spirit is the real

Father of all of God's people because the Holy Spirit causes our spiritual birth, our rebirth. We are then adopted into God's family through baptism. Paul explained our adoption in Galatians 4:3-7:

> "In the same way we also, when we were children, were enslaved to the elementary principles of the world. But when the fullness of time had come, God sent forth his Son, born of woman, born under the law, to redeem those who were under the law, so that we might receive adoption as sons. And because you are sons, God has sent the Spirit of his Son into our hearts, crying, 'Abba! Father!' So you are no longer a slave, but a son, and if a son, then an heir through God."

Adoption is different than birth. Being born brings us into the human family, but adoption brings us into God's family. I wish there was no difference between these two families, but there is. This distinction is not mine to make, but God's. Jesus recognized that there are two families of human beings. Jesus, when talking to the Pharisees, who had hatched a plan to kill Him, said to them:

> "You are of your father the devil, and your will is to do your father's desires. He was a murderer from the beginning, and does not stand in the truth, because there is no truth in him. When he lies, he speaks out of his own character, for he is a liar and the father of lies. But because I tell the truth, you do not believe me" (John 8:44-45).

Jesus recognized that some people did not self-identify as children of God. It's not that God excluded them, but that they excluded themselves from God's family. They refused to recognize it. They didn't believe it. And the result of their belief—actually, their lack of belief, was that they denied the fact of their own adoption, often denouncing the idea as ludicrous. Had God really adopted them? Paul said in Galatians 3:13-14:

> "Christ redeemed us from the curse of the law by becoming a curse for us—for it is written, "Cursed is everyone who is hanged on a tree"— so that in Christ Jesus the blessing of Abraham might come to the Gentiles, so that we might receive the promised Spirit through faith."

God called Abraham to be a blessing to the whole world:

"and in you all the families of the earth shall be blessed" (Genesis 12:3).

All the families of the earth, not just the Jewish families.

So when Christ paid the price for our sins, whose sins were included? Everybody's! Christ died to redeem the whole world. This means that each Christmas we celebrate all of the new births in God's family. It's a family reunion! But has everyone come to the family reunion? No, not yet. Sadly, not yet. God is waiting for all of His people to realize who they actually are.

The joy of Christmas is the family reunion of God's people. The lament of Christmas is that not everyone has made it to the reunion... yet. Christmas is a time of both joy and sorrow. Neither can be avoided. The experience of what is called "Blue Christmas" is real, and we all feel that, too. Life is painful because sin is real.

But on this night as we focus on the Child in the manger, so on this night we are filled with hope and anticipation for our final reunion with all of God's people. Babies are full of hope because we have hope for what they might do, who they may become in this world.

Fill us with your hope, Lord, fill us with your light, the light of Jesus Christ, that we may be beacons of your light in this dark world, in Jesus' name.

Lord, the world is dark: wars, disasters, disease, divorce, and disappointment are everywhere. Yet, the darkness we see is evidence of your presence in our lives. We recognize the dark things only because Jesus provides the light. Without Jesus we would not even see what is in the dark, because Jesus provides the light. When we enter a dark room we see nothing until the light is turned on.

We ask that You would help us to be tuned to what is important. Christmas is a time when we can get so distracted by materialism and cultural expectations that we miss the main event. Please help our hearts and minds be focused on Your Son, our Lord, this Christmas—and beyond, every day. Remind our own souls of our great salvation that comes from You alone. Help us to celebrate what is eternal over what is temporal.

Give us the desire to search Your Scriptures for more understanding of Your life and miracle birth. Bless the church with a focused heart and mind on the message of the love of Jesus. When we celebrate in ways that are common to our culture and traditions, may people be reminded of the greater gift and relationship that we have in You. May the quality of our lives make our friends want what we have in Jesus Christ. We praise You that you were born a child, that a son was given, and Your government is on His shoulders. Thank You that You are called Wonderful Counselor, Mighty God, Everlasting Father, Prince of Peace. We celebrate the victory that Your government and peace will never end. Our hope is fully in You. We give you the glory and honor and majesty forever. Amen.

Now What?

41 Now his parents went to Jerusalem every year at the Feast of the Passover. 42 And when he was twelve years old, they went up according to custom. 43 And when the feast was ended, as they were returning, the boy Jesus stayed behind in Jerusalem. His parents did not know it, 44 but supposing him to be in the group they went a day's journey, but then they began to search for him among their relatives and acquaintances, 45 and when they did not find him, they returned to Jerusalem, searching for him. 46 After three days they found him in the temple, sitting among the teachers, listening to them and asking them questions. 47 And all who heard him were amazed at his understanding and his answers. 48 And when his parents saw him, they were astonished. And his mother said to him, "Son, why have you treated us so? Behold, your father and I have been searching for you in great distress." 49 And he said to them, "Why were you looking for me? Did you not know that I must be in my Father's house?" 50 And they did not understand the saying that he spoke to them. 51 And he went down with them and came to Nazareth and was submissive to them. And his mother treasured up all these things in her heart. 52 And Jesus increased in wisdom and in stature and in favor with God and man.　　　　　　　　　—Luke 2:41-52*

12 Put on then, as God's chosen ones, holy and beloved, compassionate hearts, kindness, humility, meekness, and patience, 13 bearing with one another and, if one has a complaint against another, forgiving each other; as the Lord has forgiven you, so you also must forgive. 14 And above all these put on love, which binds everything together in perfect harmony. 15 And let the peace of Christ rule in your hearts, to which indeed you were called in one body. And be thankful. 16 Let the word of Christ dwell in you richly, teaching and admonishing one another in all wisdom, singing psalms and hymns and spiritual songs, with thankfulness in your hearts to God. 17 And

whatever you do, in word or deed, do everything in the name of the
Lord Jesus, giving thanks to God the Father through him.
                                                    —*Colossians 3:12-17*

Jesus was a remarkable child. While His childhood was normal for the most part because He was fully human, yet there was something about Him that was different. From an early age He enjoyed adult conversations. There isn't much information about Jesus as a child, but we do have this story in Luke about the time He was found talking with the Temple teachers.

He was twelve! To us twelve is that time between childhood and teenager. But not so long ago, there was no such thing as teenagers. People simply went directly from being children to being adults, without that in-between stage that we call teenager. But something happened to the old pattern. A new era suddenly dawned; not very long ago the era of the teenager dawned.

Before the twentieth century, young people were seen as either children or adults. There was no inbetween. But as the world changed, so did the way people thought about youth. In the 1950s, the idea of teenagers burst onto the scene with their own teenage style, music, and way of life. The origin of the teenager goes back farther, to changes in schooling and parenting as the nation industrialized after the Civil War.

As people moved from farms to factories, labor unions formed and advocated for young people to stay out of the workforce to ensure higher wages for adult workers. The population in America trended young because of high birth rates and immigration. The solution was to keep the young in school. This made sense because the industrial economy required workers with skills in math, physics, machinery operation, and literacy. People needed more education to work industrial jobs and high schools could provide this education. It took a while for this to develop, but by 1950 it was the norm.

The bottom line is that prior to the Industrial Revolution of the modern age, there was no such thing as a teenager. Children simply became adults and took on adult responsibilities at home and on the farm at about 12-13 years of age. This doesn't mean that people before the Industrial Age were uneducated. Many were, of course, but the people who founded the United States in the 1700s were generally more educated than people today. Books were more scarce, and therefore more valued. Most families had few books, a Bible or two, and a few other classics—and newspapers.

The printing press made books and periodicals easier to have. Back then they took reading much more seriously. Simply reading and studying the Bible, actually understanding the Bible provides a better education than most people get today. What people need today is not more knowledge. People need wisdom and discernment. Knowledge is easy, ask Google. Wisdom is more demanding.

The point is that when Jesus was found in the Temple talking with the teachers, He was a young adult, a young man and therefore responsible for adult things. The fact that His parents couldn't find Him because they didn't know where He was when it was time to leave Jerusalem and return home doesn't mean that they were irresponsible parents who "lost" Jesus in the big city. Not at all!

Jesus was twelve, and therefore was a responsible adult. He was not a child. They didn't even look for him until they were on their way home. They expected Him to take care of Himself, and be on the caravan home. And that is why the Temple teachers were willing to spend time talking to Him. He was, no doubt, holding His own as He talked theology to the theologians of His day. Not the theologians in His little Podunk town out on the edge of nowhere. But the theologians in the capital city of Israel.

Jesus' parents didn't miss Him because they thought that they had lost Him. They considered Him to be an adult who could take care of Himself. After three days, and halfway back home, they determined that He wasn't in the caravan. That seems like a long time to us, but in those days the pace of life was a lot slower. For us, a missing twelve year-old for 3 hours would warrant calling the police. But if the missing son was 30, an adult, we would feel differently.

Jesus had been caught up in conversation at the Temple with the most erudite intellectuals of His time about the most important things in the world. He was an adult and was being treated like an adult, though a young adult. Jesus' wisdom amazed the Temple teachers. Apparently He had been reading and studying the Bible, and He knew it better than they did. They were amazed that one so young knew so much.

When His parents found Him they were distressed. They were not distressed at his carelessness about not telling them where He was. They were distressed because He had mistreated them. And how did Jesus mistreat them? They thought that Jesus had shown disrespect for His father, Joseph. It should have been Joseph who introduced Him to the Temple teachers, rather than Jesus approaching them on His own. Jesus had broken traditional protocol, and that embarrassed Joseph, the father of the family.

Joseph thought it was a lack of consideration for him, and was distressed with his independent-minded son. Jesus was not concerned with traditional protocol. Joseph knew about Jesus' interest in the Bible and the Temple, and should have known where to find Him.

But it wasn't Jesus who was being inconsiderate, it was Joseph who should have known where to find Jesus. Surely Jesus and Joseph had discussed the Bible and history, and probably told Jesus that He would have to inquire about such deep concerns with the Temple teachers because Joseph was just a small town carpenter.

So Jesus was found, the family was reunited, and they went home to Nazareth. And Jesus submitted to the family structure, and honor was restored to Joseph. While Jesus may have broken, or at least stretched, Temple protocol, He honored family protocol when He returned home. And Mary "treasured up all these things in her heart" (v. 51). She remembered them.

This was Jesus' first action as an adult man. He went to His Father's house and asked some hard questions.

And on this first Sunday after Christmas the Lectionary points us to Colossians 3, where we learn how we are to live as born-again Christian adults. As adults in Christ we are to be *compassionate, kind, humble, meek, patient, and forgiving.*

Rebecca Knight in an article in the *Harvard Business Review* discusses eight essential qualities of successful leaders. They are: authenticity, curiosity, analytical prowess, adaptability, *creativity, comfort with ambiguity, resilience, and empathy.*

Comparing the lists we see some commonalities. Empathy is like compassion, and comfort with ambiguity is like patience. But Jesus was not talking about being successful, and Rebecca was not talking about being a Christian. So maybe I'm making a false comparison, but maybe not. Paul was talking about living in Christ, and Rebecca was talking about living in the world. But Paul was not avoiding the world, where Rebecca had no concern for Christ in her article on leadership.

Maybe she was a faithful Christian. I don't know. But she didn't bring Christ into her discussion of leadership. She was simply reflecting the culture and teaching of Harvard, the most influential academic institution in America. She probably agreed with Harvard, that teaching Christianity is not Harvard's responsibility. And that leadership has nothing to do with Christianity.

Paul was talking to the Christians at Colossae, and Christians everywhere, which includes us. Maybe I should forgive Rebecca for overlooking Jesus in her description of leadership qualities. After all, Jesus was not a model of worldly success. He died as a convicted criminal, and all of His followers abandoned Him. It was only after He died that His cause began to grow. But it's immediate growth was opposed by both Roman and Jewish leaders.

The leaders of the world did all they could to squelch His movement. But the leaders of the world failed! And Jesus went on to become the most effective leader in the world, in that Christianity is currently the largest religion in the world. Paul told us to

"put on love, which binds everything together in perfect harmony" (v. 14).

Love applies to everything. Love brings everything into harmony. Not some things, but everything. Paul told us to

"let the peace of Christ rule in your hearts" (v. 15).

Why? Because people who are ruled by peace and fueled by love are one people, one body, one group, one family. People who are ruled by peace and fueled by love are brothers and sisters. And for this harmony, for this oneness, we are to be thankful.

Paul told us to admonish one another in all wisdom. To *admonish* is to remind people of something forgotten or disregarded; to remind people of an obligation and responsibility. People are obligated and responsible to Jesus. This means that all people must respond to Jesus because we all have the ability to respond to Jesus. We all have that response-ability. And it is a simple responsibility: yes or no. Are you in? Or are you out?

This responsibility cannot be ignored because in the long run people are either in or out of God's kingdom. There is no middle ground. There is no one foot in and one foot out when the door is closed. So, said Paul,

> "whatever you do, in word or deed, do everything in the name of the Lord Jesus, giving thanks to God the Father through him" (v. 17).

Has America followed Jesus? Of have we followed Harvard? What about you? Are you living in the name of Jesus? In the character of Jesus? Is Jesus your hero?

BIBLIOGRAPHY

Following is a list of resources that will help guide an understanding of the tradition of the one, holy, apostolic, orthodox, reforming, and evangelical church. This is the continuing tradition of the faithful German Evangelical and Reformed churches. This perspective has been overlooked and forgotten for more than a century, but is being rediscovered today. It may not be the final word on Christ's church, but it provides serious contemporary hope for much needed renewal across the proverbial board.

Mercersburg Study Series
- *Born of Water and the Spirit: Essays on the Sacraments and Christian Formation, by John Williamson Nevin, Philip Schaff and Emanuel V. Gerhart,* Edited by David W. Layman and W. Bradford Littlejohn, Wipf and Stock, 2016
- *Coena Mystica: Debating Reformed Eucharistic Theology*, by John Williamson Nevin and Charles Hodge, Edited by Linden J. DeBie and W. Bradford Littlejohn Wipf and Stock, 2013.
- *One, Holy, Catholic, and Apostolic, Tome 1: John Nevin's Writings on Ecclesiology (1844–1849)*, by John Williamson Nevin, Edited by Sam Hamstra Jr. and David W. Layman Wipf and Stock, 2017.
- *One, Holy, Catholic, and Apostolic, Tome 2: John Nevin's Writings on Ecclesiology (1851–1858)*, by John Williamson Nevin, Edited by Sam Hamstra Jr. and David W. Layman Wipf and Stock, 2017.

- *Philosophy and the Contemporary World: Mercersburg, Culture, and the Church,* by John Williamson Nevin, Edited by Adam S. Borneman and Patrick Carey Wipf and Stock, 2024.
- *Retrieving Catholicity in American Protestantism: Essays in Church History,* by John Williamson Nevin, Edited by Michael J. Stell Wipf and Stock, 2024.
- *The Development of the Church: "The Principle of Protestantism" and other Historical Writings of Philip Schaff,* by Philip Schaff, Edited by David R. Bains and Theodore Louis Trost Wipf and Stock, 2017.
- *The Incarnate Word: Selected Writings on Christology,* by John Williamson Nevin, Philip Schaff and Daniel Gans, Edited by William B. Evans and W. Bradford Littlejohn Wipf and Stock, 2014.
- *The Mystical Presence: And The Doctrine of the Reformed Church on the Lord's Supper,* by John Williamson Nevin, Edited by Linden J. DeBie and W. Bradford Littlejohn Wipf and Stock, 2012.

Arndt, Elmer J. F.
- *The Faith We Proclaim: The Doctrinal Viewpoint Generally Prevailing in the Evangelical and Reformed Church,* The Christian Education Press, 1960.

Bahnsen, Greg L. & Butler, Michael R.
- *The Objective Proof For Christianity: The Presuppositionalism of Cornelius Van Til and Greg L. Bahnsen,* The American Vision, 2024.

Beecher, Edward, Phillip A. Ross, Editor
- *Conflict Of Ages: Or, The Great Debate on the Moral Relations of God and Man,* Pilgrim Platform, Marietta, Ohio, 2011.
- *Concord Of Ages: The Individual And Organic Harmony Of God And Man,* Pilgrim Platform, Marietta, Ohio, 2013.

Bloesch, Donald G.
- *Christian Foundation:s A Theology of Word & Spirit: Authority & Method in Theology,* Intervarsity Press Academic, 1992.

- *Christian Foundations: God the Almighty: Power, Wisdom, Holiness, Love,* Intervarsity Press Academic, 1995.
- *Christian Foundation: Jesus Christ: Savior & Lord*, Intervarsity Press Academic, 1997.
- *Christian Foundations: The Holy Spirit: Works & Gifts*, Intervarsity Press Academic, 2000.
- *Christian Foundations: The Church: Sacraments, Worship, Ministry, Mission*, Intervarsity Press Academic, 2002.
- *Christian Foundations: The Last Things: Resurrection, Judgment, Glory*, Intervarsity Press Academic, 2004.
- *Christian Foundations: Holy Scripture: Revelation, Inspiration & Interpretation*, Intervarsity Press Academic, 2006.

Borneman, Adam S.
- *Church, Sacrament, and American Democracy: The Social and Political Dimensions of John Williamson Nevin's Theology of Incarnation*, Wipf and Stock, 2011.

Calvin, John
- *Calvin's Commentaries*, 22 volumes, public domain.
- *Institutes of the Christian Religion*, public domain.

Cornelius Van Til
- *In Defense of the Faith,* vols I-VI, P&R Publications, 1967.
- *Common Grace and the Gospel*, P&R Publications, 2015.
- *A Christian Theory of Knowledge*, P&R Publications, 1957.
- *The Reformed Pastor and Modern Thought*, P&R Publications, 1971.
- *The Case for Calvinism,* P&R Publications, 1964.
- *Essays on Christian Education*, P&R Publications, 1971.

Dunn, David, and others
- *A History of the Evangelical and Reformed Church*, The Christian Education Press, 1961.

Evans, William B.
- *A Companion to the Mercersburg Theology: Evangelical Catholicism in the Mid-Nineteenth Century*, Cascade Companions, 2019.

Frame, John
- *Systematic Theology: An Introduction to Christian Belief,* P&R Publishing, 2013.

- *The Doctrine of the Christian Life (A Theology of Lordship)*, P&R Publishing, 2008.
- *The Doctrine of the Word of God (Theology of Lordship)*, P&R Publishing, 2010.
- *The Doctrine of the Knowledge of God (A Theology of Lordship)*, P&R Publishing, 1987.
- *Cornelius Van Til: An Analysis of His Thought*, P&R Publications, 1995.

Gerhart, Emanuel V.
- *Institutes of the Christian Religion*, Vols. 1 & 2, 1896, 1899.

Hart, D. G.
- *John Williamson Nevin: High Church Calvinist*, P&R Publishing, 2025.

Heschel, Susannah
- *The Aryan Jesus: Christian Theologians and the Bible in Nazi Germany*, Princeton University Press, 2008.

Littlejohn, W. Bradford
- *The Mercersburg Theology and the Quest for Reformed Catholicity*, Pickwick Publications, 2009.

Kalantzis, George and Tooley, Andrew
- *Evangelicals and the Early Church: Recovery, Reform, Renewal*, Wipf and Stock, 2011.

Maxwell, Jack M.
- *Worship and Reformed Theology: The Liturgical Lessons of Mercersburg*, Wipf and Stock, 1976.

Miller, Samuel
- *A Treatise on Mercersburg Theology: or Mercersburg and Modern Theology Compared*, independently published, 2017.

Natan, Yoel
- *The Jewish Trinity: When Rabbis Believed in the Father, Son, and Holy Spirit*, Createspace, 2003.

Nevin, John Williamson
- *The Reformed Pastor: Lectures on Pastoral Theology*, Edited by Sam Hamstra Jr. Wipf and Stock, 2006.

Owen, John
- *The Works of John Owen*, 16 volumes, public domain.

Pearcey, Nancy R.

- *Love Thy Body: Answering Hard Questions about Life and Sexuality*, Baker Books, 2019.

Poythress, Vern S.
- *Philosophy, Science, and the Sovereignty of God*, P&R Publications, 1976.
- *Symphonic Theology: The Validity of Multiple Perspectives in Theology*, Zondervan, 1987.
- *God-Centered Biblical Interpretation*, P&R Publications, 1999.
- *Redeeming Science: A God-Centered Approach,* Crossway Books, 2006.
- Redeeming Sociology: A God-Centered Approach. Crossway Books: 2011.
- *Logic: A God-Centered Approach to the Foundation of Western Thought,* Crossway Books, 2013.
- *Redeeming Mathematics: A God-Centered Approach.* Crossway Books, 2015.
- *Reading the Word of God in the Presence of God: A Handbook for Biblical Interpretation,* Crossway Books, 2016.
- *Knowing and the Trinity: How Perspectives in Human Knowledge Imitate the Trinity,* P&R Publications, 2018.
- *Redeeming Our Thinking about History: A God-Centered Approach.* Crossway Books, 2022.
- *Redeeming Reason: A God-Centered Approach,* Crossway Books, 2023.
- *Making Sense of the World: How the Trinity Helps to Explain Reality.* P&R Publications, 2024.

Rushdoony, John Rousas
- *The Institutes of Biblical Law*, vols. 1&2, Ross House Books, 1982.
- *Systematic Theology,* vols. 1&2, Ross House Books, 1994
- *The One and the Many,* Thoburn Press, 1978.
- And others.

Schaff, Philip
- *History of the Christian Church*, 8 vols., public domain.
- *The Creeds of Christendom*, 3 vols., public domain.

Schneider, Carl Edward

- *The German Church On The American Frontier: A Study In The Rise Of Religion Among The Germans Of The West, Based On The History Of The Evangelischer 1840-1866.*

Silva, Moises
- *Foundations of Contemporary Interpretation: Six Volumes in One*, Zondervan, 1996.

Von Rohr, John
- *The Shaping of American Congregationalism: 1620-1957*, The Pilgrim Press, 1992.

Wentz, Richard, E.
- *John Williamon Nevin: American Theologian*, Oxford University Press, 1997.

Wilson, Douglas
- *Mere Christendom*, Canon Press, 2023.

Yrigoyen, Charles, Jr. & Bricker, George H.
- *Catholic and Reformed,* Pickwick Publications, 1978.

www.ingramcontent.com/pod-product-compliance
Lightning Source LLC
Chambersburg PA
CBHW060040100426
42742CB00014B/2650